汉诗英译教程

A Coursebook on Chinese Verse Translation

卓振英　李贵苍　编著

图书在版编目(CIP)数据

汉诗英译教程/卓振英,李贵苍编著. —北京:北京大学出版社,2013.9
(21世纪课程规划教材)
ISBN 978-7-301-23041-1

Ⅰ.①汉… Ⅱ.①卓…②李… Ⅲ.①诗歌—英语—翻译理论—高等学校—教材 Ⅳ.①H315.9

中国版本图书馆 CIP 数据核字(2013)第 190978 号

书　　　名:	汉诗英译教程
著作责任者:	卓振英　李贵苍　编著
责 任 编 辑:	初艳红
标 准 书 号:	ISBN 978-7-301-23041-1/H · 3362
出 版 发 行:	北京大学出版社
地　　　址:	北京市海淀区成府路 205 号　100871
网　　　址:	http://www.pup.cn　新浪官方微博:@北京大学出版社
电 子 信 箱:	alice1979pku@163.com
电　　　话:	邮购部 62752015　发行部 62750672　编辑部 62759634
	出版部 62754962
印 刷 者:	北京鑫海金澳胶印有限公司
经 销 者:	新华书店
	730 毫米×980 毫米　16 开本　14.75 印张　293 千字
	2013 年 9 月第 1 版　2013 年 9 月第 1 次印刷
定　　　价:	32.00 元

未经许可,不得以任何方式复制或抄袭本书之部分或全部内容。
版权所有,侵权必究
举报电话:010−62752024　电子信箱:fd@pup.pku.edu.cn

目 录

前言 …………………………………………………………………………… 1

第一章　汉诗及其英译 ……………………………………………………… 1
　　第一节　汉诗及其社会功能 ……………………………………………… 1
　　第二节　汉诗英译及其意义 ……………………………………………… 7

第二章　汉英两种诗歌的格律要素 ………………………………………… 14
　　第一节　节奏 ……………………………………………………………… 14
　　第二节　押韵 ……………………………………………………………… 16

第三章　典籍英译的类型归属及译者必备条件 …………………………… 22
　　第一节　研究型翻译与非研究型翻译 …………………………………… 22
　　第二节　典籍英译的类型归属 …………………………………………… 25
　　第三节　典籍英译者的必备条件 ………………………………………… 26
　　第四节　小结 ……………………………………………………………… 28

第四章　汉诗英译的标准与原则 …………………………………………… 32
　　第一节　汉诗英译的不同主张 …………………………………………… 32
　　第二节　汉诗英译的标准与原则 ………………………………………… 33

第五章　诗歌的模糊性及翻译的标准和方法 ……………………………… 40
　　第一节　诗歌的模糊性 …………………………………………………… 40
　　第二节　关于翻译的标准和方法的若干探讨 …………………………… 41
　　第三节　小结 ……………………………………………………………… 47

第六章　汉诗英译方法比较研究 …………………………………………… 50
　　第一节　汉诗英译的不同方法及
　　　　　　基于原作美学特征的译作评价体系 …………………………… 50

第二节　译作比较研究 …………………………………………… 51
　　第三节　结论 ……………………………………………………… 60

第七章　译作定性评价方法的探索
　　——以秦观《鹊桥仙》的三种英译为例 ……………………………… 63
　　第一节　意象层面的比较分析 …………………………………… 65
　　第二节　意境层面的比较分析 …………………………………… 66
　　第三节　语言风格层面的比较分析 ……………………………… 68
　　第四节　格律层面的比较分析 …………………………………… 68
　　第五节　小结 ……………………………………………………… 69

第八章　汉诗英译中的总体审度 ……………………………………… 73
　　第一节　何谓汉诗英译中的总体审度？ ………………………… 73
　　第二节　《大中华文库·楚辞》英译的总体审度 ………………… 75
　　第三节　小结 ……………………………………………………… 81

第九章　汉诗英译中的决策 …………………………………………… 85
　　第一节　《大中华文库·楚辞》英译的翻译决策 ………………… 85
　　第二节　翻译策略所产生的效果 ………………………………… 86
　　第三节　小结 ……………………………………………………… 89

第十章　汉诗英译中的考辨 …………………………………………… 93
　　第一节　考辨的必要性 …………………………………………… 93
　　第二节　若干疑难的考辨 ………………………………………… 93
　　第三节　小结 ……………………………………………………… 121

第十一章　汉诗英译中的逻辑调适 …………………………………… 124
　　第一节　逻辑调适的必要性 ……………………………………… 124
　　第二节　基于东西方思维差异而进行的介入与调适 …………… 124
　　第三节　基于原版本某些因素而进行的介入与调适 …………… 131
　　第四节　基于目的语的文本要求而进行的介入与调适 ………… 132
　　第五节　小结 ……………………………………………………… 132

第十二章　汉诗英译中的移情 ………………………………………… 134
　　第一节　何谓汉诗英译中的"移情"？ …………………………… 134

第二节　移情的理论依据 …………………………………… 134
　　第三节　移情的实践依据 …………………………………… 137

第十三章　汉诗英译中的"借形传神"及变通 …………… 143
　　第一节　"借形传神"及变通的必要性 …………………… 143
　　第二节　"借形传神"及变通的可行性 …………………… 145

第十四章　汉诗英译中的风格重构及变通 ………………… 158
　　第一节　风格的可知性和可译性 …………………………… 158
　　第二节　变通的理据和方法 ………………………………… 160
　　第三节　小结 ………………………………………………… 181

第十五章　汉诗英译中的"炼词" …………………………… 184
　　第一节　何谓汉诗英译中的"炼词"？ …………………… 184
　　第二节　利用英语构词法炼词 ……………………………… 184
　　第三节　从语义、语体和搭配关系等角度炼词 …………… 186
　　第四节　从修辞的角度炼词（句） ………………………… 190
　　第五节　小结 ………………………………………………… 193

第十六章　诗、词、曲、赋及楹联的诗化译法 …………… 196
　　第一节　诗、词、曲的语体色彩 …………………………… 196
　　第二节　诗、词、曲、赋和楹联的翻译 …………………… 197
　　第三节　诗化译法的若干技巧 ……………………………… 199

第十七章　对仗英译研究 ……………………………………… 208
　　第一节　关于对仗及其英译 ………………………………… 208
　　第二节　对仗英译方法的探讨 ……………………………… 208
　　第三节　小结 ………………………………………………… 214

附录　译者及著作者姓名缩略形式与全称对照表 ……………… 220
主要参考文献 ……………………………………………………… 222

前　言

　　理论可以影响人类的思维和行为方式。有的理论不仅能启迪心智、让人明理，而且还兼备认知功能（cognitive function）、解释功能（explanatory function）、方法论功能（methodological function）、评价功能（evaluative function）及预见功能（prophetical function），可以转化为想象力、创造力和生产力。从某种意义上说，掌握了一门理论就等于获得了观察、认识和解决问题的途径和方法。

　　本教程所依托的是诗学范式的汉诗英译理论。该理论具有科学性、原创性、实用性和系统性。从狭义上说，它对于汉诗英译具有指导意义；从广义上说，它对于中译外（例如典籍外译）和外译中（例如外国诗歌、小说汉译）都具有借鉴意义。

　　教程共17章。第一章介绍了汉诗的历史、品类、功能及汉诗英译的意义；第二、三章探讨了汉英两种诗歌的格律要素及典籍英译的本质属性，并对典籍英译者的必备条件进行了论述；第四章讨论了翻译的标准和原则；第五章揭示了诗歌的模糊性；第六、七章比较、分析了不同的翻译流派及其标准和方法，并建构起基于原作美学特征的译作评价体系。以上各章的内容，连同第十二章所包含的移情论（揭示汉诗英译的心理过程）、第十三章所包含的形式论（论证"形"与"神"的同构关系）、第十四章所包含的风格论（论述风格的可知性、可译性和风格变通的理据），属于本体论的范畴。而第五章所总结的模糊化翻译法，以及第八至十六章所涵盖的总体审度、翻译决策、疑难考辨、逻辑调适、移情翻译法、借形传神法、风格重构法、炼词炼句法、诗化翻译法以及对仗英译补偿法等等，则属于方法论范畴。

　　本教程是根据"学以致用""习之、好之、乐之"和"理论与实践相结合"的理念，为翻译专业本科生、翻译硕士生、翻译方向的普通研究生和广大的翻译爱好者编写的，旨在使学习者通过学理的掌握、学养的吸收和实践的磨炼，掌握典籍英译的基本理论和基本方法，不断提高自己的审美能力、思辨能力和翻译水平。每章章首的"学习目标"对该章的主旨加以提示，章末的思考题和练习题可选用于小组讨论、课堂提问或课外作业。教学内容和方法可根据不同的教学对象灵活调适、变通。例如，本科生可侧重欣赏能力和实践能力的训练，研究生可侧重理论学习和思辨能力的培养。

编者认为，若在合适的教育阶段，施教从难从严，让学生学会"攀高山"，那么，即便学生在其今后的人生路上只需要"履平地"，他们在该阶段所学的东西也依然不失为一笔丰厚而有价值的精神财富。

本教程所引用的译诗异彩纷呈，折射出各时期不同翻译流派的特色与辉煌。译者及著作者的姓名采用夹注或夹注的缩略形式，使用者可参看附录（译者及著作者姓名缩略形式与全称对照表）及主要参考文献。附录中的内容可供课外阅读和参考。

本教程的出版得到了北京大学出版社的大力支持，浙江师范大学"重点教材建设项目"以及浙江师范大学翻译系蒋林教授负责的"翻译省级重点建设专业"为本教程的出版提供了鼎力资助。在此谨向以上单位和个人致以诚挚谢意！

编者

2013年5月1日

写于浙江师范大学

典籍翻译研究所

第一章 汉诗及其英译

学习目标

通过本章的讨论,学习者应掌握汉诗的基本知识,了解中国文化的情势和典籍英译的意义。

第一节 汉诗及其社会功能

要翻译汉诗,首先就必须对汉诗的历史、样式、流派和特点有所了解。

以汉诗为代表的中国各民族的诗歌,包括诗、词、曲、赋以及楹联等,简称汉诗。和人类其他许多民族一样,华夏民族在其发展过程中产生了适合本身语言文化的诗歌形式,成为诗的国度。汉诗反映出华夏民族的价值观和文化品格,轩然霞举,折射着东方文化的绚丽光辉,是世界文化遗产中的一笔宝贵财富。

目前所知最早的诗歌是上古时期的《弹歌》("断竹,续竹,飞土,逐宍");最早的诗歌总集是《诗经》,其创作时间跨越西周初期与春秋中叶。

《诗经》多以四字句为主,按照配乐的不同分为风、雅、颂三种类型。"风"(土风、风谣)包括"十五国风"(周南、召南、邶、鄘、卫、王、郑、齐、魏、唐、秦、陈、邻、曹、豳),是《诗经》的核心内容;"雅"("大雅"、"小雅")是正声雅乐;"颂"是用以祭祀神明祖先的颂歌。

《诗经》常见的创作手法有赋、比、兴三种。"赋者,敷也,敷陈其事而直言之者也。"(朱熹:《诗集传》)这就是说,赋是指平铺直叙的表现手法。"比",就是用喻。由于喻体事物比本体事物更加生动具体、浅显易懂,比喻的使用就有助于激发联想。"兴",就是为了渲染气氛、创造意境而先言他物,以引起所咏之辞。

《诗经》生动地展现了中国周代的社会生活,真实地反映了奴隶社会从兴盛到衰败的历史面貌。其中的诗歌,有的形象地揭示出奴隶主残酷的压迫剥削,反映了奴隶们的觉醒和反抗精神,表达出人民的正义呼声和对理想生活的向

往；有的细腻地叙述了奴隶的劳动和生活状况，包括青年男女的相互爱慕、家庭和社会的束缚给青年男女带来的痛苦以及广大妇女的悲惨命运。《大雅》中的一些诗篇则反映了周部族的起源、发展和立国的历史。

与《诗经》一样，产生于两千多年前的《楚辞》是中国诗歌乃至中国文化的源头之一。楚国一带自古就有其独特的地方音乐，古称南风、南音；也有它独特的土风歌谣，如《说苑》中记载的《楚人歌》、《越人歌》和《沧浪歌》。楚人以歌舞娱神，使大量神话得以保存，使诗歌音乐得以迅速发展。春秋以后，一向被称为荆蛮的楚国日益强大。它在问鼎中原、争霸诸侯的过程中与北方各国频繁接触，促进了南北文化的广泛交流，楚国也受到北方中原文化的深刻影响。正是这种南北文化的汇合，孕育了屈原这样伟大的诗人和《楚辞》这样异彩纷呈的伟大诗篇。

屈原（约公元前339—公元前278），名平，出生于战国时期楚国的丹阳（今湖北秭归），是我国历史上杰出的政治家和第一位伟大的爱国诗人。他的崇高精神和伟大人格，惊天地而泣鬼神。据《续齐谐记》和《隋书·地理志》载，屈原投江的时间是农历五月五日。中国民间五月五端午节包粽子、赛龙舟的习俗就源于人们对屈原的景仰。1953年，屈原被列为世界四大文化名人之一，受到世界和平理事会和全世界人民的隆重纪念。

《离骚》是屈原的代表作，也是中国古代文学史上最长的一首浪漫主义的政治抒情诗。司马迁认为："《国风》好色而不淫，《小雅》怨诽而不乱，若《离骚》者，可谓兼之矣。"（《史记》）《天问》提出了170多个问题，涉及天文、地理、历史、社会、伦理、文学（神话、传说）、哲学等许多领域，表现了诗人对传统观念的大胆怀疑和追求真理的科学精神。《九歌》是在祭歌的基础上加工而成的11篇歌谣，诗中创造了大量神与巫的形象。《九章》（9篇）叙述诗人的遭际，抨击误国害民的群小，抒发诗人爱国爱民的情怀和政治理想。《远游》叙述诗人在"遭沈浊而淤秽"而又郁结难抒之际，"悲时俗之迫阨"，想象自己遨游于神仙世界，与众仙际遇，以此表达对真理的不倦追求和对故国的深厚热爱。《卜居》、《渔父》借占卜和与渔父的对话表达诗人崇高的人生观。《大招》是招魂曲词。这些作品闪耀着人道主义的光辉，表现了诗人忧国忧民、以天下为己任的使命感和刚正不阿、对祖国无限忠诚的崇高品格。

屈原以美人、鲜花象征"美政"的理想和高洁的品行，以臭物、萧艾比喻奸佞或变节的小人，使忠与奸、美与丑、善与恶形成鲜明的对照，产生言简意赅、言有尽而意无穷的艺术效果。他的作品形式上参差错落、灵活多变。采用大量典故和经过提炼的楚地方言，不但辞藻华美，富于乡土气息和艺术表现力，而且充满了积极的浪漫主义精神。其想象之大胆、奇特,古今罕有。"屈原辞赋悬日月,楚王台榭空山丘。"(李白:《江上吟》)诗人伟大的爱国主义和人文主义精神将彪炳千秋。

《楚辞》突破了《诗经》的表现形式,极大地丰富了诗歌的表现力,对汉赋的形成和后代的诗歌创作产生了深刻影响,为中国的诗歌创作开辟了一片新天地。

《诗经》的代表作是国风一类,而《楚辞》的代表作则是《离骚》,所以后世常用"风骚"指代所有的诗歌。《诗经》与《楚辞》对中国的文学和文化产生了深远的影响,成为其后产生的赋、古风、近体诗、词、曲和楹联等诗歌形式的源头活水。

赋是一种介于诗歌和散文之间的边缘文体,发源于《楚辞》,盛行于汉朝。它与诗、词的最大区别是不像诗那么讲究简练,在字数、长短等方面没有那么严格的限制。赋有骚体赋、四言诗体赋和散体赋(大赋)等类别。赋讲究用典铺陈,借景抒情,在句式上一般以四、六字句为主,错落有致;追求骈偶、华丽的辞藻和细腻的描写,具有诗的节奏和声律特征。有一部分赋(文赋)吸取了散文的特点,格式相对宽松。由于过分注重形式,赋在唐代的古文运动之后便逐渐失去了活力。

配乐演唱的乐府诗也是在汉代时形成的。乐府诗相当于现在的歌词,有"曲"、"辞"、"歌"、"行"等类别,其中较著名的有《上邪》、《陌上桑》、《木兰辞》、《孔雀东南飞》等。三国时期以建安文学为代表的诗歌作品,例如曹操的《短歌行》、《薤露行》、《蒿里行》、《苦寒行》等,吸收了乐府诗的营养,为后来格律更为严谨的"近体诗"奠定了基础。唐朝以后仍然有相当多的诗人以乐府曲名创作。虽然随着乐曲古谱的逐渐散失,古乐府逐渐失去了影响力,但以歌配词的做法仍然得到传承和发展,形成了后来的词。

古体诗(古风)指的是唐朝以前不配乐的诗,它与近体诗(格律诗)、乐府诗构成了狭义的古诗三大类别。近体诗是南北朝时期出现、至唐朝而成熟的诗体,其特点是讲究格律,即从字数、平仄、用韵、对仗等方面来规范诗作。

唐朝(618—907)是中国诗歌发展的黄金时代,可谓云蒸霞蔚,名家辈出。《全唐诗》收编的诗歌多达四万余首,其形式、内容和风格丰富多彩。唐诗继承了汉魏民歌和乐府的优良传统,大大发展了歌行体的样式。在五言、七言古诗的基础上发展起来的近体诗,把我国古典诗歌的音节和谐、文字精练的艺术特色,提高到一个全新的境界,为古代抒情诗找到一种最为优美的形式。

近体诗有两种,一种叫做绝句,一种叫做律诗。绝句和律诗又各有五言和七言之别。唐诗的基本形式有五言古体诗、七言古体诗、五言绝句、七言绝句、五言律诗和七言律诗。

相对而言,古体诗对音韵格律的要求比较宽松,一首诗的句数可多可少,篇章可长可短,韵脚可以变换。近体诗对音韵格律的要求则比较严,一首诗的句数有限定,平仄声须遵循一定的规律,韵脚不能随意转换;其中律诗还要求中间的四句(颔联与颈联)构成对仗。

唐诗题材广泛,从自然现象、政治事件、劳动生活、社会风习直至个人的思想情感,包罗万象。其中有的从侧面反映当时的社会状况和阶级矛盾,揭露现实的黑暗;有的歌颂正义战争,反对侵略,抒发爱国的思想;有的描绘山河的秀丽多娇,表达对大自然的热爱;有的抒写个人的抱负和遭际,诉说人生悲欢,表达儿女爱慕之情,等等。在创作方法上,既有现实主义的流派,也有浪漫主义的流派,而许多伟大的作品,则又是这两种创作方法相结合的典范。著名诗人李白、杜甫分别被誉为诗仙和诗圣。诗集《唐诗三百首》家喻户晓,从前一直被当做儿童的主要启蒙书籍。

骈文是另一种韵文的体裁,初期主要强调对偶,到了南北朝吸收了汉赋的特点,开始注重用韵,体例越来越拘束,常常空有其表。

词即唱辞。隋、唐的歌者杂用胡夷里巷之曲(少数民族和民间的歌谣曲谱),如"菩萨蛮"、"苏幕遮"等,配以歌词,于是便形成一种新兴的歌诗。词有小令、中调、长调。相对来说,长调字数多韵疏。词中的诗句看似长短不齐,而实际上有其定格。一般须依声填词、依乐分片(阕)、依拍造句、依调用字。因其"出身卑微",形似简陋,语近粗俗,加上创作者的社会地位往往比较低下,词在开始时颇受歧视。唐代元和之后,文人中填词的逐渐增多。他们的作品精致凝练、细腻华美,使词逐渐脱离其原始状态,确立其作为正式文人文学体裁的地位。

开始时,词专写爱情。到了宋代,范仲淹、欧阳修赋予词以新的内容,拓展了词的题材,而柳永则创造了"长调",丰富了词的形式。在前人的基础上,苏轼扩大了词的思想境界,使之升华为可以表达各种思想、描绘各种社会生活的文学样式。词逐步与音乐分离,改变了其作为音乐的附庸的地位。以苏为代表的豪放派迎来了词的黄金时代,对中国的诗歌乃至中国文学产生了深远的影响。苏逝世后,诗文革新运动即行分化。黄庭坚、陈师道建立江西诗派,周邦彦创立格律派,而秦观和贺铸则各树一帜。

爱国题材在南宋初年便为进步文学所垂青。辛派诗人如陆游、辛弃疾、陈亮、刘过、刘克庄等代表着豪放派的主流,其作品在思想上忧国忧民,在风格上热情奔放,在艺术上炉火纯青。该时期的著名诗人还有岳飞、张元干、张孝祥、范成大和杨万里等。伟大的女词人李清照代表婉约派,著名诗人陈以义代表江西诗派,也参加了南宋爱国主义交响乐的大演奏,发出了惊天地、泣鬼神的音符。

乐府产生的时代远早于词;乐府曲名有别于词牌名;乐府是先有曲,后有文字,反之,早期的词牌则一般是为了配合原有的诗作。尽管如此,由于乐府与词的亲缘关系,人们有将词称为乐府的。例如,苏轼的词集就有《东坡乐府》的别称。

词曾一度趋向衰微,后又繁荣滋长,至今仍受青睐。

自元代开始,文学创作的主流逐渐转移到戏曲、小说等形式。元曲是配乐的,也讲究节奏和用韵。元曲包括元杂剧(由套数组成的曲文,间以宾白和科范,用于舞台演出)和散曲(包括小令、带过曲和套数,用作清唱的歌词)。

在体制上,元曲包含:1)宫调(中国古代音乐的调式),如"仙吕宫"、"南吕宫"、"中吕宫"等,各具声情;2)曲牌(俗称"曲子",即对各种曲调的泛称,如《点绛唇》、《山坡羊》等,各有其曲调、唱法);3)曲韵(平仄通押,不避重韵,一韵到底);4)平仄(在用字的平仄上比诗词更严,对末句的平仄更是注重);5)对仗(对仗要求比较自由,可平仄相对,也可平声相对,即平声对平声,仄声对仄声);6)衬字(在曲律规定的字数之外所增加的字)。

就散曲而言,其形式和词很接近。不过,在格律上词严而曲松;在语体上词雅而曲俗。散曲按体式可分为小令(又叫叶儿,体制短小)和散套(由多支曲子组成,要求一韵贯串始终),曲牌近乎俚俗(例如《叨叨令》、《山坡羊》等)。

元杂剧所具有的叙事功能使其逐渐脱离韵文的局限,因而在成就上远远超过了散曲。由于可以添加衬字或增句,在韵律上又允许平仄通押,曲有定格而不呆板,比诗词具有更大的灵活性。元曲既承袭了诗词的清丽婉转,又泼辣、大胆,可以咏志抒怀,反映社会生活,具有较强的战斗性,深为人民群众所钟爱。例如,关汉卿的《窦娥冤》通过窦娥蒙冤的事件叙述和人物形象刻画,控诉了社会的黑暗,表现了十分强烈的反抗精神,惊天地而泣鬼神。关汉卿、马致远、白朴、郑光祖并称"元曲四大家"。

元曲题材广泛,语言通俗,形式活泼,风格清新,手法多变,深刻地揭露了社会现实,是中国文学百花园中的奇葩。

楹联有偶语、俪辞、联语等通称。楹联言简意赅,雅俗共赏,有"诗中之诗"的美称。早在秦汉时期,民间就有在过年时悬挂桃符的习俗,即把具有避邪驱鬼法力的"神荼"、"郁垒"的名字写在两块桃木板上,分别悬挂于门的两侧,以求安康。由于这种渊源关系，古人便称春联为"桃符"。"对联"之称则始于明代。对联有四言、五言、六言、七言等句式，讲究平仄、对仗、用典，具有诗歌的特点。它语句凝练，与书法珠联璧合，可构成绚丽多彩的独立语篇。古人有以对对子的方式比拼才智，或是考验一个人是否有灵性和才学的。

楹联有各种类别。根据贴挂的位置，有门联、中堂联和楹柱联等；根据用途，有春联、贺联、挽联、赠联、自勉联、行业联、言志联等；根据对偶形式，则有言对、事对、正对、反对、工对、宽对、流水对、回文对和顶针对。通常使用比喻、夸张、反诘、双关和设问等修辞手法，谐音、嵌字、隐字、复字、叠字、偏旁、析字和拆字等用字技巧，并列、转折、选择和因果等逻辑结构。

楹联与诗、词、曲、赋、骈文一样，属于文学范畴，是我国独特的文化瑰宝。对联还传入越南、朝鲜、日本、新加坡等周边国度。

孔子说："小子何莫学夫《诗》？《诗》可以兴，可以观，可以群，可以怨。"（《论语·阳货》）这是孔子对诗歌的社会功能的高度概括，开创了中国文学批评史的源头。

所谓"兴"，据舜所说："诗言志，歌永言，声依永，律和声"（《尚书·尧典》）；据庄子说："诗以道志"（《庄子·天下篇》）；据孔安国注，就是"引譬连类"；据朱熹注，就是"感发意志"。这就是说，诗是可以用比兴的方法抒发思想感情，从而感染、影响读者的。

所谓"观"，据郑玄注，是"观风俗之盛衰"；据朱熹注，是"考见得失"。这就是说，诗歌是反映社会现实生活的，因此通过诗歌可以帮助读者认识风俗的盛衰，民心的向背和政治的得失。《孔丛子·巡狩篇》记载："古者天子命史采歌谣，以观民风"；《汉书·食货志》记载，周朝朝廷派出专门的使者在农忙时到全国各地采集民谣，由周朝史官汇集整理后给天子看，目的是了解民情。朝廷根据诗歌所反映的人心向背，在必要时修改法令，调整政策。

所谓"群"，据孔安国注，指"群居相切磋"；据朱熹注，是"和而不流"。这就是说，诗可以帮助人沟通感情，互相切磋砥砺，以提高自身的修养和群体的凝聚力。

所谓"怨"，孔安国注曰："怨刺上政。"即是说，诗可以批评指责执政者为政之失，抒发对苛政的怨愤。

孔子的话也可以解释为，诗歌具有表达功能、认识功能、政治功能、凝聚功能和社会矫正功能。此外，诗歌也有其教育功能和测试功能。按照诗教的传统，人们用诗歌来修身养性、教育子女、培养人才；诗歌还可以用来检视个人的气质和才思——民间用以交友、择婿，朝廷以此录用官吏（例如，白居易的《赋得古原草送别》便是应试的命题诗作)。

第二节　汉诗英译及其意义

一、典籍的英译"就时间论,西人居先"。

英国对中国古典文学的介绍是从间接翻译开始的。法国耶稣会士杜赫德根据传教士们所提供的材料编成《中华帝国全志》,于 1735 年出版。该书收有《诗经》数首。英国很快就出版了该书的两种英译本:一种是 R. 布鲁克斯(R. Brookes)的节译本,书名改为《中国通史》,1736 年出版;第二种是爱德华·凯夫(Edward Cave)的全译本,从 1738 年到 1744 年陆续出版。(马祖毅,1997:222—223)其后,威廉·琼斯爵士(Sir William Jones,1746—1794)也尝试过诗经的翻译。19 世纪的里雅各(James Legge,1815—1935)、德庇时(J. F. Davis,1795—1890)和翟理思(Herbert Allen Giles,1845—1935)被合称为"19 世纪英国汉学的三大星座",他们都翻译过中国诗歌,且成就斐然。继之而起且从事《诗经》、《楚辞》、陶(渊明)诗、唐诗等诗歌翻译的汉学家中,杰出的有亚瑟·韦利(Arthur Waley,1888—1966)、戴维·霍克斯(David Hawkes)和伯顿·沃森(Burton Watson)等。加拿大、新西兰、澳大利亚、日本等国的汉学家中,从事汉诗英译的有 D. Bryant,Rewi Alley(1897—1987),Hugh Dunn(1923—　)和小畑熏良等。(马祖毅,1997:223—228)

琼斯爵士(Sir William Jones,1746—1794)在翻译《卫风·淇奥》时,对该诗颇为欣赏,并开始注意汉诗的美学特征。他认为:"这首诗非常庄严,又非常简洁,每行只有四个字,因此省略是常有的事,但风格上的晦涩,却增加它的壮丽。……所以这首诗,可以说是远古文明最有价值的瑰宝。这也可以证明,诗在任何民族,任何时代,都被重视,而且在任何地域,都采用同样的意象。"(马祖毅,1997:227)这些议论带有比较诗学的色彩。

德庇时爵士主张:"为了真正欣赏中国诗歌和其他诗歌,韵文正是迻译它们的形式。"(《中国诗歌》)(马祖毅,1997:233)翟里斯采取直译押韵的诗体形式。诗体派后来的代表人物是 John Turner。

里雅各开始倾向于散译,认为应当尽可能贴近字面,不增译,不意释,但后来也推出自己的《诗经》韵译本。

韦利在其《中国诗一百七十首》中所附"翻译方法"专文里,说他的方法是逐字逐句直译,采用不押韵的自由形式,认为用韵势必害义。吕叔湘先生对此颇为赞同:"不同语言有不同之音律,欧洲语言同出一系,尚且各有独特的诗体,以英语与汉语相去之远,其诗体自不能苟且相同。初期译人好以诗体翻译,即令达意,风格已殊,稍不慎,流弊丛生。故小畑、Waley、Bynner 诸氏率用散体为之,原诗情趣,转为保存。此中得失,可发深省。"(马祖毅,1997:243)茅盾先生也认为,对于格律"不如不管,而用散体去翻译"。(《中国翻译》,1986:11)

韦利的学生霍克斯在 1959 年由牛津大学出版的 *Ch'u Tz'u: The Song of the South: An Ancient Chinese Anthology* 中"采取介乎逐字逐句与自由翻译之间的中间道路",在译文中加进大量注释(annotations)。他认为,韵固然重要,义更须优先。(《中国翻译》,1986:235)

逐字翻译派的代表人物是 Wills Barnstone,Burton Watson 属于散体派,Ezra Pound 属于仿译派。

艾黎(Rewi Alley)译诗,通常牺牲韵和节奏,被当做现代派的代表。他认为,任何纯粹的直译都不会是正确的翻译,应当抓住精神的传达。赵朴初先生颇有同感,说:"诗歌语言之美总是和一个民族的语言特征分不开的,是不可能翻为另一种语言文字的。"建议译者研究艾黎的办法。

诸多外国汉学家出于对学术和中国诗词的热爱,努力克服文化、语言的种种障碍,在黑暗中苦苦摸索前行。他们不仅留下了十分珍贵的语料,而且开创了汉诗英译及其研究的伟业,促进了中西方文化交流。

二、汉诗是中国典籍的组成部分,其英译的意义必须从典籍英译的意义谈起。

一个民族的生存发展既有赖于其政治、经济、军事实力,又有赖于其文化活力。这里所谓的文化是从狭义上说的,它指一个民族的意识形态,包括价值观、天人观、信念、信仰、态度、语言、风俗习惯等,以及相关的组织、机构;它既反映经济与政治,又作用于经济与政治。文化活力不但指某一文化实体本身延续和发展的能力,还指其与他文化相互依存的能力和对于他文化的影响力。

文化活力是综合国力的重要因素之一,它与民族兴亡息息相关。楼兰古国灭亡之后,其文化遂成历史;玛雅人公元前 3 世纪即有象形文字和高度发达的农业、数学、历法,他们建立起来的国家 10 世纪衰落,16 世纪灭亡,其文化也随之消亡。西方列强在殖民时期实行文化扩张(包括语言传播),日本侵略者在占领台湾时期甚至限制中国人说汉语,之所以如此,也正是由于它们看到了文化活力的重要性。

　　文化活力的强弱是可以进行量化测定的。目前可以接受的量化方法之一就是看某个特定民族被翻译为外文的文化典籍数量在其总量中所占的比例。在文化典籍的被译量方面，建国仅二百余年的美国远远高于具有七千年文明史的中国。这主要是由于美国综合国力强大，但与其重视对外宣传和在该项工作的巨大投入也有一定关系。据统计，2007年我国图书、报纸、期刊累计进口2亿多美元，累计出口仅有3700多万美元；在版权贸易方面，2008年中国引进图书版权15776种，输出图书版权2440种。根据韦努蒂（Lawrence Venuti）在 *Rethinking Translation：Discourse，Subjectivity，Ideology* 前言所提供的数字，英美输入的翻译著作远远低于其他国家，仅占2%至3%。这足以说明，东西方文化落差巨大。近年虽有所改观，但局面并无根本变化。为了中国的国家安全和文化安全，对于这个事实我们千万不能掉以轻心！

　　值得庆幸的是，首先，我们有七千年的文明史，文化积淀丰富厚重。河姆渡考古发现说明，我们的祖先最迟在七千年前就种植水稻；早在几千年前，我们就有《周易》这样的哲学巨著问世，老子就提出辩证法，主张博爱，指出宇宙"大象无形"（参看《道德经》），孟子就提倡"民为贵，社稷次之，君为轻"（《孟子·尽心下》）的思想，我们的祖先就笃信"天人合一"的理念，注意环境保护和生态平衡。就"天人合一"而言，不但思想深刻，而且制度完善。《吕氏春秋》记载，在环保方面人们一年四季都必须有所遵循。孟春"乃修祭典，命祀山林川泽。牺牲无用牝，禁止伐木，无覆巢，无杀孩虫胎夭飞鸟，无麛无卵，……无变天之道，无绝地之理，无乱人之纪"；仲春"无作大事，以妨农功。是月也，无竭川泽，无漉陂池，无焚山林"；季春"田猎毕弋，……馁兽之药，无出九门"；孟夏"无起土功，无发大众，无伐大树"；仲夏"令民无刈蓝以染，无烧炭，无暴布，……游牝别其群"；季夏"乃命虞人，入山行木，无或斩伐"；孟秋"命百官，始收敛，完堤防，谨拥塞，以备水潦"；仲秋"凡举事无逆天数，必顺其时，乃因其类"等等。这些简单的事例说明，我们民族在思想上、行为上都为世界文明的发展和人类共同家园的保护作出过无与伦比的贡献。其次，在华夏民族的历史上，每当民族危亡、道德沦丧、礼崩乐坏、大厦将倾的时候，就必有仁者出。先知先觉鸣钟警世，奔走呼号，启发民心民智，使华夏民族万众一心，共赴国难，最终化险为夷。几千年来文明与国家同在，这其中必有值得我们自豪、自尊的道理，自强、自立的根据。

　　今天，金融危机、生态危机、精神危机和价值危机正深刻影响着人类社会的健康发展，人类的命运又一次面临严峻的挑战。如何应对这些问题和挑战？对此存在不同的态度和战略。文化霸权主义者、文化殖民主义者试图通过削弱第三世界的文化活力,实现文化吞并,以长久掌握霸主的话语权,而世界上的有识之士则站在全人类生存与发展的高度,检视东西方哲学,以融合、筛选、提炼出一种超越种族、国家、地理界限的新世纪人类精神,使各族文化共存互补,营造和谐的世界,造福子孙后代。我们应抱着"国家兴亡,匹夫有责"的历史责任感,思考一下作为一个中国人,自己在修身养性方面该做些什么,在重新建构民族的核心价值体系方面自己又能做些什么。在这方面,我们作为外语学习者和工作者,同样是可以有所作为的。典籍外译——包括汉诗英译——就是我们可以做的一项有意义的工作。

典籍英译的意义主要有以下几方面:

(1) 中国学者翻译自己民族的典籍,是以中国自己的概念来诠释中国思想的一种方式。法国哲学家于连(François Jullien)认为:"现在到了对中国思想进行重新检索的时候了。这种检索不是用西方的哲学概念对中国思想传统进行重新诠释,也不是回到过去,而是以中国自己的概念来诠释中国思想。一方面避免堕入虚假的普世主义的旋涡,另一方面以重新检讨过的中国思想光华来丰富世界思想,从而避免陷入民族主义的陷阱。"(王岳川,2008:11)萨义德(Edward W. Said)、斯皮瓦克(Gayatri C. Spivak)和霍米·巴巴(Homi K. Bhabha)等人的后殖民理论批判了文化霸权主义,认为翻译是文化建构的工具,既可用以殖民化,也可用以抵御殖民化。他们为我们开展典籍翻译,以消解、抵御政治霸权和文化殖民的影响提供了理据。

(2) 典籍外译的过程也是新经典的创造和建构的过程。任何民族的典籍都是符号化了的民族文化,是具有学术或艺术生命力的开放的系统。中国典籍的外译赋予了典籍以新的生命力、生命形态和生存空间。这将会悄然显现华夏民族的本来形象,维护中国的文化安全,巩固中国文化在世界上的地位和身份,促进各国各民族之间的相互理解,增强华夏民族的文化活力。

中华民族勤劳智慧,热爱和平,对世界文明作出了卓绝的贡献;华夏文化源远流长,博大精深;作为华夏文明精髓的典籍(包括汉、壮、藏、蒙、回等等历代各领域的权威性著作)浩如沧海,灿若明珠,是全人类共同的宝贵精神财富。和《诗经》、《楚辞》一样,壮族《布洛陀史诗》、藏族文化宝典《格萨尔王传》、蒙古民间叙事长诗《嘎达梅林》都是中华各族人民所创造的诗歌经典,都让我们为自己民族的辉煌文化感到自豪。由于英语是世界上广泛应用的语言,典籍英译自然构成文化传播的重要方面。它对于弘扬民族文化、促进东西方文化融汇、保持中国固有的文化身份,显然有着十分重大的现实意义。中国要生存、发展,就必须加强文化的传播与交流。在这种传播与交流中,典籍英译不可或缺。

(3) 典籍外译还将作为民族核心价值体系建构的一个工作层面,启迪国人检视本族文化的价值,树立民族自豪感和自尊心,实现自我文化认同,并在对于传统的继承与对于文化的创新中重塑民族的灵魂。所谓民族的核心价值体系,就是该民族所共同尊奉和信仰的核心哲学思想体系,包括价值观、天人观、道德观和伦理观等。它具有稳定性、规约性、生发性和普遍性,能够衍生出信念、信仰、态度、语言习惯和风俗习惯等等,并制约着它们的发展与变化。一个人没有信仰是可悲的,因为那就等于没有灵魂,没有正确的言行价值准则和判断真、善、美与假、恶、丑的标准;一个民族没有共同的信仰是危险的,因为它对内没有凝聚力,对外没有影响力,难以形成可攻可守的文化战略,思想上撑不起一面能够指引和鼓舞大众的鲜明旗帜。

由于典籍外译作品既能使人接受优秀传统文化的熏陶,又有助于外语和翻译的学习与研究,因此拥有广大的华人读者群。在耳濡目染、潜移默化之中,读者的灵魂将得以升华。

(4) 在学术上,典籍英译及其研究将通过探讨典籍英译的特殊性,揭示翻译的普遍性,推进译学研究。近年来,典籍英译研究成就斐然,专著、论文质优量大,所探讨的很多学术问题是前人未曾涉及的,所作出的解答是十分富于创造性的。典籍英译及研究这一生机勃发的方面军在中国译学理论建设中的奉献将是丰厚而宝贵的。

《楚辞·渔父》描述了屈原与渔父的对话,表现了两种人生观的碰撞。其中有这样的诗句:

> 吾闻之,新沐者必弹冠,新浴者必振衣;
> 安能以身之察察,受物之汶汶者乎!
> 宁赴湘流,葬於江鱼之腹中。
> 安能以皓皓之白,而蒙世俗之尘埃乎!

陆游《鹊桥仙》一词则表现了淡泊名利、超然物外的境界:

> 一竿风月,
> 一蓑烟雨,
> 家在钓台西住。
> 卖鱼生怕近城门,
> 况肯到、红尘深处?
> 潮生理棹,

潮平系缆,
潮落浩歌归去。
时人错把比严光,
我自是、无名渔父。

在物欲横流、人心不古的险恶环境中,保持"皓皓之白",尤为可贵。在学习汉诗英译的同时以诗歌陶冶情操,使自己与"红尘深处"保持一段安全距离,令我们的精神家园少一些粗俗、丑恶,多几分高雅、善良,不亦乐乎?学会汉诗英译和典籍英译,近可修身养性、完善自我,远能安身立命、报效祖国,不亦乐乎?既然如此,那就让我们来习之、好之、乐之!

思考题

1. 什么是民族的文化活力?为什么说典籍英译与我国的文化活力息息相关?
2. 典籍英译的意义何在?
3. 你懂得什么民族语言?对民族典籍有何了解?
4. 你是否在挖掘、整理和翻译民族典籍方面具有民族、地缘、专业技能等优势?你准备为民族典籍的英译和传播做些什么?

练习题

1. 请以"⌒"代表平声、"⌣"代表仄声,标出下面这首七绝的平仄:
 水光潋艳晴方好,山色空蒙雨亦奇。
 欲把西湖比西子,淡妆浓抹总相宜。
 ——苏轼

2. 律诗的3、4句称为颔联,5、6句称为颈联。按格律,颔联、颈联都必须使用对仗。试分析下面两首诗的对仗:
 (1) 登高
 风急天高猿啸哀,渚清沙白鸟飞回。
 无边落木萧萧下,不尽长江滚滚来。
 万里悲秋常作客,百年多病独登台。

艰难苦恨繁霜鬓，潦倒新停浊酒杯。

　　　　　　　　　　　　　　　　——（唐）杜甫

2) 赴戍登程口占示家人（其二）

　　力微任重久神疲，再竭衰庸定不支。
　　苟利国家生死以，岂因祸福避趋之！
　　谪居正是君恩厚，养拙刚于戍卒宜。
　　戏与山妻谈故事，试吟断送老头皮。

　　　　　　　　　　　　　　　　——（清）林则徐

3. 上面第二首诗有以下两种不同英译。凭直觉你喜欢哪种？

(1) Oral Compositions to My Family upon Leaving for the Frontier (No. 2)

I couldn't have been able any longer to sustain
The vital post, which has tir'd this unworthy person out.
Whate'er's in th' interest of the state I'll do with might and main,
And personal weal or woe is not to be car'd about.
Demotion only shows His Majesty's favour, and life
In th' frontier will perfectly suit my mortal dim and dull.
Let me, on leaving, retell a story to my dear wife
And read aloud the poem therein 'bout "forfeiting th' old skull".
(zzy,1996:317)

(2) Before Going into Exile

Weary for long with feeble strength and duty great,
Mediocrity exhausted, could I not sink low?
I'd risk life and brave death to do good to the state.
Could I but for myself seek weal and avoid woe?
The banishment just show the royal favor high;
My border service is good to do what I can.
I tease my wife with a story of days gone by:
Why not try to chant verse to see off your old man?
(xyz,2000:295)

第二章　汉英两种诗歌的格律要素

学习目标

　　翻译诗歌，无疑必须对有关诗歌的格律有所了解，否则便难以透彻理解原作的艺术含义，最大限度地再现或重构原诗的美学价值。格律（prosody or metrical rules）是诗歌在节奏（rhythm/cadence）、押韵（rhyming）、诗节（stanza）与诗句（行）长短（line length）等方面的规定。能使诗歌获得音乐美和形体美的两大格律要素是节奏和押韵。通过本章的讨论，学习者应对格律有更多的了解和更深的认识。

第一节　节奏

　　汉诗的基本单位是句，若干句构成一首诗。汉诗是利用字在音长（duration）和声调（tone）上的差异，以平声字与仄声字互协的方式实现节奏的。"顿"，类似音乐中的"拍"，是基本的节奏单位。若以粗体代表韵，斜体代表破格（即本该平声而用了仄声，反之亦然），"＿"和"￨"分别代表平仄声，隔字符"/"代表顿，那么，王之涣《登鹳雀楼》一诗的格律就可以这样来表示：

　　　　白日／依山／尽，黄河／入海／流。
　　　　欲穷／千里／目，更上／一层／楼。

　　有时，为了充分发挥文采或自由表达思想，诗人在万不得已的情况下可以"破格"，即不依常格。破格的诗句叫"拗句"。破格是有条件的。"一三五不论，二四六无情"指的是，一行诗的第一、第三、第五个字可以破格。（这个口诀易记，但是不够严谨）若一行五言诗因破格而除了韵脚之外仅存一个平声字，那就是犯了"孤平"的大忌，按要求必须进行"拗救"，即在合适的仄声位置补上平声。这可以通过本句自救，也可以通过对句相救。

汉诗还有另一格律因素，那就是对仗。例如"天"对"地"，"高"对"低"，"动"对"静"。律诗的颔联和颈联是要求对仗的。此外，对仗在绝句、骈文、辞赋、对联中也得到广泛的运用。上面这首绝句中的首联就用了对仗——虽然这并非格律的要求。

英诗的基本单位是行(line)，若干行构成一个诗节(stanza)，若干诗节构成一个诗章(canto)。也有些英诗是不分诗节的，这种诗体称作连续体(continuous verse)。

英诗是利用音节的重读(stressed)与非重读(unstressed)，按一定规律实现节奏的，基本节奏单位是音步(foot)。音步有单音步(monometer)、双音步(dimeter)、三音步(trimeter)、四音步(tetrameter)、五音步(pentameter)、六音步(hexameter)、七音步(heptameter)、八音步(octameter)。分析诗歌的格律，将它划分成音步，辨别出是何种音步，并计算出音步的数量，这种音步划分程序就叫音步分辨(scansion)。

常用音步及其例子如下：

(1) 抑扬格(the iambus)，即由一个轻读音节与一个重读音节构成一个音步，例如：The val/iant nev/er taste/of death/but once (Shakespeare, *Julius Caesar*)

(2) 抑抑扬格(the anapaest)，即二轻一重构成一音步，例如：In the morn/ing of life,/when the cares/are unknown (Thomas Moore, *In the Morning of Life*)

(3) 扬抑格(the trochee)，即一重带一轻，例如：Then the/little/Hia/watha learned of/every/bird its/language (Longfellow, *The Song of Hiawatha*)

(4) 扬抑抑格(the dactyl)，即一重带两轻，例如：Touch her not/scornfully; Think of her/mournfully (Thomas Hood, *The Bridge of Sighs*)

英诗也有类似汉诗破格的情况，称为"变格"(variations in rhythm)。变格也有规律可循：扬抑格与扬抑抑格都是下降的节奏，可以相互替代(substitution)；同理，作为上升的节奏，抑扬格与抑抑扬格也可以相互替代。

第二节　押韵

押韵具有使结构完美、层次清晰、音响和谐、形象丰满、意义彰显的功能。诗有诗律,词有词谱。一般来说,汉诗(包括词、曲、赋等)是按格律规定押韵的。例如,《忆江南》的词谱是:

平平仄,
仄仄仄平**平**。
仄仄平平平仄仄,
平平仄仄仄平**平**。
仄仄仄平**平**。

白居易的词:

江南好,
风景旧曾**谙**。
日出江花红胜火,
春来江水绿如**蓝**。
能不忆江**南**?

就是按词谱规定的韵律,在二、四、五行分别用谙、蓝、南作为韵脚的。

英诗用韵的主要方式是头韵(alliteration)和尾韵(rhyme)。什么是头韵和尾韵呢? 我们可以举些浅显的例子加以说明:习语 as *fit* as a *fiddle* 和 with *might* and *main* 分别是用单词的开头辅音 f 和 m 押了头韵;而谚语 Harm s*et*, harm g*et* 和 No p*ains*, no g*ains* 则是押了尾韵。在 Harm s*et*, harm g*et* 这个谚语中,单词 *set* 与 *get* 的元音及其后接的辅音相同,而元音前的辅音(s 和 g)则不同,这种韵就叫单音节韵,属于阳性韵;阴性韵则有双音节韵和三音节韵。双音节韵要求押韵词的相同重读音节之后带有一个发音相同的轻读音节,例如 b*orrow* 与 s*orrow*;三音节韵则要求押韵词的重读音节后带有发音相同的两个轻读音节,例如 bea*utiful* 与 d*utiful*。

上文所讨论的称为完全韵(perfect rhyme),其他的押韵方式还有:

A. 不完全韵(imperfect rhyme),包括:

a. 全同韵(identical rhyme),即词或音节发音完全相同的押韵方式,如 see — sea, blue — blew。

b. 眼韵(eye rhyme),即听觉上不构成韵脚而拼写上却看起来像是押韵的押韵方式,如 blood — stood,swallow — shallow,have — grave,watch-catch。

c. 近似韵(approximate rhyme),例如雪莱(P. B. Shelly) *Song to the Men of England* 中的两行"Wherefore, Bees of England, *forge* /Many a weapon, chain and *scourge*",以及胡德(T. Hood)的 *The Bridge of Sighs* 中的"Look at her *garments*/Clinging like *cerements*;/Whilst the wave *constantly*/Drips from her clothing;/Take her up *instantly*, Loving, not loathing"等诗行中,forge 与 scourge, garments 与 cerements, constantly 与 instantly 押的就是表现在音质方面的近似韵。此外还有表现在重音方面的近似韵,这里指的是以下各种情况:(1) -y, -ment, -ite 等结尾的罗曼斯语词汇可以承受格律重音,与相应的重读音节押韵,例如 sea — liberty, bent — instrument, infinite — night;(2)日耳曼语词汇的派生词尾 -ing, -er, -ess, -ly 等,在中古英语中可以与重读音节押韵,在现代英语中,-ly 作为例外,依然具有这种功能,例如,下面诗句中的 be 与 invisibly 是押韵的:

> Never seek to tell thy love,
> Love that never told can *be*;
> For the gentle wind doth move
> Silently, invisib*ly*.
> (Blake, *Love's Secret*)

B. 辅音韵(consonance),例如 be*st* — wor*st*;

C. 似韵(pararhyme),例如 *mill* — *meal*;

D. 准韵(assaonance 又译为"腹韵"),例如 m*a*d—h*a*t, f*i*sh—sw*i*m, str*ea*m—gr*ee*n, rh*y*me—t*i*ght;

E. 回逆韵(reverse rhyme),例如 *mad*—*dam*;

F. 同源词韵(paregmenon),例如 *success* — *succeed*;

G. 后缀韵(homeoteleuton),例如 shoot*ing* — aim*ing*, sick*ness*—busi*ness*。

英诗同样有自己的韵式(rhyme scheme)。以四行诗(the quatrain/the four-linestanza)为例,其韵式有联韵(couplet rhyme,即 a a b b)、套韵(alternate/interlaced rhyme,即 a b a b)、间韵(intermittent rhyme,即 a b c b)、抱韵(enclosing rhyme,即 a b b a)等多种。

若要进一步了解汉英诗歌的格律,学习者可参考王力先生所著的《诗词格律》和吴翔林先生所著的《英诗格律及自由诗》。

思考题

1. 汉英诗歌在节奏、押韵方面有何异同？

2. 音乐美是人类的共同审美取向，汉英两种语言的不少谚语、俗话也反映出这种取向。试举例说明之。

3. 王维《山居秋暝》的不同英译是如何在形式（格律）上与原作寻求近似（approximation to the original in form）的？

原作：

空山新雨后，天气晚来秋。
明月松间照，清泉石上流。
竹喧归浣女，莲动下渔舟。
随意春芳歇，王孙自可留。

译文 1: *An Autumn Eve during My Stay in the Mounts*

The rain has lent a new charm to the heights,
And autumn's so real in the eve of day.
A serene moon through tall pines shifts its light,
A limpid spring on rough rocks winds its way.
A bustle from the bamboos does announce
The girls' return from bleaching, and the leaves
Of lotus for a fishing boat make way,
Which seems to slide and bounce.
Though flowers may wither, and fall the leaves,
Princes would yearn to hither stay.
(zzy,1996:104)

译文 2: *An Autumn Evening in the Hills*

Through empty hills new washed by rain
As dusk descends the autumn comes;
Bright moonlight falls through pines,
Clear springs flow over stones;
The bamboos rustle as girls return from washing,
Lotus stir as a fishing boat casts off;

Faded the fragrance of spring,

Yet, friend, there is enough to keep you here.

(yxy & gy,2001:36)

练习题

1. 标出刘禹锡《乌衣巷》这首诗中每个字的平仄声：

  朱雀桥边野草花，乌衣巷口夕阳斜。

  旧时王谢堂前燕，飞入寻常百姓家。

2. 上面这首诗的首行按格律应是"仄仄平平仄仄平"，但首字"朱"却是平声字。是诗人错了吗？请解释。

3. 以下是 Burns 的诗 *A Red, Red Rose* 的第一个诗节。试分辨其音步。

  O my love is like a red, red rose

  That's newly sprung in June;

  Oh, my love is like a melodie

  That's sweetly played in tune.

4. 你喜欢杜甫《春望》一诗的哪种英译？为什么？

原作：

  国破山河在，城春草木深。

  感时花溅泪，恨别鸟惊心。

  烽火连三月，家书抵万金。

  白头搔更短，浑欲不胜簪。

译文 1：*The Panorama in Spring*

The mounts and rivers still exist, the capital has fallen, tho!

Untended grass and trees—a dismal spring scene does the city show.

Affected by the times I shed tears at the sight of flowers fair;

To this sep'ration-stricken heart the birds can only add despair.

The flames of war have rag'd for three months, causing sufferings untold; A letter trav'lling far from home is worth ten thousand taels of gold.

Repeated scratches out of trouble now have made my white hair thin—

'Tis so infirm and thin that it can hardly hold a pin.
(zzy,1996:126)

译文 2: *Spring—Looking into the Distance*

The state is destroyed; hills, rivers remain;

Spring: within the city wall, grass, trees, are thick.

Emotion, fitting to the season; flowers bring a rush of tears;

I hate being cut apart; the song of birds quicken my heart.

Beacon fires burn incessantly; their flames connect this Third

Moon with that of last year;

A letter from home would be worth ten thousand ounces of gold.

I scrathe my white head; the hair is shorter than ever;

It is matted; I should like to knot it, but cannot succeed in

thrushing through the jade hair-pin.

(F. A., from xyz, 1992:232)

译文 3: *Spring View*

The country torn apart, what though the mountains and rivers are as before?

And the greenery — too profuse for a city in spring.

Grieving over the times, the flowers are bedewed with tears.

Loath to part, the birds are stricken to the heart.

War hasbeen blazing for three months;

A letter from home is worth ten thousand pieces of gold.

My white head cannot bear scratching,

The hair already too thin to hold a pin.

(lwj,1985:66)

译文 4: *Spring—the Long View*

Even though a state is crushed

Its hills and streams remain;

Now inside the walls of Chang'an

Grasses rise high among unpruned trees;

Seeing flowers come, a flood

Of sadness overwhelms me; cut off

As I am, songs of birds stir

My heart; third month and still

Beacon fires flare as they did

Last year, toget news

From home would be worth a full

Thousand pieces of gold;

Trying to knot up my hair

I find it grey, too thin

For my pin to hold it together.

(R. A., 2001:71)

第三章 典籍英译的类型归属及译者必备条件

学习目标

本章旨在帮助学习者深化对于翻译的类型与本质的认识,明确个人修养的方向。

第一节 研究型翻译与非研究型翻译

随着对事物认识的深化,人们会根据事物的不同性质与特征,将它们加以分门别类。分类行为标志着人类对事物(现象)本质认识的深化和飞跃。以翻译研究为例,英国当代翻译家、翻译理论家彼得·纽马克(Peter Newmark)根据文本功能和翻译目的的关系,在德国学者莱斯(Reiss)和诺德(Nord)研究的基础上,将文本划分为三种基本形式,即表达型文本(Expressive text)、信息型文本(Informative text)和呼唤型文本(Vocative text),不但在指导实践方面产生了积极的作用,也推进了翻译研究。这表明,翻译理论界对于翻译对象有了进一步的认识。

各种翻译的差异是客观存在的。"文学翻译"、"科技翻译"是根据翻译对象的内容所进行的分类,而"口译"、"笔译"则是根据场合及目的语的语言形式等因素所进行的分类。我们可以根据翻译活动本身在性质方面的差异,将翻译划分为研究型和非研究型两种。前者复杂,后者单纯;前者以意象翻译为主,后者以专业性概念的双语替换为主;前者除了涉及逻辑思维,还涉及非逻辑思维,例如类比、想象、灵感、顿悟、联想、直觉等,后者涉及逻辑思维,但不涉及或较少涉及非逻辑思维;前者的研究性工作所占的比例大,后者的研究性工作所占比例小;前者的译者主体性强,因而译者发挥创造力、想象力的空间大,后者的译者主体性弱,译者发挥创造力、想象力的空间小;前者所生产出来的翻译文本译者个性明显,后者所生产出来的翻译文本较少带有译者个性的痕迹,或者译者个

性表现微弱。

我们以汉诗和算术等式的翻译为例,来考察二者的区别。

叶绍翁《游园不值》诗题及"春色满园关不住,一枝红杏出墙来"两句有以下几种译法:

Shut without the Garden
A gardenful of spring can't be shut up, though. Within sight
A twig of apricot flowers is flaming out o'er th' wall!
(zzy,1996:256)

Visiting a Garden When Its Master Is Out
The ravishing beauties of the garden could not be contained:
A bough of glowing apricot blooms stretched out of the wall.
(sdy,1997:459)

A Closed Garden
The garden cannot shut up the full blooming spring;
An apricot stretches out a branch o'er the wall.
(xyz,2000:183)

由于诗句的翻译涉及移情审美和意象重构,译者的个性存在差异,译文各具特色。光是诗题的英译就给读者以不同的感受,译文所建构的"春色"与"红杏"就更不用说了,其模糊美、动态美、色彩美之强弱是不同的。

再以《诗经·采薇》(节选)为例:

昔我往矣,杨柳依依。
今我来思,雨雪霏霏。
行道迟迟,载渴载饥。
我心伤悲,莫知我哀。

其不同译法如下:

(1)
My native willows green and gay
Did wave me farewell in the past;
Now that I'm on my home-bound way,
The sleet is falling thick and fast.
Stricken with both hunger and thirst,

I'm staggering at a pace slow;
And worst of all, my heart does burst
With such sorrow as none could know!
(zzy,1996:17)

(2)

When I set out so long ago,
Fresh and green was the willow.
When now homeward I go,
There is a heavy snow.
The homeward march is slow;
My hunger and thirst grow.
My heart is filled with sorrow;
Who on earth will ever know!
(wrp,1995:693)

(3)

Long ago, when we started,
The willows spread their shade.
Now that we turn back
The snowflakes fly.
The march before us is long,
We are thirsty and hungry,
Our hearts are stricken with sorrow,
But no one listens to our plaint.
(AW,from web & wyx,79)

(4)

At first, when we set out,
The willows were fresh and green;
Now, when we shall be returning,
The snow will be falling in clouds.
Long and tedious will be our marching;
We shall hunger; we shall thirst.
Our hearts are wounded with grief,

And no one knows our sadness.

(sms,from cted,1986:1—2)

"杨柳依依"有"My native willows green and gay/Did wave me farewell"、"Fresh and green was the willow"、"The willows spread their shade"、"The willows were fresh and green"等不同译法,杨柳所负载的情感意义不同;"雨雪霏霏"有"The sleet is falling thick and fast"、"There is a heavy snow"、"The snowflakes fly"、"The snow will be falling in clouds",等不同译法,"雨雪"的意象与所传递的情感信息不同;从译文的韵律、情感、文体色彩看,四种译法也各有千秋。之所以如此,是因为译者对于原文的理解、研究能力、翻译策略、知识结构等等方面存在着差异。译者个性明显,这正是研究型翻译的特点。词语的选择涉及扩散思维和聚敛思维。翻译过程体现了张今教授所总结的"外国语思维和本族语思维的统一,对原作语言形式的感知与对艺术境界感知的统一,语言分析与逻辑分析的统一,思想分析与艺术分析的统一,作者与译者审美经验的统一,逻辑思维与形象思维的统一"(韩家权、柏敬泽,2003:21)。可以说,研究型翻译也是审美活动与审美创造的统一。

而科技翻译则属于非研究型翻译。以等式"二加二等于四"($2+2=4$)为例,不论其英译是"Two plus two is four",还是"Two and two make(equal) four",都是数学概念的双语替换,没有歧义,不需要文字考证、原作者研究或版本研究,不存在意象重构等创造性思维活动,因而也就没有给译者以操控或表现个性的机会。

第二节 典籍英译的类型归属

根据研究型翻译的界定,典籍英译(包括汉诗英译)就具有研究型翻译的特征,属于研究型翻译的范畴。由于源文本(原作)有多种版本;由于原作者、原作相关信息湮没或模糊;由于原文因错简或部分文字亡佚,或因年代久远,或因语言文化变迁,文字意义难以确定,因而,翻译活动的创造性贯串始终。有赖于译者研究的问题很多,诸如:

(1) 在典籍英译中,为了制订正确的翻译策略,翻译出成功的译作,就必须对作者的思想、生平,作品的内容、风格、形体、类别、版本和时代背景,现有英译的各种版本,相关的翻译方法论以及决定预期翻译文本文化定位的社会文化因素等等进行一番深入细致的研究,通过文化历史观照、文本内证及外证、互文观照以及作品与文本的互证对文本进行语义诠释,通过解码、解构、解析、整合对文本进行"文化解读",(刘宓庆,1999:70—71)以便对作品的总意象(total concept)及预期翻译文本的文化定位等等做到心中有数。这就是说,典籍英译必须进行总体审度,而总体审度所涵盖的作者研究、文本研究、版本研究、译文本文化定位研究、社会文化因素研究等等,都属于研究活动。

(2)在进行翻译决策的时候,对遵循的标准和采用的策略(译文语言形式、文体、文化语义表达等)需要研究。

(3)在进行考辨的时候,需要采用"训诂、移情推理、考据、文化历史观照、文本内证及外证、互文观照以及诗人与文本的互证等方法",对话语的形式和含义加以研究。

(4)在使用目的语构建原作所表现的风格、情感、意象、意境的时候,也需要对词、句、章法、语言形式等等加以研究。

(5)正是由于如此,它才比非研究型的翻译具有更大的挑战性和译者介入(或操控)空间,更需要译者发挥自己的才能、学识和创造性。更大的挑战性,是指它难度更大,对译者的研究能力、双语能力、东西方比较文化知识等方面要求更高、更严格;更大的介入空间,主要是指在在总体审度、翻译决策及风格、意象、意境的再现与重构等等方面译者有较大的发挥个性(包括治学态度、治学方法、知识结构、心理结构、才华学识、创造能力等)的自由度。

第三节　典籍英译者的必备条件

译者属于翻译学科的研究对象之一,译者研究是翻译本体论的组成部分。

在人才奇缺、青黄不接的情况下,培养和造就一支德才兼备的典籍翻译队伍,已经成了我国翻译界的当务之急。提出译者必备条件,是为了明确译者修养及翻译人才培养的目标与方向。"德才兼备"可以具体化为以下内容:

一、志存高远

人生的志向和使命并不是与生俱来的,而是由个人自己选择的。有的人来到世上,浑浑噩噩地在地球上啃掉上几口就走了,留下了垃圾;有的人则以其崇高的使命感和聪明才智,努力创造、奉献,留下了真、善、美。典籍英译者必须继承"以天下为己任"的优良传统和强烈的社会责任感,选择后者。崇高的理想能给人以巨大的推动力,是成功的重要因素。"非志无以成学"(诸葛亮,《诫子书》);"人患志之不立,亦何忧令名不彰学"(刘义庆,《世说新语·自新》)。

二、以德为本

在物欲横流的社会里,有的人误入歧途,舍义取利,成了拜金主义的牺牲品;在享乐主义的氛围中,有的人好逸恶劳,虚度年华,沦为醉生梦死的寄生虫。在商品经济的时代,道德的修养就尤为重要,高尚的品格就弥足珍贵。"士有百行,以德为首"(陈寿:《三国志·魏书·诸夏侯曹传》);"士虽有学,而行为本焉"《墨子·修身》;钱冠连教授认为,"要想学品高,就得人品好","做人的品格与做学问、搞创造的品格之间存在着正负对应关系"(张后尘,1999:39)。所有这些都是至理名言。治学必先治德,德不高则难成大器。这是古今学者的共识。

三、学贯中西

由于典籍内容涵盖政治、经济、历史、天文、地理、哲学等学科,典籍英译难度大,译者要有所作为,就不但要具备广博的东西方比较文化知识,雄厚的英汉语言和相关学科功底,开拓创新的能力以及文人的才情,而且必须具备娴熟驾驭翻译理论和灵活运用翻译技巧的能力。总而言之,就是要做到学贯中西。

要达到这种境界,就必须谦虚好学。山不辞坯土,故能成其高;海不厌涓滴,故能成其深。谦者知不足,"知不足者好学"(林逋:《省心录》)。"不疾学而能为魁士名人者,未之尝有也。"(吕不韦:《吕氏春秋·劝学》)谦虚好学的一个重要方面是要做到尊师重道。古人认为,尊师对于求学者十分重要。"疾学在于尊师,师尊则言信矣,道论矣。"(吕不韦:《吕氏春秋·劝学》)师的含义可以是广义的,先闻道者为师。"无贵无贱,无长无少,道之所存,师之所存也。"(韩愈:《师说》)"三人行,必有我师焉。择其善者而从之,其不善者而改之。"(《论语·述而》)从这种意义上说,学术前辈、同事、同行以至于学生都有值得学习的地方。

四、光明磊落

"知之为知之,不知为不知,是知也。"(孔子:《论语·为政》)"言不信者,行不果。"(墨翟:《墨子·七患》)"大丈夫行事,当礌落落,如日月皎然。"(《晋书·石勒载记下》)近年揭露出来的学术腐败现象说明,当今的学术界并非一尘不染的世外桃源;蒙混学位者有之,买卖文章者有之,剽窃抄袭者(包括近年揭发出来的一些博士生导师)有之,嫉贤妒能、飞扬跋扈的学棍学霸亦有之。这些前车之覆,足为后车之鉴。

五、坚忍不拔

郑燮赞美岩竹云:"咬定青山不放松,立根原在破岩中。千磨万击还坚劲,任尔东西南北风。""凡是有所'立'、有所成就的有志之士,无不具有这种'择善固执,锲而不舍'的钻研精神。"(刘重德,1997:5)认定一个目标之后,就要以坚忍不拔的精神为之奋斗。这种精神是典籍英译者所应当具备的。少了它,就可能对这项工作望而却步,或是浅尝辄止,半途而废。

六、治学严谨

一个合格的典籍英译者仅有良好的道德品格修养是不够的,必须做到德才兼备。"苟可以为天下国家之用者,则无不在于学。"(王安石:《上仁宗皇帝言事书》)工欲善其事,必先利其器。所谓"器"就是学问与才能。

古文难懂,古事悠悠。如果没有一丝不苟、"上下而求索"的精神,就不可能译出形神兼备的典籍精品。严复"一名之立,旬月踯躅",典籍译者必须具备这种严谨的治学态度。

七、开拓创新

在典籍英译的理论与实践的许多方面,目前还没有现成的路径,尚有广阔的处女地需要开垦,诸多的课题需要研究。若要有所突破,有所创新,译者和研究者就必须具备开拓的精神与能力。"如果只是鹦鹉学舌,人云亦云,或者只是比猫画虎,依样画葫芦,何来真知灼见?何来创造发明?"(刘重德,1997:5)

总而言之,典籍英译任重道远,志高者方敢为之,德高者方肯为之,才高者方能为之。

第四节 小结

本章将翻译划分为研究型与非研究型两种。首先,这种划分可以深化我们对于翻译本质的认识,并给予译者以应有的社会定位。研究型翻译是一种创造性劳动,应当得到承认和尊重。其次,翻译类型的划分有助于提高译者的学理修养和自我意识,指导翻译实践。其三,翻译类型的划分可以指导翻译人才的培养。譬如说,科技翻译翻译人才的培养就要强调有关专业知识的学习。

本章还对典籍英译者提出了"德才兼备"的标准,并将其具体化为志存高远、以德为本、学贯中西、光明磊落、坚忍不拔、治学严谨和开拓创新等译者必备条件。这些必备条件是作为培养的目标和个人努力的方向提出来的,要求很高,但并非高不可攀。只要我们百折不回,就能够一步步地接近它。只有达到这些条件,才能胜任典籍英译的使命;只有具备这些共性,才能谈得上译者的个性。

思考题

1. 本书将翻译划分为研究型和非研究型两种。你同意这种划分吗?这种划分有何意义?你能否为这种划分提供更多的理据?

2. 典籍(汉诗)英译者的素质要求很高。对于这种要求你是望而却步呢,还是打算不断完善自我以求接近它?你将如何把自己的追求与民族、人类的生存发展统一起来?

3. 评论刘禹锡《乌衣巷》的英译:

原作:

　　朱雀桥边野草花,乌衣巷口夕阳斜。
　　旧时王谢堂前燕,飞入寻常百姓家。

译文 1: *The Black Coat Lane*

The Rose-finch Bridge appears desolate 'mdst wild grass and plants;
The Black Coat Lane's obscure 'gainst th' setting sun, which westward slants.
The swallows, which us'd to construct their nests at th' splendid domes Of th' Wangs' and th' Xies', are now darting into common folk's homes.

(zzy,1996:157)

译文 2: Black Coat Lane

Wild nameless flowers by the Cinnabar Bird Bridge
Are aglow in the last sun-beams in the Black Coat Lane.
The swallows 'fore the Wang and Xie noble mansions
Now fly into the nobodies' homestalls.
(sdy,1997:413)

译文 3: Blacktail Row

Grass has run wild now by the Bridge of Red-Birds;
And swallows' wings, at sunsetin Blacktail Row
Where once they visited great homes,
Dip among doorways of the poor.
(W. B. , from lsx, 1980:63)

练习题

1. 本章所引《诗经·采薇》(节选)几种译法中,你最喜欢哪种?请简单罗列出你的理据。

2. 叶绍翁《游园不值》里的红杏具有动态美、色彩美。不同英译者是如何重构这些美学特征的?

原作:
　　应怜屐齿印苍苔,小扣柴扉久不开。
　　春色满园关不住,一枝红杏出墙来。

译文 1: Shut without the Garden

My clog-prints on greenish moss must have incurr'd the spite:
I knock at th' wooden gate, but there's no answer after all.
A gardenful of spring can't be shut up, though. Within sight
A twig of apricot flowers is flaming out o'er th' wall!
(zzy,1996:256)

译文 2: Visiting a Garden When Its Master Is Out

I repine at pressing clog-teeth prints on the deep green moss;
The brushwood door when knocked as I wait long doth not ope at all.

The ravishing beauties of the garden could not be contained;
A bough of glowing apricot blooms stretched out of the wall.
(sdy,1997:459)

译文 3: *A Closed Garden*
The green moss cannot bear the sabots whose teeth sting;
The wichet gate is closed to me who tap and call.
The garden cannot shut up the full blooming spring;
An apricot stretches out a branch o'er the wall.
(xyz,2000:183)

3. 自选唐诗一首(如白居易的《鹦鹉》:"竟日语还默,中宵栖复惊。身囚缘彩翠,心苦为分明。暮起归巢思,春多忆侣声。谁能拆笼破,从放快飞鸣。")并将其翻译成英语。保存译稿,在日后的学习过程中不断加以修改。

第四章 汉诗英译的标准与原则

 学习目标

了解汉诗英译的历史和各家之说,并认定翻译的标准和原则,以便在实践中有所遵循。

第一节 汉诗英译的不同主张

美国诗人 Robert Frost 说过:"Poetry is what gets lost in translation."中国也有学者认为,诗歌玄妙精微,是经不起翻译的。闻一多先生说过:"你定要翻译它,只有把它毁了完事!……'美'是碰不得的,一粘手它就毁了。"(《中国翻译》1987:245)郭沫若先生主张,译诗者应该是诗人。古汉语专家 A. C. Graham 则声称,"We can hardly leave translation to the Chinese, since there are few exceptions to the rule that translation is best done into, not out of, one's own language",(A. C. Graham, 1977:137)认为中国学人与本国典籍的英译无缘。

尽管如此,中国学术界还是不乏敢于攀登险峰的人。而且,在典籍英译方面"大有后来居上之势"(刘重德:2002,贺信)。20世纪,在汉诗英译方面影响较大的有苏曼殊(1884—1918)、初大告、蔡廷干、黄雯、林同济、孙大雨(1905—)、林文庆(1869—1957)、祝德光、董同龢(1911—1963)、林语堂、翁显良(1924—1983)、黄新渠(1930—)、黄龙(1925—)、吴钧陶、刘重德(1914—)、许渊冲、杨宪益、戴乃迭、楚至大、吴锡陶(1927—)、黄新渠(1930—)、赵甄陶等学者。十分可喜的是,近年涌现的中青年学者在典籍翻译的实践和学术研究方面成就斐然,令人瞩目。

许渊冲教授认为,根据翻译时采用的方法,可以把译者分为直译、意译、仿译、改译、逐字翻译、散体翻译、诗化翻译等等不同流派。"中国译诗者早期初大

告是直译派,蔡廷干是意译派,林语堂是仿译派。后期散体派有杨宪益,逐字译者有黄雯,诗体译者有许渊冲,现代派有林同济,改译派有翁显良。"(杨自俭、刘学云,1994:91)

长期以来,流派并存,各执己见,其主要分歧乃在于翻译的标准、原则和方法论。

鉴于理论研究偏于粗浅零散、缺乏自成体系的汉诗英译理论的状况,学者们对一系列课题逐一进行了探讨,并建构了一个比较完整的概念体系。

第二节　汉诗英译的标准与原则

相对于实践而言,汉诗英译的理论研究起步较晚。早期的探讨出现在各家诗集的序言或后记中,主要谈论译者自己译诗的体会。20 世纪有关诗词翻译研究的论文很少,专著就更不用说了。

近年来,学术刊物上偶有论文发表,也出过论文集。《中国翻译》编辑部、中国对外翻译出版公司所编《诗词翻译的艺术》汇集了苏曼殊、郭沫若、茅盾、郁达夫、闻一多、刘半农……黄新渠等三十余位诗词译者的论文四十余篇,作者们对于有关问题仁者见仁,智者见智。1979 年,许渊冲教授提出了"三美"的译诗标准,认为译诗必须传达原诗的意美、音美、形美。(杨自俭、刘学云,1994:91)有的学者对此持有异议。刘英凯教授引用 Arthur Waley 所说过的"韵脚的限制必然损及语言的活力,必然损及译文的信度,如果一个译者用了韵,就不可能不因声损义",得出了"韵体译诗是弊大于利"的结论,认为"事实上无韵翻译的实践""已经取得了举世公认的成就"(杨自俭、刘学云,1994:91)。1989 年,刘重德教授在《外国语》5、6 期载文,主张"写诗讲求形音义三美,而译诗决不可只满足于'达意',必须力求传神,首先是必须保留原诗的意义(meaning)和意境(artistic conception);其次,在此前提下,还应该字斟句酌地使译诗具有一定的诗的形式和一定的韵律、节奏";认为他提出的文学翻译信达切三原则"也同样适用于译诗"(刘重德,1994:29,39)。

逐字对译(metaphrase)和散文化意译(prose paraphrase)都曾起过积极的作用。然而,它们都难以使原诗的美学价值得到较全面的再现。

诗歌的思想内容与艺术形式的结合比其他文学样式更紧密,有些诗歌甚至把诗的形式作为表现意象的重要手段。因此,以英文散文或无韵诗的形式翻译中国的古典诗词是不够理想的。诗歌的翻译必须兼顾内容与形式,以形神兼似作为翻译的标准;而要达到传情传神的境界,就必须采用诗化翻译法(versified translation),遵从以诗译诗、全值再现原诗美学价值的原则,最大限度地迁移或再现原诗的形式美、音韵美、节奏美、情感美、意境美和风格美。

诗化翻译法比意译等方法多了一个颇具挑战性的步骤,即诗化(versification)。由于诗歌富于个性,诗歌语言具有极强的艺术性,诗的意象、意境、韵致微妙而难以捉摸;由于汉语复杂而富于表达力,汉诗形式多样且内容广泛;由于汉英两种语言,东西方两种文化及两种思维方式存在着较大的差异,因此,翻译过程中的理解、双语思维转换及形诸散文已特别困难,诗化就更不必说了。译者不仅要有雄厚的汉语汉诗和英语英诗功底,扎实的东西方比较文化知识以及诗人的才情,而且必须具备驾驭翻译理论和运用翻译技巧的能力。诗化是有法可依的,对此将另章加以探讨。

思考题

1. 各种译法中,你赞同哪种?为什么?

2. 有人认为,汉诗英译不必顾及格律因素,只要译出原诗意境就是成功的译作。你同意这种说法吗?为什么?

3. 仔细研读李清照《声声慢》及其英译的过程稿,并指出译稿是如何逐步趋于"最大限度地迁移或再现原诗的形式美、音韵美、节奏美、情感美、意境美和风格美"的:

原作:

寻寻觅觅,冷冷清清,凄凄惨惨戚戚。乍暖还寒时候,最难将息。三杯两盏淡酒,怎敌他、晚来风急。雁过也,正伤心,却是旧时相识。

满地黄花堆积,憔悴损,如今有谁堪摘。守着窗儿,独自怎生得黑?梧桐更兼细雨,到黄昏、点点滴滴。这次第,怎一个愁字了得。

第一稿:

At a loss I feel, at a loss
In lonely solitude
and woeful melancholy.
The turn of cold and warmth
Is the most miserable time.
How can two or three cups of light wine

Counteract the chill of swift evening winds?
It is heart-wrenching
to see the wild geese,
acquainted in the north, southward fly.

Chrysanthemums flourish here and there,
But frustrated, whoe'er would care to pluck them?
Sitting alone at the window
How can I pull through before night falls?
At dusk the drizzle drips and
drops on Chinese parasols.
On such an occasion what one has to bear
Is more than sorrow.

第二稿:
Fumbling and searching, at a loss I feel,
At a loss in such lonely melancholy
and plaintive solitude as seem unreal.
Th' turn of cold and warmth is, incredibly,
The most miserable time to endure.
Of th' chill of evening winds how can I cure
Myself with a few cups of wine impure?
'Tis heart-renching to see th' wild geese in th' sky,
My acquaintances of old, southward fly.

Chrysanthemums now flourish here and there,
But who would care to pluck them, feeling blue?
Sitting alone at th' window in despair,
Ere nightfalls I know not how to pull through.
At dusk drips and drops on the leaves of Chinese parasols
the drizzle
On such an occasion what one has to bear
Is more than sorrow.

第三稿:

Fumbling and searching, at a loss I feel,
At a loss in such lonely melancholy
and plaintive solitude as seem unreal.
Th' turn of cold and warmth is, incredibly,
The most miserable time to endure.
Of th' chill of evening winds how can I cure
Myself with a few cups of wine impure?
'Tis heart-wrenching to see th' wild geese in th' sky,
My acquaintances of old, southward fly.

Chrysanthemums now flourish here and there,
But who would care to pluck them, feeling blue?
Sitting alone at th' window in despair,
Ere night falls I know not how to pull through.
Now dripping and dropping incessantly
On the Chinese parasols is the rain.
Alas, much much more than anxiety,
At such a time, is what one must sustain.

 练习题

1. 物质生产与精神生产的共同点之一就是,两者的终端产品都会因为有无深加工、深加工技术的优劣或深加工工序的多寡而产生价值差异。汉诗英译属于精神生产,译作就是精神产品。试绘出诗化译法与非诗化译法的生产流程图,并比较说明它们在再现原作美学价值方面产生的差异。

2. 分辨出萨都剌《念奴娇·登石头城》一词的韵体译法和非韵体译法。

原文:

　　石头城上,望天低吴楚,眼空无物。
　　指点六朝形胜地,惟有青山如壁。
　　蔽日旌旗,连云樯橹,白骨纷如雪。

一江南北,消磨多少豪杰。

寂寞避暑离宫,东风辇路,芳草年年发。
落日无人松径里,鬼火高低明灭。
歌舞尊前,繁华镜里,暗换青青发。
伤心千古,秦淮一片明月。

译文 1: *An Ascent of the Gate Tower of Rocky City*
  —To the Tune of "Charming Is Niannu"

Atop the Rocky City I gaze
As far as Wu and Chu merge with the skies;
The world, which seems devoid of content, comes in sight.
Of the Six Dynasties what is still to be seen?
Only wall-like mountains green remain on the historic site.
The masts of galleys, which might have touch'd the clouds,
And the banners, which might have hidden the sun,
Have just left behind bones snow-white.
How many heroes, north and south of the river,
Had been ruin'd or reduc'd to a hopeless plight?

Each year in spring, with grasses growing lush
On its corridors, the royal summer resort,
Now deserted, presents a sorry sight.
And after sunset, along the abandon'd paths below pines,
Will-o'-the-wisp ghastly rolls on, now dim, now bright.
Ere exquisite wine cups the youth of men of th' hour
Had faded away, and in mirrors th' raven locks
Of princely souls, sapp'd by song and dance, had turn'd white.
Forever gone is the heart-rending past, but lo,
O'er the Qinhuai River the moon, as before, is shining bright!
(zzy,1996:277—8)

译文 2: *Bai Zi Ling*

Over the walls of the Stone City,

The skies of Wu and Chu hang low:

An expanse of blank nothing.

Pointing at the strategic spots of the Six Dynasties,

One now sees only green mountains instead,

Thrusting up like walls.

The battle banners darkening the sun;

The battleship sails reaching the clouds:

White bones were scattered about like snow.

North and south of the River,

How many heroes have been ground to dust?

In the peaceful Summer Palace

The east wind sweeps down the royal road.

Sweet grass turns green each spring;

The sun sets on no one in the footpaths in pinewoods;

Only will-o'—the wisps float around.

Song and dance and the wine jug:

In the mirror of fast living,

Dark hair imperceptibly fades.

Among heartbreaking tales of a millennium,

The Qinhuai River is tonight bathed in bright moonlight.

(gjh, 1999: 186—7)

译文 3: *Tune: Niannujiao*

Ascending the Walls of the Stone City

On the walls of the Stone City,

Looking that the southern sky is low,

Nothing else can the keen observer see.

Pointing to scenic spots and historic sites of the Six Dynasties,

The green hills are still there, like heavy walls.

War banners shelter the sun,

Galleys, in close formation, well depoyed,

White bones piled up like fallen snow.

Numberless horses, wars must have destroyed.

The Summer Palace is lonely,
Royal carriages wore out the road,
Fragrant grass grows every year.
The setting sun rays are the quiet paths with pine trees,
Jack-o'-lantern gave and shut off light.
For all the sensual pleasures of high life,
One's hair turns white from what was black as jet,
The moon o'er the Qinhuaihe must have seen,
Too much not to be filled with long regret.
(mxy,1997:199)

第五章　诗歌的模糊性及翻译的标准和方法

学习目标

深化对于诗歌模糊美的认识，了解和掌握翻译的标准及模糊化译法的各种技巧。

第一节　诗歌的模糊性

有的诗句、诗篇含蓄隽永，意蕴丰富，读者可以有不同的理解，仁者见仁，智者见智。刘勰称这种诗歌特点为"隐"，他说，"隐也者，文外之重旨者也"，"隐以复意为工。"（《文心雕龙·隐秀篇》）他还把"隐"与"晦塞"作了区分，指出"晦塞为深，虽奥非隐。"本文为了语言上的便利，将以"模糊性"指称"隐"。

造成模糊性的原因有二。其一是诗歌本身的多义性，例如刘禹锡《竹枝词》"道是无晴却有晴"一句中的"晴（情）"。结构主义美学对此的阐释是：诗歌文字形式的对等，即使是语音上的对等，都会导致语义对等；语义对等造成语义上的歧义，因而使象征性、多义性和复杂性成为诗歌的特质。其二是，诗歌在流传中被赋予了新的意义，即增殖义。从接受美学的角度看，审美过程是能动的再创造过程，一方面是审美对象的审美特征之心灵化；另一方面是审美主体的审美能力之外化。以诗论之，历代无数的审美主体（读者，译者或评论家等）把自己富于个性、民族性和时代性的审美体验赋予了诗作，对其作出特殊的解释，创造出更加生动丰满的艺术形象和更加深邃广博的意蕴意境。这些赋予和阐释积淀下来，被后代所继承并获得艺术生命力。例如，叶绍翁《游园不值》里的"春色满园关不住，一枝红杏出墙来"本来是写红杏探头墙外的盎然春色，现用以比喻新生事物无法遏制。

模糊性构成诗歌的混沌美，它与清晰性的互寓与对立统一又构成一种和谐美。模糊与清晰都反映了客观世界的本质，也反映了人类的审美取向和情感特

征。由于文学——特别是诗歌中——存在着形象大于思想的规律,模糊性就显得分外重要。

模糊性诗歌往往采用象征、比喻、烘托、暗示和大幅度跳跃等表现手法,给人以雾中看花、月下观景、虚虚实实、婉曲深微的审美感受。严羽在《沧浪诗话》中把这类诗歌比作"空中之音,相中之色,水中之月,镜中之象",谓其"无迹可求","言有尽而意无穷"。这类诗歌的翻译涉及混沌美的再创造,其难度是可想而知的;探讨这类诗歌翻译的规律,其意义也是不言自明的。

第二节 关于翻译的标准和方法的若干探讨

模糊性使诗歌的翻译具有特殊性和挑战性。它向我们提出了两个新问题:一、模糊性诗歌的翻译标准是什么?二、采用什么译法才能较为理想地达到这一标准?

对于第一个问题,现成的翻译理论尚未提供明确的解答。以"信、达、雅"(或"信、达、切")论之,在多义并存的情况下,译者该"信"哪一种意义?根据奈达(Eugene A. Nida)的理论,理想的翻译不仅要在译语中找到"顺乎自然的对等语"(a natural equivalent),而且还要找到"最切近的对等语"(the closest equivalent)。然而,原诗旨重意复,译语应与哪种意旨"切近"和"对等"?不解决标准这一令人困惑的问题,诗歌翻译的理论研究就难以有重大的突破。

我们知道,模糊性是语义上的差异构成的。本章第一部分所举的两个例子中,"晴"与"情"、"春色关不住"与"新生事物不可遏制"都构成差异。

恩格斯说过,"一切差异都在中间阶段融合","辩证法不知道什么绝对分明和固定不变的界限,不知道什么无条件的普遍有效的'非此即彼!',它使固定的形而上学的差异互相过渡,除了'非此即彼!',又在适当的地方承认'亦此亦彼!',并且使对立互为中介。"(徐长山、王德胜,1994:330)

编者认为,译者的任务正是寻找能使差异得以互相过渡的接合点,使译语具有语义兼容性,达到"亦此亦彼"或"花非花,雾非雾"的混沌美艺术境界,同时又最大限度地保持或再现其他的诗歌美学价值。

有了标准,译者就有目标和方向,读者和批评家就有衡量译作的尺度。然而,不解决第二个问题即方法的问题,不找到"通幽处"的"曲径",标准便失去其实践意义。

语言是个概念系统,不同的语义代表不同的概念。概念不是绝对和固定不变的。根据外延有无重合及重合的多少,概念间可有全同、交叉、属种、矛盾、反对等五种关系。在诗歌的某一特定模糊语义单位的翻译中,我们可以直接从译文语言中寻找"模棱两可",即具有语义兼容性的语符,也可以适当地使某一语义概念的边界延展至与另一个语义概念相交迭,从而构成"亦此亦彼"的特殊概念,以负载多种含义。这种方法姑且称为"模糊化翻译法"。

下面就让我们通过对汉诗的不同英译的比较分析来检验模糊化翻译法的可行性和优越性,同时对模糊化的一些技巧作出归纳。为节省篇幅,这里仅摘取有关诗句及其英译。

【例1】昔我往矣,杨柳依依。今我来思,雨雪霏霏。

——《诗经·采薇》

A译:
My native willows green and gay
Did wave me farewell in the past;
Now that I'm on my homebound way,
The sleet is falling thick and fast.
(zzy,1996:17)

B译:
Long ago we set out
When willows were rich and green.
Now we come back
Through thickly falling snow.
(tr. BW, from xyz,1992:56)

C译:
When I left here,
Willows shed tear,
I come back now,
Snow bends the bough.
(xyz,1992:56)

"杨柳"在中国诗词中有"送别"的联想意义,但在英美文学中则没有。为此,A译把联想意义显化,构造成"亦柳亦人"的新概念,使杨柳的双重意义得以再现。B译少掉了"送别"的联想意义。C译把杨柳人格化,这种手法本身可取,问题是化之失当:说"杨柳垂泪",这与说"蚯蚓飞翔"一样不合情理,也有悖"依依"之含义。

后两句里的"雨雪"象征"凄苦"。A 译里的"sleet"具有这种兼义性,而"snow"的这种兼义性稍差。西方人企盼的"white Christmas"是有雪的圣诞节,白雪产生的联想也可以是"圣洁"。再说,"sleet"也更切合"雨雪"的字面义。

【例2】欲穷千里目,更上一层楼。

——王之涣:《登鹳雀楼》

A 译:
Aim higher and up the tower take another flight
To acquire a vision broader than one thousand li.
(zzy,1996:97)

B 译:
Wish you an endless view to cheer your eyes?
Then one more storey mount and higher rise.
(ctg, from gzz,1994:17)

这两句诗原来是说望远须登高,现被赋予激励人们奋发向上之义。A 译"Aim higher"既含"立志更高远"之意,又与"更上一层楼"的原意相合;"目"被抽象化而译为"vision",兼有"眼光"和"远见"之义;"tower","another flight"比"one more storey"更具象征性。B 译"Wish you an endless view to cheer your eyes?"("你想不想……一饱眼福?")格调不够高,难以包容积极向上的意蕴。再说,所用疑问句型也不及 A 译的祈使句富于感召力。

【例3】春蚕到死丝方尽,蜡炬成灰泪始干。

——李商隐:《无题》

A 译:
The silkworm ceases not to spin her thread before she's dead;
Unless burnt to ashes endless tears a candle'll shed.
(xyz,1992:188)

B 译:
A silk-worm exhausts its silk-threads, before it die;
A candle gutters on, till its tear-drops run dry.
(xzj,1990:343—344)

诗句原来寓指爱情坚贞、至死方休,现用以表达为人民为正义鞠躬尽瘁、死而后已的高尚情怀。A 译以人称代词指蚕,且显化了"蚕"与"烛"的主观意识

("cease not"表达了"蚕"的志向;"Unless burnt to ashes"表达了"烛"的决心),使之具有了人的特性。人与蚕、烛的语义差异得以"互相过渡",因而译语指爱情或利他主义精神皆可。B 译未运用意识化的手法使"蚕"、"烛"在语义上朝"忘我的人"的概念适当延伸,其兼义功能就不如 A 译。

【例 4】孤舟蓑笠翁,独钓寒江雪。

——柳宗元:《江雪》

A 译:

On board a boat a man alone is busy with his rod and line
Despite the driving snow, with which his hat and palm-bark cloak abound.
(zzy,1996:151)

B 译:

A little boat, a bamboo cloak,
An old man fishing in the cold river-snow.
(tr. WB, from gzz,1994:189)

诗中的人物形象既是寒江独钓的渔翁,又是政治改革失败后坚强不屈的诗人自己。A 译以"渔翁"为主语,突出了他的主体地位,"... busy with his rod and line / Despite the driving snow"又显化了人物形象矢志不渝与不畏艰险的气质,模糊了"渔翁"与诗人的差异。B 译把舟、竹衣(本应为蓑衣——编者注)、渔翁置于三个等立的名词短语中,主次不明,渔翁的气魄又未加以显化,难以激发多义联想,"渔翁"仅是渔翁而已。

【例 5】两岸猿声啼不住,轻舟已过万重山。

——李白:《早发白帝城》

A 译:

The jabbering of apes along the banks still seems to last,
Oho, ten thousand sweeps of mounts my swift boat has flash'd past!
(zzy,1996:115)

B 译:

Let the apes wail. Go on.
Out shoots my boat. The serried mountains are all behind.
(tr. wxl, from xyz,1992:218)

C译：
The screams of monkeys on either band
Had scarcely ceased echoing in my ear
When my skiff had lift behind it
Ten thousand ranges of hills.
(tr. xtxl,from gzz,1994:68)

这两句诗原以猿声反衬舟行之疾,现被赋予新义,用以比喻进步事物不顾反对咒骂而发展前进。A译:"jabbering"(急促而含混地说、闲聊或猿猴等吱吱喳喳地叫)比B译:"wail"(恸哭)及C译"screams"(尖叫)语义更广,更能包容"猿啼"和"反对或咒骂"两种意义。

【例6】采得百花成蜜后,为谁辛苦为谁甜?

——罗隐:《蜂》

A译：
You are collecting pollen with such haste,
And yet the honey you make who will taste?
(zzy,1996:193)

B译：
After all flowers are touched and honey's made,
They know not for whose sweet life they all toil?
(gzz,1994:258)

诗中的"蜂"隐喻劳苦大众。A译通过对"蜂"("You")说话及使用"with such haste"("如此匆忙地")这一短语而把蜂人格化,使之亦蜂亦人、人犹如蜂,合乎诗意。B译"They know not for whose sweet life they all toil?"("它们不知道为谁的甜蜜生活而辛劳?")一句中的"蜂"就很难说有无意识可言了。

【例7】野火烧不尽,春风吹又生。

——白居易:《赋得古原草送别》

A译：
The prairie fires may burn and lick;
When breezes blow they'll yet revive.
(zzy,1996:161)

B译：
Wild fire for its spread cannot burn it up
Spring breezes at once revive it again.
(xyz,2000:268)

"草"是进步力量的象征。A译里的"草"是主动的、人格化了的，其生命力得到恰当的表现；而B译里的"草"是被动的，是"春风"使其"再生"，这与诗的原义与增殖义都不甚相符。

【例8】夜来风雨声，花落知多少？

——孟浩然：《春晓》

A译：
The winds shatter'd and the rains splatter'd yesternight;
How many flowers have dropp'd in a wretched plight?
(zzy,1996:99)

B译：
But now I remember the night, the storm,
And I wonder how many blossoms were broken.
(tr. wb & kkh,from gzz,1994:268)

诗从听觉入手写春声春色，抒发爱春惜花的情感。香花在中国往往象征真、善、美，这里引用的诗句便自然被引申为对于受到摧残迫害的进步人士的同情。A译的拟声词把"声"具象化，以形容"风雨"的狂烈，并以"in a wretched plight"（"困苦地"）把花人格化、心灵化。"有感觉的花"这一新概念可以包容诗的增殖义。B译"But now I remember..."（"现在我可想起……来了。"）及"I wonder..."（"我想知道……"）的轻松语气限制了"花落"的含义，阻塞了诗句与"迫害进步力量"这类重大事件的语义关联。

【例9】旧时王谢堂前燕，飞入寻常百姓家。

——刘禹锡：《乌衣巷》

A译：
The swallows, which us'd to construct their nests at th' splendid domes

Of th' Wangs' and th' Xies', are now darting into common folk's homes.

(zzy,1996:157)

B 译:

Where once the swallows knew the mansions of the great,

They now to humbler homes would fly to nest and mate.

(tr. ctg,from gzz,1994:177)

诗人借写飞燕而言世事变迁,盛衰无常。"燕"是历史的见证。A 译一般过去时和现在进行时、"splendid domes"和"common folk's homes"在语法意义和结构(位置对称)上都指向变迁的客观性,为"燕是见证"的联想提供了必要的语境因素,再现了"燕"这一意象的语义双重性。B 译虚拟形式"would fly"不论表示假设还是表示主观意愿,都不指向今昔变迁的客观性,"mate"("交配")一词的使用又淡化了"燕"的意象,降低了原诗的格调,破坏了原诗的意境。总之,B 译未能为"燕"与"见证"这两个语义概念的接合提供有利的语境因素。

第三节 小结

在以上各例中,A 译通过运用人格化、意识显化、心灵化、抽象化、选用具有语义兼容性的语言符号和创造激发多义联想的语境等模糊化技巧,构造成"会送别的杨柳"(见例1)、"有意识的蚕、烛"(见例3)、"有感觉的花"(见例8)和"隐喻奋发向上的登楼"(见例2)等特殊概念;每个特殊概念都是使诗歌某一语言单位的多种意义得以"互相过渡"的桥。比较分析说明,模糊化翻译法不但可行,而且较之其他译法具有相对的优越性。这种方法的可行性和优越性又转而说明,混沌美的艺术境界并不是高不可攀的。

思考题

1. 诗歌、绘画等艺术有其共通之处。谈谈你对绘画中模糊美与清晰美的感受和认识。

2. 你对"模糊化翻译法"的各种技巧是否赞同?是否有什么补充?

练习题

1. 比较元稹《行宫》的不同英译在"白头宫女"、"宫花寂寞红"及诗题"行宫"的文化意义处理方面的异同：

原作：

　　寥落古行宫，宫花寂寞红。
　　白头宫女在，闲坐说玄宗。

译文 1：*The Imperial Resort*

The ancient palaces present a rueful sight；

'Tis vainly that are blooming flowers red and bright.

Those white-hair'd ladies，who've surviv'd their mental pain，

Now sit at ease recalling Xuanzong and his reign.

(zzy，1996：1992：172)

译文 2：*At an Old Palace*

Deserted now the Imperial bowers

Save by some few poor lonely flowers.

One white-haired dame，

An Emperor's flame，

Sits down and tells of by-gone hours.

(H. A. G.，from xyz，1992：289)

译文 3：*The Ancient Travelling Palace*

Empty and falling down is the ancient traveling palace.

The palace flowers put forth their red blooms in silent neglect.

Inside a white-haired palace woman

Idly mumbles of the glorious days of Hsuan Tsung.

(S. J.，from xyz，1992：289)

译文 4：*At an Old Palace*

Deserted now imperial bowers.

For whom still redden palace flowers？

Some white-haired chambermaids at leisure

Talk of the late Emperor's pleasure.

(xyz,1992:289)

2. 诗中"寥落古行宫,宫花寂寞红"两句以花喻人,"寂寞"的似乎是花,实际上却是人。以上各种译作对于这种"模棱两可"是如何再现的?

3. "闲坐说玄宗"一句中,到底宫女们在"说"玄宗什么事情,诗人并没有挑明,因此"说"的内容是模糊的。试分析各种译法是如何处理这种模糊性的。

4. 举例说明你熟知的某些汉诗或英诗所蕴含的模糊性。

第六章 汉诗英译方法比较研究

学习目标

汉诗英译有哪些不同的方法？它们之中孰优孰劣？何以优？何以劣？学习者应掌握有关的学理，提高自己的鉴赏能力。

第一节 汉诗英译的不同方法及基于原作美学特征的译作评价体系

汉诗浩如烟海，灿若明星，折射着博大精深的华夏文明，是世界文化宝库中的珍贵遗产。汉诗英译对于弘扬民族文化、促进中外的融汇交流有着十分重大的意义。

汉诗英译难。然而，中外学者却知难而进。他们呕心沥血，前赴后继，摸索出了各种不同的方法，做出了各自的宝贵贡献。在为香港中文大学的《翻译词典》撰写的 "Development of Verse Translation" 词条中，许渊冲教授罗列了直译、意译、仿译、改译、逐字翻译、散体翻译、诗化翻译等方法。本章根据译品形式，概而言之，将这些方法分为三种，即非诗化译法（Non-Versified Translation）、韵体译法（Rhymed Versification）和非韵体译法（Unrhymed Versification）。后两者是诗化（Versification）翻译方法的分支。

对于以上三种译法，仁者见仁，智者见智。倾向于非诗化译法的翁显良教授主张，应该"在再现原作意象的前提下有伸缩变化的自由"，"在格律问题上不必作茧自缚，实行自度曲可也"。（杨自俭、刘学云，1994:49—54）。赞同非韵体译法的刘英凯教授引用 Arthur Waley 所说过的"韵脚的限制必然损及语言的活力，必然损及译文的信度，如果一个译者用了韵，就不可能不因声损义"，得出了"韵体译诗是弊大于利"的结论，认为"事实上无韵翻译的实践"已经取得了举世公认的成就。"（杨自俭、刘学云，1994:49—54）。主张韵体译法的许渊冲先生

则提出了"三美"(即意美、音美、形美)的原则(杨自俭、刘学云,1994:90—91),押韵就是其中的内容之一。

诗的神(意象、意境、韵味、神思等)与诗的形(诗体、节奏、音韵、语言等)有着密不可分的同构关系;神寓于形,形之不存,神将焉附?因此,汉诗英译的最高境界应是形神兼似;因此,要评判诗歌翻译的成败优劣,就要看译作在多大程度上迁移或再现原诗的形式美、音韵美、节奏美、情感美、意境美和风格美。

诗的神(意象、意境、韵味、神思等)与诗的形(诗体、节奏、音韵、语言等)有着密不可分的同构关系;神寓于形,形之不存,神将焉附?因此,汉诗英译的最高境界应是形神兼似;因此,要评判诗歌翻译的成败优劣,就要看译作在多大程度上"迁移或再现原诗的形式美、音韵美、节奏美、情感美、意境美和风格美"(卓振英,1997:44)。

本章将借助基于原诗美学特征的评价体系,对《登鹳雀楼》的六种英译进行比较研究,以探讨各种译法的优劣。比较研究采用定性分析与"半定量分析"相结合的方法,以定性分析为主,以半定量分析为辅。所谓半定量分析,即是运用模糊数学的理论和方法,确定译文对原作"信"的隶属度。(杨自俭、刘学云,1994:461)

本论域(全集合)U 包含八个模糊子集:A1(节奏美)、A2(结构美)、A3(音韵美)、A4(意象美)、A5(意境美)、A6(模糊美)、A7(语言美)和 A8(风格美)。元素 X(即集合中的个体)对模糊集合 A 的隶属度,即 X 有几分属于 A,取(0,1)之间的某一实数值,$\mu_A(X)$表示。半定量分析旨在给出模糊量以供参考,尽管各模糊聚类的内容有主次轻重之分,仍不设权重值。

第二节 译作比较研究

王之涣《登鹳雀楼》原诗如下:

> 白日依山尽,黄河入海流。
> 欲穷千里目,更上一层楼。

三种不同译法各选译作两首,A、B 译为非诗化译法,C、D 译为非韵体译法,E、F 为韵体译法:

X1(A 译): *Climbing the "Building of Storks"*

Lingeringly the sun is sinking behind the mountains

While the Yellow River is rolling into the sea.
To have a full view of an expanse of a thousand li,
Let us climb one storey higher.
(czq,from wzk,1989:215—6)

X2(B 译): *Upward*!

Westward the sun, ending the day's journey in a slow descent behind the mountains. Eastward the Yellow River, emptying into the sea. To look beyond, unto the farthest horizon, upward! upward another storey!!
(tr. wxl,from xyz,1992:195)

X3(C 译): *At Heron Lodge*

Mountains cover the white sun,
And oceans drain the golden river;
But you widen your view three hundred miles
By going up one flight of stairs.
(tr. WB,from lybs:?,378)

X4(D 译): *On Ascending Kuan Ch'iao Tower*

The sun is diminishing behind the mountains,
While Yellow River keeps flowing to the sea;
Exhausting my eyes to a thousand li further,
I am ascending one more storey of the tower.
(ljm,1989:66)

X5(E 译): *Ascending the Stork Tower*

Ling'ring is the setting sun about the mountain height,
Surging is the Yellow River eastwards to the sea.
Aim higher and up the tower take another flight
To acquire a vision broader than one thousand li.
(zzy,1996:107)

X6(F 译): *On the Stork Tower*

The sun beyond the mountains glows;
The Yellow River seawards flows.

You can enjoy a grander sight
By climbing to a greater height.
(*xyz*,1992:195)

现在,让我们从以下八个层次,对不同译作与原诗美学特征的隶属度(近似度)作一比较研究。

一、节奏美

汉诗的节奏是由平声字与仄声字的规律性交替来实现的。这首五言绝句所遵循的平仄规律是:

仄仄平平仄,平平仄仄平。(平)平平仄仄,仄仄(仄)平平。

第三句首字"欲"与第四句第三个字"一"分别为仄、平声,这是格律所允许的。这样,朗诵起来抑扬顿挫,声调铿锵,可以像唱歌或奏乐一样打拍子。节奏反映了物质运动的规律和人类的一种审美取向,它赋予诗歌以音乐美。无节奏不可言诗。

六种译作各行(句)音节数(以括号内数字显示)、重读、非重读音节(各以"—"、"*"表示)排列情况、节奏分析及隶属度如下:

A 译:— * * * — — * * — * — *(13)/ — * — * — * — — * — * *(12)/ * — * — — * * — * * — * — (14)/ — * — — — — *(8)

该译轻重音节排列无一定节奏格式,即无法按一定规律把一个诗行划分为一定数目在时值上大致相等的音步,不具备诗歌节奏。$\mu_{A1}(X_1)$ 为 0.10。

B 译:— * * — — * * — * — * — * — *(20)/ — * * — * — * — * * — *(14)/ * — * — * — * — * — * — * — * — * — *(21)

英诗常用节奏有抑扬格(*the iamus*)、抑抑扬格(*the anapest*)、扬抑格(*the trochee*)、扬抑抑格(*the dactyl*)、扬扬格(*the spondee*)、抑抑格(*the pyrrhic*)等。该译不属于其中任何一种,但作为散文,读起来节奏感比 A 译强。$\mu_{A1}(X_2)$ 为 0.20。

C 译:— * — * — —(7)/ * — * — * — * — *(9)/ * * — * — — — * —(10)/ * * — — — * —(8)

第二行为抑扬格,最后一个轻读音节可视为"超音步音节"(hypermetrical syllable)。但其他各行未能与之协调,也难以看做变格(variations in rhythm)。不过节奏感强于 B 译。$\mu_{A1}(X_3)$ 为 0.40。

D 译:*—*—*—*—*—(12)/ *—*—*—*—*— (11)/ *—*— —*—*—(12)/ ——*—*——*—*—(13)

第一行较有规律性,基本上呈抑扬格,第二音步可视为抑抑扬格替代(anapestic substitution)。但其他各行则较散漫,不合节奏规律。$\mu_{A1}(X_4)$ 为 0.40。

E 译:—*—*—*—*—*—(13)/ —*—*—*—*— —*—(13)/ —*—*—*—*—*—(13)/ —*—(13)

每行第一个音节都是单音节音步(monosyllabic foot),它可以替代任何一种音步;第二行的介词"to"及第四行作为不定式符号的"to"由于处在"扬音部"的位置而获得了格律重音。不会影响译作抑扬格七音步(iambic heptameter)的节奏类型。$\mu_{A1}(X_4)$ 为 0.80。

F 译:*—*—*—(8)/ *—*—*—(8)/ *—*— *—(8)/ *—*—*—*—(8)

这是严整的抑扬格四音步(iambic tetrameter)。$\mu_{A1}(X_{16})$ 为 0.85。

二、结构美

文艺美学家瑞恰兹(A. Richards)认为,好诗是各方面平衡的结果,对立的平衡是最有价值的审美反应的基础。(胡经之、王岳川,1994:212)汉诗的对仗所构成的对称美是无与伦比的。从外部形态看,全诗四句,每句五个字,可排列成正长方形。从内部结构看,诗的首联构成工对:"白日"对"黄河","依山"对"入海","尽"对"流";尾联构成流水对,"欲穷"对"更上","千里目"对"一层楼",十分巧妙。除了对仗,首联与尾联以及各联上下句的音节数目和平仄声也造成对称。对称是构成本诗结构美的重要因素。英诗少用对仗,故对仗不构成格律因素,但翻译时可以作为一种修辞手段来对待。

A 译一、二行用了平行句式,有几分形似。但各行音节数参差不齐,且不合音步律,除了行首字母大写,结构上缺乏诗歌这一文学体式的其他特征,其实质是分行散文。$\mu_{A2}(X_1)$为0.20。

B译前两句采用平行结构,有些形似,但译作取散文形式,连诗行这一特征都没有显现出来。$\mu_{A2}(X_2)$为0.20。

C译与A译大同小异,外形比A译更接近原作。$\mu_{A2}(X_3)$为0.35。

D译各行音节数目差别不大,外形有些近似英诗四行诗体(*quatrain*),但一二行句型各异,缺乏对称感,又不合音步律。$\mu_{A2}(X_4)$为0.30。

E译与一、二行是平行句式,也具备诗歌的形态与结构。但七个音步嫌多。$\mu_{A2}(X_5)$为0.80。

F译与E译大同小异,其音步数更接近英诗中的四行诗体。$\mu_{A2}(X_6)$为0.85。

三、音韵美

诗人在二、四句用了同韵字"流"和"楼",使之押韵。押韵在结构上使诗歌各行有机地结合在一起;在音响上造成声音的呼应回环与和衷共鸣,增加诗歌的音乐美;在修辞上加强语气和效果,给人以更深刻的印象和更丰满的感受。押韵是汉诗的一大特色。自诗经以来,我国诗歌几乎没有不押韵的,不论其为古风、格律诗、民谣、辞赋还是散曲。

A译二、三行是押韵的。虽然英语四行诗体中并不存在 $a\,b\,b\,c$ 这种韵式,但这毕竟能产生一定的音响效果。$\mu_{A3}(X_1)$为0.20。

B译不押韵,$\mu_{A3}(X_2)$为0。

C译不押韵,$\mu_{A3}(X_3)$为0。

D译不押韵,$\mu_{A3}(X_4)$为0。

E译押韵,韵式为套韵(*interlaced rhyme*)*abab*,读起来声韵铿锵。$\mu_{A3}(X_5)$为0.85。

F译押韵,韵式为联韵(*couplet rhyme*)*aabb*,读起来朗朗上口。$\mu_{A3}(X_6)$为0.85。

四、意象美

所谓意象,即是主观心意与客观物象在语言文字中的融汇与具现。《周易》就有"观物取象"、"立象以尽意"之说。荣格的原型理论则认为,艺术意象是意识与无意识瞬间沟通的结晶。意象不是人或物体形象的简单复制,它是经过思维的取舍与加工的,是诗人独特的审美感受的产物。例如这首诗里"依山尽"的"白日"与"入海流"的"黄河"两个意象既反映出大自然的雄浑壮观,具有动态美、色彩美及苍劲美,又饱含着诗人对祖国山河的无比热爱。白日的刺眼、炎热,黄河的浑浊、狂野,都被诗人舍弃了。

A译对"黄河"这个意象的再现比较成功,但"sinking"一词描写"白日"容易产生"沉沦"的联想义,不够理想。$\mu_{A_4}(X_1)$为0.60。

B译对"白日"和"黄河"这两个意象的描画比较生动;但"鹳雀楼"这一重要意象缺失。$\mu_{A_4}(X_2)$为0.50。

C译"Mountains cover the white sun"(山遮白日)影响了"白日"的视觉效果;以"golden river"(金色的河)译"黄河",使之失去了原有的地理特征,欠准确;"oceans drain the golden river"中的"drain"有"排水、排尽、剥夺、饮"等义项,不论海洋是饮吸、排尽"金河水"还是使"金河水"徐徐流出,都使黄河从主动变为被动,失去了奔流的磅礴气势。$\mu_{A_4}(X_3)$ 0.50。

D译"diminishing"一词意为"缩小",有伤意象美;"behind the mountains"(山那边)削弱了"白日"的视觉效果;"Yellow River keeps flowing to the sea"不够形象化。末行"I am ascending"说的是,诗人自己正在登楼,而原作中登楼者的身份和人数却是不确定的。$\mu_{A_4}(X_4)$为0.50。

E译采用下义词"Ling'ring"、"Surging"去描绘"白日"与"黄河",下义词即具体词,具体词生动简捷,富于描写性。$\mu_{A_4}(X_5)$为0.85。

F译所用下义词"glows"形象生动;不足的是,"beyond the mountains"(山那边)影响了"白日"的视觉效果的再现。"a grander sight"和"a greater height"具有较强的兼义性。$\mu_{A_4}(X_6)$为0.85。

五、意境美

诗人采用虚实结合的手法,创造出一种形神兼备、情景交融的艺术境界,它有言外之意、弦外之音,能诱发读者想象,使之获得蕴藉隽永、韵美无穷的美感。这种艺术境界便是意境。意境美和意象美都包含了情感美。诗中的"山"、"海"、"白日"与"黄河"融入了诗人的情感,寄托了诗人热爱大自然和祖国河山的思想感情,情与景浑然一体;"更上一层楼"虽言登高望远,却使我们联想到进取和积极向上,含蓄深远。真可谓诗中有画,象外有象,熔情景于一炉。

A译末行"Let us"的行为主体似不包括读者(Let us ≠ Let's,前者用于向受话者提出请求,后者用于建议对方一同采取某一行动或进入某种状态),缩小了诗歌感召力的涵盖面，与原作含义有一定差距。$\mu_{A5}(X_1)$为0.55。

B译"*horizon*"（地平线、眼界、范畴……）有较强的兼义性；"*upward*"的重复有强调的效果，有助于生成激励人们奋发向上的含义。$\mu_{A5}(X_2)$为0.70。

C译"*By going up one flight of stairs*"说的是"爬上一层楼"，原作中"更"的含义未能得到再现；"*stairs*"过于具体而削弱了兼义性。$\mu_{A5}(X_3)$为0.45。

D译由于意象扭曲变形（分析见上文）而破坏了情感美和意境美；有关登楼的陈述除了"登楼"，难以发掘到其他隐含。$\mu_{A5}(X_4)$为0.45。

E译"*Aim higher*"及"*take another flight*"可兼指登楼及积极向上，"*vision*"兼有视力、洞察力、想象力、美景、绝好的人或事物等义项，具有较强的兼义性。三、四行使用祈使句，有助于再现原作所蕴涵的感召力，其内容对人对己都能适用。$\mu_{A5}(X_5)$为0.85。

F译三、四行中的"*height*"可兼指高处及高度，"*sight*"可兼指景象及目光，这两行诗既指登楼远眺，又喻站得高看得远的哲理。不足的是，"*You*"虽是泛称代词，它的使用拉大了诗人与读者的心理距离。$\mu_{A5}(X_6)$为0.80。

六、模糊美

模糊数学问世以来，人们对客观世界的模糊性有了更深的认识。它和精确性是互寓的，都反映了世界的本真和人类的情感与思维特征。结构主义美学认为，诗歌任何文字形式的对等，即便是语音上的对等，都会导致语义对等；语义对等造成语义上的歧义，因而使象征性、多义性和复杂性成为诗歌的特质。（胡经之、王岳川，1994:242）

在这首诗里，除了上面谈到的融情于境及"登楼"的多义性，模糊性也表现在"千里"、"一层"这两个数量词上。"千里"、"一层"的表面意义是精确的，而深层含义"远大"、"新的高度"则是不精确的，这是一种对立的统一，是瑞恰兹所说的"中和"与"包容"。（胡经之、王岳川，1994:212）

模糊性诗歌的翻译是有一定的方法可以遵循的。在诗歌的某一特定模糊语义单位的翻译中，我们可以直接从译文语言中寻找"模棱两可"，即具有语义兼容性的语符，也可以适当地使某一语义概念的边界延展至与另一语义概念相交迭，从而构成'亦此亦彼'的特殊概念，以负载多种含义。

A译"*a full view*"用"*of an expanse of a thousand li*"加以修饰，限定了概念的范畴，使概念的边缘更加清晰；末句则划分出登楼者与不登楼者；数词"*one*"比不定冠词"*a*"更强调数量"一"。这些都削弱了词语的兼义性，影响了模糊美的再创造。$\mu_{A6}(X_1)$ 为 0.20。

  B 译 "*To look beyond, onto the farthest horizon*" 带有"超越"的意味；如上文所述，"*horizon*"的兼义性较强。$\mu_{A6}(X_2)$ 为 0.70。

  C 译 "*But you widen your view three hundred miles*" 不是把"千里"理解为夸张，而是把它换算为"三百英里"，使之更接近精确性而远离模糊性；"*one flight*" 被 "*of stairs*" 所修饰，这等于多了一个定义项而使概念趋于清晰，减弱了象征性。$\mu_{A6}(X_3)$ 为 0.50。

  D 译把登楼者明确为"我"，并使用现在进行时，这就减弱了"激励人们奋发向上"的深层含义及其感召对象的普遍性。$\mu_{A6}(X_4)$ 为 0.45。

  E 译 "*flight*" 有"飞翔、航程、楼梯的一段"等义项，有较强的兼义性和象征性；"*a vision broader than one thousand li*" 具有不确定性，有助于模糊美的重构。$\mu_{A6}(X_5)$ 为 0.80。

  F 译三四行中的 "*sight*" 有"奇观、视力、眼界、风景"等义项，"*height*" 有"高处、顶点、鼎盛时期"等义项，兼义性强。$\mu_{A6}(X_6)$ 为 0.80。

七、语言美

  词语的语体色彩有口语、书面语和诗歌用语三种。一般来说，诗歌语言比较高雅、锤炼。我们只要把这首诗中的"更上"与"再往上爬"、"欲"与"如果要"作一番比较便可明了。英语里 *dome, skyscraper, building* 这三个单词也可以说明词汇层的语体差别。

  A 译用 "*rolling*" 一词描绘黄河，十分生动。不过题目及末行的 "*climb*" 不如 "*ascend*" 高雅；"*Building of Storks*" 不如 "*Stork Tower*" 恰切，因鹳雀楼是塔楼而不是一般的楼房。$\mu_{A7}(X_1)$ 为 0.50。

  B 译副词的使用比较巧妙，但通篇着意不用一个谓语动词，就是祈使句也是仅用副词 "*upward*"，这就未免过于胶柱鼓瑟且流于口语化，而原作却是运用谓语动词去表现心与物的多维动态美的。$\mu_{A7}(X_2)$ 为 0.45。

  C 译题目 "*At Heron Lodge*" 中的 "*Heron Lodge*" 乃"苍鹭居"而非"鹳雀楼"，不准确；"*going up*" 属口语语体；第三行 "*But*" 的使用牵强，其所表示的转折关系是原文所没有的；"*three hundred miles*" 未能再现"千里"这一夸张，因英文习惯上一般用 "*hundreds of ...*"、"*thousands of ...*"、"*a hundred and one*" 等等构成量的夸张，而不用 "*three hundred*"（"三百"）。$\mu_{A7}(X_3)$ 为 0.45。

  D 译把 "*Exhausting my eyes ...*" 这一分词短语作为目的状语，是一种语法错误。如果理解为伴随状语,则与原作相违。"Yellow River"这一地理名词之前未加冠词"the",欠规范。$\mu_{A7}(X_4)$为 0.45。

E 译用词高雅,如"Ling'ring"、"Surging"、"acquire"、"vision"等;一、二行是两个倒装的平行句式,三、四行采用祈使句式,语言形式活泼,修辞效果好。$\mu_{A7}(X_5)$为 0.75。

F 译流畅简洁。不足的是,原诗夸张("千里")这一修辞格未在译作中得到再现。$\mu_{A7}(X_6)$为 0.75。

八、风格美

诗意含蓄,格调高远,风格自然、酣畅、豪放,具有风格美。

A 译"Lingeringly the sun..."中的头两个单词以一个重音带四个轻音,读起来有些佶屈聱牙;"sinking"一词有违豪放的风格;末行("请让我们再爬上一层去")缺乏原作的力感 $\mu_{A8}(X_1)$为 0.50。

B 译散文化、口语化的文体特征与原作风格差别较大(分析见上文)。$\mu_{A8}(X_2)$为 0.40。

C 译中的"Exhausting"词义为"使精疲力竭;用尽"等,传达的是一种疲劳感,"山遮白日"产生的是一种阴暗感,这都与原作豪放轻松的风格和乐观积极的情调不符 $\mu_{A8}(X_3)$为 0.40。

D 译首行颇有感伤的情调;二行难觅热爱山河之情怀;"Exhausting my eyes..."隐含吃力艰苦;"I am ascending..."丢失深层含义,属于减值翻译。所有这些都不甚合乎热情奔放、含蓄蕴藉的文体风格。$\mu_{A8}(X_4)$为 0.40。

E 译一、二行再现了黄河白日的雄浑,有奔放、酣畅之气,三、四行赋予译作以双重含义,兼豪迈、含蓄之风。不过与 F 译相比,尚嫌不够简洁。$\mu_{A8}(X_5)$为 0.75。

F 译所使用字符最少,论简洁酣畅而有余;但诗人的参与意识及原诗夸张手法未能再现,论蕴藉含蓄则不足。$\mu_{A8}(X_6)$为 0.75。

以上分析可得下表:

隶属 隶属度元素 子集 模糊子集	X1(A译)	X2(B译)	X3(C译)	X4(D译)	X5(E译)	X6(F译)
A1(节奏美)	.10	.20	.40	.40	.80	.85
A2(结构美)	.20	.20	.35	.35	.80	.85
A3(音韵美)	.20	0	0	0	.85	.85
A4(意象美)	.60	.50	.50	.50	.85	.85
A5(意境美)	.55	.70	.45	.45	.85	.80
A6(模糊美)	.20	.70	.50	.45	.80	.80
A7(语言美)	.50	.45	.45	.45	.75	.75
A8(风格美)	.50	.40	.40	.40	.75	.75

由上表统计出，$X1$ 至 $X6$ 的总分 m 分别为：八、5、一、5、第三节 5、第三节 0、6.45、6.50；八个模糊子集的平均值 $m/8$ 分别为：0.356、0.394、0.381、0.375、0.806、0.813。按译作质量自优至劣的次序排列，应是：F 译、E 译、B 译、C 译、D 译、A 译。按照类别统计，韵体译作 F 译、E 译的平均值为 0.810，非韵体译作 D 译、C 译的平均值为 0.378，非诗化译作 A 译、B 译的平均值为 0.375。韵体译作的平均值最高。

第三节　结论

　　一般说来，以诗译诗的方法，即诗化译法，要比非诗化译法优越。这是因为，诗歌是按照符合人们普遍审美要求的一定艺术原则构成的，节奏、音韵、形态、等格律要素都是具有一定艺术含义的符号。非诗化译法舍弃这些要素，是一种减值翻译的方法，难以使原诗的美学价值得到较全面的再现。依此法译出的作品，缺失的原诗美学特征太多，读起来味如嚼蜡。而诗化译法遵循的是较高的标准，其本身就有着很强的生命力，因为这种形式具有较为全面地再现或保持原作诗歌美学价值的潜在功能，比其他方法（诸如逐字对译和散文化意译）优越。至于按照诗化的方法译出来的作品是否成功，那就不仅要看译者是否有雄厚的汉语汉诗和英语英诗功底，扎实的东西方比较文化知识以及诗人的才情，而且还要看其是否"具备驾驭翻译理论和运用翻译技巧的能力。"非韵体译法的 C 译和 D 译之所以比非诗化译法的 B 译还差，其原因盖在于此。

　　诗化译法中的韵体译法又比非韵体译法前进了一步。就其本体而论，此法追求的是更高的境界，遵循的是更高的标准，较之后者多了押韵这一要求，因而具有更为全面地再现原诗美学价值的潜在功能;从传播学和接受美学的角度看,按照这种以文艺美学、汉英比较诗学及翻译学等有关理论(如等效理论)为支撑的全值再现原则翻译出来的文本,作为媒介和审美客体,更加适合受众(读者)——特别是以英语为母语的受众—的阅读心理和审美取向。

比较研究说明,Arthur Waley 关于"韵脚的限制必然损及语言的活力"和译文的信度、用了韵"就不可能不因声损义"的说法是不足为据的。我们不应宥于前人即使是名人的某些过时言论而裹足不前。近些年来,韵体翻译的方法论研究日趋广泛深入,成就斐然;许渊冲、汪榕培等等学者运用此法译出的《诗经》等作品臻于形神兼似,受到国内外学界的普遍赞誉。如果说,借助非诗化译法只能满足于拼凑有序的瓷片,借助非韵体译法只能汲汲乎有所缺损的瓷瓶,那么,借助韵体译法就有可能把完整的艺术品奉献于世。

思考题

1. 古人说,"尽信书不如无书"。学习本章之后你对此有什么新的体会?
2. 本章关于韵体译法的优越性的论述能使你信服吗?你是否有新的论据加以补充?
3. 本章是对不同流派翻译思想的总结与批判。你觉得持论公允吗?

练习题

1. 根据所学的新知识,对你所译的唐诗(第三章的练习3)进行修改、润色,同时保留初稿和二稿。
2. 比较分析李白《望庐山瀑布》的不同英译在押韵等格律要素的重构等方面的异同:

原作:
　　日照香炉生紫烟,遥看瀑布挂前川。
　　飞流直下三千尺,疑是银河落九天。

译文 A: *Watching the Waterfall in the Lushan Mountains*
Around the sunlit Incense Burner glows a purplish haze;
The waterfall afore the stream afar attracts my gaze:

With torrents plunging down three thousand feet, it flies and flies
As if it were the Milky Way descending from the skies!
(zzy,1996:117)

译文 B: *Sighting the Cataract of Mount Lu*
The sun shining on the Incense-burner Peak
Issueth purple smoke to wreathe round,
Seen afar the cataract seemeth hung from the cliff top
To the water front of the Mount.
The flying torrent for three thousand feet
Ceaselessly dashing down headlong.
Is taken to be the Silvery Stream falling from
The ninth heaven to the ground.
(sdy,1997: 235)

译文 C: *Watching the Waterfall at Lushan*
In sunshine Censer Peak breathes purple vapor,
Far off hangs the cataract, a stream upended;
Down it cascades a sheer three thousand feet —
As if the Silver River were falling from Heaven!
(yxy & gy,2001:100)

译文 D: *Viewing the Waterfall at Mount Lu*
Sunlight streaming on Incense Stone kindles a violet smoke;
Far off watch the waterfall plunge to the long river,
Flying waters descending straight three thousand feet,
Till I think the Milky Way has tumbled from the ninth height of Heaven.
(Burton Watson, from gzz, 1994:64)

第七章 译作定性评价方法的探索
——以秦观《鹊桥仙》的三种英译为例

学习目标

了解定性评价的各个层面和分析方法。

构建合理的汉诗英译评价体系,以便相对客观地对译作作出具有真知灼见的评价,以指导实践,这是汉诗英译研究的重要课题之一。本书第六章对不同翻译方法进行的比较研究,采用的是定性与半定量分析相结合的研究方法;在这里,我们不妨对基于原作美学特征的定性研究方法作一尝试。

以"七夕"为题材的诸多吟咏之中,最为脍炙人口的当推秦观的《鹊桥仙》:

纤云弄巧,飞星传恨,银汉迢迢暗度。
金风玉露一相逢,便胜却人间无数。
柔情似水,佳期如梦,忍顾鹊桥归路?
两情若是久长时,又岂在朝朝暮暮!

这首词通过描写牛郎织女的"七夕"之会,颂扬了纯真专一的男女之爱,表达了词人对爱情的严肃态度和高尚理想。它委婉含蓄,清丽秀雅,曲尽衬托、比喻之妙,笔端流淌着一种恬静淡逸的惜别情思,使读者感受到一种升华了的情感美。

要把这样一首词译为英文,并最大限度地保持或再现原作的美学价值,包括意境美、风格美、式样美、音韵美和节奏美,绝非易事。本章拟就三种不同的英译进行分析和比较,以探索对古诗词英译进行评价的不同层面及分析方法。三种译文如下:

第一种译文(以下简称甲译):QUEQIAOXIAN
    Clouds have their peculiar flair and skill;
    They can change their size andshape, as they will.

Stars have qualities more wonderful still;
The hopes of their fellows, they can fulfill.
In those celestial regions, high above,
As links for one star to approach her love;
They help "Lassie" to cross the Milky Way,
To see her "Laddie" once a year, this day.
Their love is like heavenly dew for gods to drink.
To the human level, it would never sink.
One rendezvous between them is of more worth
Then countless such as we have on this, our earth.
Their love is constant, as water is, in its flow.
Their lover's meeting is short, as sweet dreams go.
How she bears the sight of Magpie Bridge without a tear,
Which marks their separation for another year!
Since their affection is something that endure,
Must they bill and coo as daily renewer?
(xzj,1986:67—68)

第二种译文（以下简称乙译）：TUNE:" IMMORTAL AT THE MAGPIEBRIDGE"

Clouds float like works of art;
Stars shoot with grief at heart.
Across the Milky Way the Cowherd meets the maid.
When autumn's Golden Wind embraces Dew of Jade,
All the love scenes on earth, however many, fade.
Their tender love flows like a stream
Their happy date seems but a dream.
How can they bear a separate homeward way?
If love between both sides can last for aye,
Why need they stay together night and day?
(xyz,1992:384—5)

第三种译文（以下简称丙译）：*Celestial Beings on the Magpie Bridge*

Her yearning in th' clouds th' Girl Weaver subtly weaves,
While the shooting stars display how th' cowherd grieves.
Across the Milky Way they meet
But once out of a year's so many eves!
Howe'er, no secular love can e'er compare
With th' holy sentiments they for a time share.
Their keen affection is like a long long stream;
Their meeting as short as a transient dream.
Their hearts may bleed now that they part
At th' Magpie Bridge—men are inclined to deem.
But nay, so long as undying love will stay,
Whereat should they be bound up each night and day?
(zzy,1996:227)

第一节 意象层面的比较分析

一、"鹊桥仙"

这是词牌名,指的是牛郎织女的"七夕"之会,与词的题材和情思关系密切,且构成意象。甲译采用音译法,难以再现原作意象。乙、丙用意译法较为可取;乙译"Immortal"一词如改用复数则效果更佳。

二、"纤云弄巧,飞星传恨,银汉迢迢暗度。"

这是客观物象"纤云"、"飞星"和"迢迢"、"银汉"以及主观心意"巧"、"恨"和"暗度"所构建成的意象群,可谓情景交融,先声夺人,一开篇就让读者感受善织云锦的织女的相思之苦,感情真挚的牛郎的哀怨之深和他们之间的相见之难。

甲译用了8行笔墨予以处理,除了行文拖沓之外尚有三点不足:仅写星云之美而失却了它们的烘托作用;说飞星帮助"女孩"过银河去探"男孩",主动的似乎仅仅是女方,且为之造桥的竟是"星"而不是鹊,这与原词及传说大相龃龉;以"Laddie"及"Lassie"指称牛织也不够明确。

乙译"Clouds float like works of art;/Stars shoot with grief at heart./

Across the Milky Way the Cowherd meets the Maid",以"the Maid"指称织女,也较含混,且未能表现借云弄巧、借星传恨者为何人及其相见之难。

丙译"Her yearning in th' Girl Weaver subtly weaves,/While the shooting stars display how th Cowherd grieves./Across the Milky Way they meet but once out of a year's so many eves!"忠实地以飞星和纤云作为阳刚及阴柔的情感表达方式,牛织的译法比甲、乙妥帖,三、四两行既隐含怨叹又体现出原作的含蓄之风,可谓恰到好处。

三、"柔情似水,佳期如梦"

这两个比喻以虚幻的手法表现了相会的情景和会短情长的矛盾心态:委婉温馨,情思秀逸。

甲译"Their love is constant, as water is, in its flow./Their lover's meeting is short, as sweet dreams go."基本上忠实地再现了原作的思想内容,烘托出哀婉的相思情味。

乙译"Their tender love flows like a stream;/Their happy date seems but a dream."亦然,不过其中的"but a dream"有产生歧义的可能,即"只是一场梦"(不现实)。

丙译"Their keen affection is like a long long stream;/Their meeting as short as a transient dream."以重复强调了"长"又点明了"如梦(般短暂)",似更准确而富于表现力。

第二节 意境层面的比较分析

词人采用虚实结合的手法,熔情、景、理于一炉,创造出蕴藉隽永、韵味无穷的艺术境界。虽写天上的神仙,却又诱发读者联想地上的凡人,并以牛织相会这一特定的时空和情景为支点,去俯视无限的人间众生相,真是象外有象,景外有景。

除了上文所提及的情景之外,词人所抒发的情怀对于意境的创造起了重要的作用。

一、"金风玉露一相逢,便胜却人间无数。"

这两句把牛织的感情与"人间无数"作了比较(但不是对比)。

甲译"Their love is like heavenly dew for gods to drink./To the human level it would never sink./One rendezvous between them is of more worth/Than countless such as we have on this, our earth."说"他们的爱像可供神仙饮用的天上的露水",这一比喻是原文所无的,也不甚妥当。原文"金风玉露"指的是时间,这可参照李商隐《辛未七夕》"由来碧落银河畔,可要金风玉露时"二句。再者,"sink"一词的使用把神仙的爱与凡人的爱对立起来,也不合适。

"一相逢"者本是牛织,乙译"When autumn's golden Wind embraces Dew of jade,/All the love scenes on earth, how ever many, fade."却误把风与露当做行为主体。

丙译"Howe'er, no secular love can compare/With th' holy sentiments they for a time share."较为忠实原文,不过未能点明时在金秋,也是一憾。

二、"忍顾鹊桥归路?"

这是从一般人的心理角度提出的设问,它既委婉地表现了牛织之间的惜别,又巧妙地为下文的转折作了铺垫。

甲译"How she bears the sight of Magpie Bridge without a tear,/Which marks their separation for another year!"言只及"她"而不及"他",这正如以单人舞的形式去表现双人舞的内容一样,是无法再创造出原作的意象和意境的。再者,说织女"忍住了眼泪",这既不够忠实,又说明不了其思想境界有何超绝处。

乙译"How can they bear a separate homeward way?"不论在思想内容还是语言形式方面都是比较贴切的。

丙译"Their hearts may bleed now that they part/At th' Magpie Bridge—men are inclined to deem."用插入语对设问的心理角度加以明确,也为下文由"But, nay"引起的转折作了铺垫,与原作有异曲同工之妙。

四、"两情若是久长时,又岂在朝朝暮暮!"

在这里,词的意脉空际转身,幻化出了超凡脱俗的境界。词人的情思与牛织融为一体,竟难分"何者为我,何者为物(客体)"了。

三种译法都使用了修辞问句,富于表达力。其他方面则各有千秋:甲译"bill and coo"比较生动,但嫌俗嫌露;乙译"for aye"比较高雅,丙译转折比较自然,语言也不俗。

第三节 语言风格层面的比较分析

原词行文自然酣畅、委婉含蓄、简约有力,具有一种素净之美。上片以凄迷冷清的情景烘托气氛,下片以精辟的比喻、巧妙的设问和掷地作金石声的感慨层层递进,勾勒出一份清秀隽永的浓郁相思情。

甲译 1—4 行对于星、云的描绘略嫌浮华;9 行以露喻爱,而露具有"短暂"的联想意义,不甚妥当;倒数第二行"... is something that endure"中的"endure"一词本该加词尾"-s",为了押韵而违犯了语法规则;行内不必要的停顿过多,阻滞了语言的自然流畅。

乙译基本上合乎原作风格,但个别地方语体不一。例如,"for aye"是比较古雅的用语,但以"Their happy date"译"佳期"则有偏俗之嫌,因为"date"作"约会"解时是美国英语的一种非正规用法。

丙译颇具原作委婉含蓄的文风,如前 4 行的描述;行文也流畅自然。

第四节 格律层面的比较分析

原词分上下片,每片 5 句,三、五句押韵。两片各行字数及节奏一一对应。

一、样式

甲译共 18 行,上片译为 12 行,下片译为 6 行,不分诗节。英诗这么多行而不分诗节的殊不多见,因而使人有译文流于拖沓之感。

乙译共 10 行,分为两个诗节,近似英诗的五行体。

丙译共 12 行,分为两个诗节,近似英诗 6 行体。乙、丙皆得形似之妙。

二、节奏

甲译各行音节数无一定规则,少的 10 个音节,多的(倒数第四行)13 个音节。

乙译两个诗节各行的音节数目分别为 6、6、12、12、12;8、8、11、10、10。欠严整。

丙译两诗节各对应诗行的音节数目相等。

乙、丙两译的基本节奏形式为抑扬格。这就是说,其中有变格的现象。根据英诗格律,变格不仅是允许的,而且有助于避免单调平板。

三、押韵

甲、乙、丙的押韵格式分别为:a a a a b b c c d d e d f f g g h h;a a b b, c c d d d;a a b a c c,d d e d f f。三种译文读来都比较上口,特别是后两种,声韵铿锵、力透纸背、忠实得体、节奏明快;在结构上、修辞上和音响效果上更加美妙。

第五节 小结

从总体上看,丙译佳于乙译,乙译佳于甲译。丙译相对而言更多地保持和再现了原作的诗歌美学价值,更臻于形神兼似的诗译境界。

本章说明,采用基于原作美学特征的定性评价方法,从若干层面对译作进行分析或比较研究,是可行的。

杨宪益夫妇以格律诗的形式翻译出的《九歌》,有人曾笑之为"Easter Egg",认为缺乏活力。对于此种嘲笑,编者不敢苟同。抛开具体某一译品的成败优劣不论,以诗化的形式翻译中国古诗词,其本身就有着很强的生命力,因为这种形式具有较为全面地再现或保持原作诗歌美学价值的潜在功能,比其他方法(诸如逐字对译和散文化意译)优越。它在理论和实践两个方面都不断地得到完善和发展。译者们分别发表于 1996 年、1992 年和 1986 年的丙、乙、甲三种译作一译胜过一译,这也可以作为这种完善和发展的佐证之一。

丙译有几点可供借鉴:

其一,译者对原作的思想内容、艺术形式和相关文化背景是作过一番研究和审度的,否则就不可能产生比较忠实得体的译作,也难以避免其他译作所出现的错误和不当。

其二,兼顾到中英两种文化和语言的差异及以英语为母语的读者的特点,采用了恰当的翻译方法。例如,原文文字并未交代"一相逢"的主语、何人"弄巧"、为谁"传恨"及究竟是什么"胜却人间无数",译者打破表层结构,挖掘深层含义,对汉语的"无主句"和原文隐而不露的内容分别作了增补及显化处理。

其三,用词古雅,例如疑问词"whereat",起衔接作用的"But nay",以及既与"weaves"和"grieves"押韵又点明牛、织相会时间的"eves"等,使译作与原作在语言风格方面基本上相切合。

3. 批评应以发展学术为出发点,实事求是,以理服人。古人有"举贤不避亲"一说。只要我们抱着实事求是的态度,去对待所有的研究对象,追求真理,那么,对于他人的学术观点的长短处,就不妨指陈得失;对于自己的研究成果的优缺点,也不必讳言、护短。

最近又见到两种译文,兹收录于此,以供读者参照:

Que Qiao Xian

The fleecy clouds affect patterns delicate;
The flying stars communicate their grief e'er so deep,
Crossing the expansive Milky Way they meet.
Alas! That single meet amid celestial winds and dews
Surpasses countless meets on earth.
Sweet tenderness overflows their hearts,
Short rendezvous passes like a dream:
Mournfully she contemplates her homeward way
Across the magpie-bridge!
Yet if two hearts are ever steadfast,
Though parted, they are together
Night and day!
(hhq,2001:131)

Tune: Queqiaoxian

Clouds float like works of art,
Stars bring the grief of love.
Across the Milky Way, the Cowherd meets the Maid.

When the golden autumn's wind encounters with dew of jade,
Their meeting is better than many times on earth.
Their tender love flows like a stream,
Their happy date seems as sweet dreams.
How she bears the sight of Magpie Bridge without a tear!
If the affection on both sides can endure,
Why need they stay together night and day?
(mxy,1997:105)

思考题

1. 建立汉诗英译的评价体系有何意义?
2. 唐太宗问魏征:"人主何为而明,何为而暗?"魏征答道:"兼听则明,偏信则暗"。学习者应广开言路,拓展视听,做到持论公允,而不可为本教程的观点所囿。对于秦观《鹊桥仙》的不同英译,评价纷纭。请从"知网"上搜索具有相反看法的批评文章,仔细研究其立论的理据。

练习题

1. 从本书附录中任选一首诗、词、曲、赋,对其英译予以评价。
2. 对所选诗、词、曲或赋的英译提出你的改进意见,并说明你的理据。
3. 试比较林则徐赴戍登程口占示家人(其二)的不同英译。

原作:

力微任重久神疲,再竭衰庸定不支。
苟利国家生死以,岂因祸福避趋之!
谪居正是君恩厚,养拙刚于戍卒宜。
戏与山妻谈故事,试吟断送老头皮。

译文1: *Oral Compositions to My Family upon Leaving for the Frontier* (*No.2*)

I couldn't have been able any longer to sustain
The vital post, which has tir'd this unworthy person out.

Whate'er's in th' interest of the state I'll do with might and main,
And personal weal or woe is not to be car'd about.
Demotion only shows His Majesty's favour, and life
In the' frontier will perfectly suit my mortal dim and dull.
Let me, on leaving, retell a story to my dear wife
And read aloud the poem therein 'bout "forfeiting th' old skull".
(zzy,1996:317)

译文 2: *Before Going into Exile*

Weary for long with feeble strength and duty great,
Mediocrity exhausted, could I not sink low?
I'd risk life and brave death to do good to the state.
Could I but for myself seek weal and avoid woe?
The banishment just show the royal favor high;
My border service is good to do what I can.
I tease my wife with a story of days gone by:
Why not try to chant verse to see off your old man?
(xyz,2000: Gems 295)

第八章 汉诗英译中的总体审度

学习目标

了解总体审度的意义和范畴,掌握审度的方法。

第一节 何谓汉诗英译中的总体审度?

在汉诗英译中,为了制订正确的翻译策略,翻译出成功的译作,就必须对作者的思想、生平,作品的内容、风格、形体、类别、不同版本(如果有的话)和时代背景,现有英译的各种版本及其翻译模式和特点,相关的翻译方法论以及决定预期翻译文本文化定位的社会文化因素等等进行一番深入细致的研究,通过文化历史观照、文本内证及外证、互文观照以及作品与文本的互证对文本进行语义诠释,通过解码、解构、解析、整合对文本进行文化解读,以便对作品的总意象(total concept)及预期翻译文本的文化定位等等做到心中有数。这就是汉诗英译中的总体审度。

忽略总体审度,名家高手也难免败笔,这样的例子实在不少。

杜甫"漫卷诗书喜欲狂"一句本来形容妻子的情感与动作,译为"I gather up books and poems","I can well say I am wild with glee"(xzj,1990:153),竟成了诗人的感情与动作。

王维"此物最相思"一句,原意指朋友之情,在历史沿用中衍生出来的意义是广义的爱,译为"The best reminder of love between woman and man"(xzj,1990:77),变成了狭义的男女之爱。

贺知章"儿童相见不相识"一句,分别被译为"And my children, meeting me, do not know me"(tr. WB, from lsx,1980:5),"Seeing my kids, I don't know who they are./Neither do they recognize me, their pa"(xzj,1990:34),"My very children do not know my face"(tr. H.A.G, from xyz,1992:182)和"My children, whom I meet, do not know who am I"(xyz,1992:182),误将诗

人故乡的儿童当做诗人的亲生子女。

以上各例,如果分别参照上句"试看妻子愁何在";弄清《相思》一诗又题为《江上赠李龟年》;审明贺知章是天宝三载辞官回越州老家时写《回乡偶书》的,时年八十六岁,那么,其中的错误就可以避免,诗歌的思想内容就可能得到真实再现。

根据总体审度,编者建议将(1)至(5)例有关诗句译为:"... My wife and son, wild with glee, /Are packing up books—no trace of care can I see"; "The token best of love sincere indeed"; "The native children, in whose eyes I am a stranger entire, /Politely smile on meeting me: 'Where comest thou?' they inquire,"以避免内容上的误差扭曲。

诗的韵致、风格和境界也不可不予以审察,否则,诗译就不可能"传神"。《登鹳雀楼》中有"黄河入海流"一句,它融入了眼前景与意中景,绘出大自然的壮丽雄浑,抒发了诗人的山河之爱。把它译为"The muddy Yellow river seawards flows"(xzj,1990:32),便以"浑浊"(muddy)破坏了原诗的意象美和情感美。又有"欲穷千里目,更上一层楼"二句,表达了进取的精神和高瞻远瞩的襟怀,流传的过程中又被赋予"站得高方能看得远"的哲理,寓意深远。译为"If more distant views are what you desire, /You simply climb up a storey higher"(xzj,1990:32),淡化了诗人的主体意识,降低了原诗的思想深度和艺术高度,未能再现原诗意境。又以元稹《行宫》英译为例,H. A. Giles 和 Soame Jenyns 都把"白头宫女"译为单数("An Emperor's flame","a white-hair palace woman"),未能像原作那样反映玄宗之荒淫;"闲坐说玄宗"一句,Jenyns 和另一译家分别译为"Idly mumbles of the glorious days of Hsuan Hsung"和"Talk of the late Emperor's pleasure"(xyz,1992:289),前者失之于有誉无贬,而后者不仅未能表达原诗的哀怨与盛衰之叹,且失却了原诗含蓄的风格,平添了一种浅陋与粗俗。秦观《鹊桥仙》一词中的"飞星传恨",有的学者译为"Stars have qualities more wonderful still"(xzj,1986:67),根本无"恨"可言;"佳期"一语,也有人译为"their happy date"(xyz,1992:385),一改原诗之优雅。上述种种信息迁移方面的不当或者失误,与忽略总体审度不无关系。我们应当引以为戒。

上文所涉及的《登鹳雀楼》、《行宫》二首唐诗及宋词《鹊桥仙》有关诗句,编者作了如下试译,仅供参照。

　　　　白日依山尽,黄河入海流。欲穷千里目,更上一层楼。

　　　　　　　　　　　　　　　　　　　——(《登鹳雀楼》)

Ling'ring is the setting sun about the mountain height,
Surging is the Yellow river towards the vast sea.
Aim higher and up the tower take another flight
To acquire a vision broader than one thousand Li.
寥落古行宫,宫花寂寞红。白头宫女在,闲坐说玄宗。

——《行宫》

The ancient palaces present a rueful sight,
'Tis vainly that are blooming flowers red and bright.
Those white-hair'd ladies, who've surviv'd their mental pain,
Now sit at ease recalling Xuan-zongand his reign.
纤云弄巧,飞星传恨
Her yearning in th' clouds th' girl Weaver subtly weaves,
While the shooting stars display how th' Cowherd grieves.
柔情似水,假期如梦
Their tender feeling is like a long long stream,
Their rendezvous is like a transient dream.

以上分析说明,以总体审度的尺度衡量英译是否保持、再现或在多大的程度上保持了原诗的节奏美、音韵美、形式美、风格美、情感美和意境美同样是可行的。这就是说,总体审度是译作的评价指标之一。下文将以楚辞英译为例,对总体审度的范畴和方法加以描述。

第二节 《大中华文库·楚辞》英译的总体审度

楚辞英译中的审度主要包含以下范畴:

一、作者和时代背景

屈原(约公元前339—公元前278)是我国历史上杰出的政治家和第一位伟大的爱国诗人。他明于治乱,娴于辞令,在担任三闾大夫、左徒期间坚决主张联齐抗秦,积极辅佐怀王变法图强。然而,由于与楚国腐朽贵族集团发生了尖锐的矛盾,屈原遭到上官大夫子兰等人的排挤、诬陷和楚王的疏远,一再遭到放逐,在极度悲愤中自沉汨罗江。屈原是《楚辞》的代表作家,流传下来的作品凡

26篇。他崇高的人文精神和伟大人格,惊天地而泣鬼神。司马迁说,屈原"虽与日月争光可也"(《史记》)。1953年,屈原被列为世界四大文化名人之一,受到世界和平理事会和全世界人民的景仰和隆重纪念。

二、原作的内容及其版本

　　刘向编定的《楚辞》16卷原本已佚,今存最早的《楚辞》注本是东汉王逸的《楚辞章句》。《楚辞章句》以刘向《楚辞》为底本,除了对楚辞做了较完整的训释之外,还提供了有关原本的情况。南宋洪兴祖在《楚辞章句》的基础上作了《楚辞补注》,南宋朱熹著有《楚辞集注》,清初王夫之撰有《楚辞通释》,清代蒋骥有《山带阁注楚辞》,等等。当代学者也有不少楚辞研究方面的著作。

　　《离骚》是屈原的代表作,也是中国古代文学史上最长的一首浪漫主义的政治抒情诗;《天问》提出了170多个问题,涉及天文、地理、历史、社会、伦理、文学(神话、传说)、哲学等许多领域,表现了诗人对传统观念的大胆怀疑和追求真理的科学精神;《九歌》是在祭歌的基础上加工而成的11篇歌谣,诗中创造了大量神与巫的形象;《九章》叙述诗人的遭际,抨击误国害民的群小,抒发诗人爱国爱民的情怀和政治理想;《远游》叙述诗人在"遭沈浊而淤秽"而又郁结难抒之际,"悲时俗之迫阨",想象自己遨游于神仙世界,表达对真理的不倦追求和对故国的深厚热爱;《卜居》、《渔父》借占卜和与渔父的对话表达诗人崇高的人生观;《大招》是招魂曲词。

　　屈原深刻揭露了楚国政治的黑暗、贵族集团的腐朽和楚王的昏庸,同时对战争造成的"民离散而相失"(《哀郢》)寄托了深切的同情;为了实现崇高的理想,他不怕"路修远以多艰","虽九死其犹未悔"(《离骚》)。他所"上下而求索"的"美政",就是"举贤授能",即不分贵贱,把真正有才能的人选拔上来,反对世爵世禄,限制旧贵族对权位的垄断;"循绳墨而不颇",即修明法度,以法律为准绳,限制旧贵族的种种特权;"察笃夭隐,孤寡存只","田邑千里,人阜昌只。美冒众流,德泽章只。先威后文,善美明只",即明赏罚,重民生,施福利,德、法相济,富民强国。屈原的作品表现了诗人对传统观念的大胆怀疑、对真理的不倦追求和对祖国的无限忠诚,闪耀着人道主义的光辉。

　　由于楚辞的写作年代久远,又经历了复杂的文化变迁,其中不少章句的解读众说纷纭,悬而未决。

三、原作的艺术形式和风格

屈赋、楚辞体、骚体都用以指战国时楚地出现的一种新诗体。楚辞之称始于汉代。《史记·酷吏列传》记载:"买臣以'楚辞'与助(庄助)俱幸。"金开诚《屈原辞研究》指出:"楚人称之为'辞',以别于《诗三百篇》之'诗'。"楚辞是一种诗体,这应是无可非议的。

屈原将对理想的热烈追求融入了艺术的想象和神奇的意境之中,其想象之大胆、奇特,古今罕有。他以一系列比兴手法来表情达意,以美人、鲜花象征"美政"的理想和高洁的品行,以臭物、萧艾比喻奸佞或变节的小人,使忠与奸、美与丑、善与恶形成鲜明的对照,产生言简意赅、言有尽而意无穷的艺术效果。

他的作品形式上参差错落、灵活多变;采用大量典故和经过提炼的楚地方言,辞藻华美,极富于乡土气息和艺术表现力。

四、楚辞在文学史和文化史中的地位

与《诗经》一样,产生于两千多年前的《楚辞》是中国诗歌乃至中国文化的源头之一。《楚辞》突破了《诗经》的表现形式,极大地丰富了诗歌的表现力,对汉赋的形成和后代的诗歌创作产生了深刻影响,为中国的诗歌创作开辟了一片新天地。

司马迁说:"《国风》好色而不淫,《小雅》怨诽而不乱,若《离骚》者,可谓兼之矣"(《史记》)。朱熹对楚辞褒贬参半。他所说的使"天性民彝之善""交有所发"是不错的:楚辞闪耀着人文精神之光辉,具有呼唤、启迪人性真善美之感召力。然而,从现在的观点看来,他所谓"过于中庸"者,乃蔑视传统道德观念,敢于超越叛逆也;所谓"流于跌宕怪神,怨怼激发"者,乃疾恶如仇,气势磅礴,融神话与现实于一炉也;所谓"不知学于北方,以求周公仲尼之道,而独驰骋于变风变雅之末流"者,乃富于创新精神,开百代之文风也。

五、现有的英译

虽然在楚辞外译的历史中,英译起步较晚,却呈现出蓬勃发展的势头。自从1879年派尔克在《中国评论杂志》发表了《离骚》英译以来,楚辞英译便层出不穷。1884年,翟理斯教授在上海出版了《中国文学精华》,其中有《卜居》、《渔

父》和《山鬼》的英译。1895 年,理雅各在《亚洲学刊》发表了《离骚》英译。1918 年,韦利在孔斯答勃尔出版《中国诗歌一百七十首》,其中有《国殇》。1919 年,韦利在阿伦与昂汶公司出版的《中国文学译作续编》上译介了《大招》。1928 年,比亚拉斯《华北分会学刊》发表了《屈原的生平和诗作》,其中有《东皇太乙》、《山鬼》、《惜颂》、《卜居》、《渔父》及《天问》前 12 行的英译。1929 年,林文庆在上海出版了英译《离骚》。1947 年,纽约出版了白英和西南联大师生合译的《白驹集》(古今中国诗选),其中有《九歌》、《九章》、《卜居》、《渔父》、《招魂》、《天问》。1953 年,杨宪益、戴乃迭夫妇在外文出版社出版了他们选译的《楚辞》。1955 年,韦利出版了《九歌》。1959 年,霍克思在牛津大学出版《楚辞》全译本,该译本 1985 年由企鹅出版公司再版。近年国内出版的英译本则有许渊冲英译、杨逢彬编注的《楚辞》(湖南出版社,1994)、孙大雨的《屈原诗选英译》(上海外语教育出版社,1996)和杨宪益、戴乃迭的《楚辞选》(外文出版社,2001)等。

尽管他们的译品瑕瑜互见,但是,这些走在前面的巨人们弘扬了华夏文化,探索了翻译的路径,为产生更好的译作准备了条件。

六、决定预期翻译文本文化定位的社会文化因素

翻译是受社会文化制约的。汉诗英译是东西方文化交流的需要,也是华夏民族增强文化活力以求生存、图发展的需要。

汉诗英译有普及型和学术型之别。林语堂所译《论语》属于普及型,而《大中华文库》是之前新闻出版总署立项的重大翻译出版工程,翻译、出版的目的是弘扬华夏文化、满足文化层次较高的中外读者欣赏、收藏和研究的需要,其汉诗的英译属于学术型翻译。目前《大中华文库》已确立其典籍英译精品的地位。楚辞英译必须适应这一情势。

七、汉诗翻译方法研究在当今的建树

楚辞是骚体诗,而诗歌是按照符合人们普遍审美要求的一定艺术原则构成的,节奏、音韵、形态等格律要素都是具有一定艺术含义的符号。汉诗英译的方法有多种。非诗化译法舍弃这些要素,是一种减值翻译的方法,难以使原诗的美学价值得到较全面的再现。诗化译法中的韵体译法比非韵体译法前进了一步,它所追求的是更高的境界,遵循的是更高的标准,较之后者多了押韵这一要求,因而具有更为全面地再现原诗美学价值的潜在功能。从传播学和接受美学

的角度看,按照这种以文艺美学、汉英比较诗学及翻译学等有关理论(如等效理论)为支撑的全值再现原则翻译出来的文本,作为媒介和审美客体,更加适合受众(读者)——特别是以英语为母语的受众——的阅读心理和审美取向。目前,汉诗英译研究(特别是诗学范式汉诗英译研究)已形成较完善的理论系统,在翻译标准、原则、诗歌美学(如诗歌的模糊性)、总体审度、风格变通与重构、借形传神、炼词、移情、诗化、对仗翻译、译作评价体系和译者必备条件等方面都有较深入的探讨,可以借鉴和参考。

八、现有各种译本的特点

在版本、选材方面,杨宪益、许渊冲、霍克斯等译家各有所好、各有所据,篇数也有差异,后者仅译 17 篇。首先,中外译家的思想与精神就值得推崇与学习。他们热爱中国文化,并为其传承与弘扬而呕心沥血;其次,他们尽其所能,力图再现原作的美学特征,这种治学态度也是值得仿效的。霍克斯在其 *The Songs of the South* 中就写了大量很有价值的注解(annotations)。不足之处在于:

(1) 在文化语义(内容)处理方面,基本完全依照某种白话版本对原作的解读,缺乏自己的研究和见解,文化语义的传递也值得斟酌。外文出版社 2001 年版的《楚辞选》把鄂渚译为 the Beach,江湘译为 the river,辰阳译为 Southern Star,溆浦译为 poolside,桑扈译为 the recluse;湖南出版社 1994 年版的《楚辞》则把鄂渚、方林、江湘、溆浦、吴榜分别译为 the River Bank,the Wood,the Bay,the town,Oars,把重华、接舆、桑扈、比干、伍子等专有名词译为普通名词 ancient Kings,one Sage,one Saint,Good Ministers,another,把为屈原拉车的"青虬"、"白螭"分别译为 blue dragons,white snakes 和 green-horn Serpents,dragons white,竟是龙蛇混杂。在西方,snake 与 Serpent 容易使人联想到恶人、撒旦;再说,屈子也羞与虫蛇为伍。

(2) 在艺术形式上,有的将楚辞译为无韵诗,例如《思美人》:

> Thinking of a Fair One,
> I brushed back my tears and long stand gazing,
> Sundered from friends to plead for me, for the road is blocked,
> I can frame no message to send to him,
> And my burning wrongs, in tumult,

Are choked within and cannot find an outlet.
Until the dawn I pour out my inner heart;
But my will is thwarted and cannot reach its object.
(David Hawkes,1985:173)

"押韵与节奏一样,使诗歌富于声乐美。汉诗更重押韵,可谓无韵不成诗。"(卓振英 b,2003:25)因此,这种译法是否可取,值得商榷。

有的译本是按英雄双行体或四行诗体翻译的,韵式基本上始终如一,缺乏变化。例如:

THE YOUNG FATE

Mingled with Anise, Autumn Orchids late
In Clustersgrow before the Palace Gate;
Green are their Leaves, their tender Sprigs are white;
Their Fragrance floods my Senses with Delight.
Each Mortal has a Loved One of his own,
Then why should she, the Goddess, sigh alone?
Fresh spring the Autumn Orchids' tender Shoots;
Green are their Leaves and purple are their Roots.
Young Gallants throng the Palace to Entrance,
But I alone am favoured by her Glance.
(yxy & gy, 2001: 51—52)

有的译本套用四行诗节,若遇到六行的诗节,就作为两个四行诗节处理,这样,由于其中一个诗节少了两行,就用两个省略号代替:

THE YOUNG GODDESS OF FATE

Autumn orchids, oh! and the flower sweet
Like silver stars, oh! grow at our feet.
Their leaves are green, oh! and blossoms white;
Fragrance assails us, oh! left and right.
... ,
... .
All women have, oh! fair ones they love.
Why are you sad, oh! lonely above?

Autumn orchids, oh! are lush with shoots;
Their leaves so green, oh! with purple roots.
The fair ones fill, oh! the hall with glee.
Why is amorous look, oh! but cast on me?
(xyz,1992:43)

这同样不甚可取,因为楚辞不同于诗经,它可有各种行数的诗节。省略号可能会产生误导,使读者以为被省略处已经亡佚,或因不堪入目而被译者略去。

至于《渔父》一篇,除了渔父所唱四行外,以上所引译本都把它译为散文。这样一来,楚辞里就既有诗又有散文,这是不太适宜的。当然,原诗美学价值的保留与再现,并不是做好总体审度就能办得到的。译作成败还取决于翻译决策是否得当。

第三节　小结

汉诗英译中的总体审度好比战争中综观天时、地利、人和及敌我双方的力量对比。只有做到全局在胸,才能制订出正确的战略部署,克敌制胜;只有掌握一首诗的全貌及内涵、外延,才能缩小译者与作者的心理距离,确切领悟字里行间的寓意,确定正确的翻译策略与方法,使译作与原作具有异曲同工的艺术效果。

翻译汉诗(典籍)——从四行小诗到鸿篇巨制——都必须首先进行一番仔细的研究,按照总体深度的要求,审时度势,把握总意象,以便制订出恰当的翻译模式和策略,选择恰当的翻译技巧。切不可率尔操笔。

思考题

1. 总体审度那么费劲,有必要吗?为什么?
2. 说出审度应包含的主要范畴。
3. 陆游的《卜算子》颂扬了梅花的孤傲骨格。它的不同英译中,是否有哪种英译有失于风格的总体审度?你认为"梅"该用什么人称才比较合适?

原作：

　　驿外断桥边，寂寞开无主。
　　已是黄昏独自愁，更着风和雨。

　　无意苦争春，一任群芳妒。
　　零落成泥碾作尘，只有香如故。

译文 1: *The Diviner — Ode to the Plum Flower*

By the broken bridge beyond the post thou bloom'st
In solitude, expecting none to flatter.
At dusk the rains spatter, when thou suffer'st lonely cares,
And the blasting winds do boom and thee shatter.
As thou hast ne'er vi'd with the favour'd in spring,
What matters if they should thee envy and blame?
Thou may'st wither, fall and be ground to dust, thy fragrance,
However, will remain as before the same!
(zzy, 1996: 241)

译文 2: *Pu Suan Zi — To the Mei Flowers*

Beyond the post and by the broken bridge
In solitude you blow and unloved.
The deepening dusk has only brought you sadness,
Which to increase the winds and rains
Are lashing you so merciless!
You have no heart to vie with spring hues;
Their envying you affects you not.
Anon ground to dust
You shall vanish in the earth,
Yet your wonted scent forever lives.
(hhq, 2001: 221)

译文 3: *Ode to the Mume Blossom*
Tune: "Song of Divination"

Beside the broken bridge and outside the post hall
A flower is blooming forlorn.

Saddened by her solitude at nightfall,
By wind and rain she's further torn.

Let other flowers their envy pour.
To spring she lays no claim.
Fallen in mud and ground to dust, she seems no more,
But her fragrance is still the same.
(xyz,1990:327)

 练习题

1. 对王昌龄《出塞》一诗进行审度：
   秦时明月汉时关，万里长征人未还。
   但使龙城飞将在，不教胡马度阴山。
2. 以审度的理念对上面这首诗的以下各种译法进行分析并加以评论：

译文 1: *Far Away on the Frontier*
As in th' Han and th' Qin Dynasties th' same fortes and the same moon;
How are men on th' expedition able to come home soon?
Were the Flying General who'd struck th' Dragon Town with fear
Still alive, th' Hun steeds would've been kept 'yond Yinshan—th' frontier!
(zzy,1996:102)

译文 2: *Army Life*
The age-old moon still shines o'er the ancient Great Wall,
But our frontier guardsmen have not come back at all.
Were the winged general of Dragon City here,
The Tartar steeds would not dare to cross the frontier.
(xyz,from gzz,1994:29)

译文 3: *Over the Border*
The moon goes back to the time of Qin, the wall to the time of Han.
And the road our troops are travelling goes back three hundred miles....

Oh, for the winged General at the Dragon City —
That never a Tartar horseman might cross the Ying Mountains.
(W. B. , from lsx, 1980:27)

3. 根据新理论和新知识,修改自己所译的古诗(词)。

第九章 汉诗英译中的决策

学习目标

  为何翻译？预期的读者是谁？如何翻译？翻译之先、之中及初稿完成之后该做些什么工作？诸如此类的问题译者都必须在总体审度的基础上做出决定和选择。通过本章的学习，了解决策的范畴、思路和并掌握决策的方法。

第一节 《大中华文库·楚辞》英译的翻译决策

  中西方近年兴起的文化翻译学及翻译研究各流派，如多元系统理论（polysystem theory）、描写译学（descriptive translation studies）、操控学派（manipulation school）等等，都认识到翻译是一种社会文化活动，翻译的过程是译者作决定的过程。多元系统论认为："文化对翻译的制约既表现在拟译文本的选择上，也表现在翻译策略的确定中。"（王东风，2000:2）
  描写学派提出了是什么社会文化因素影响着译者对材料及翻译模式的选择的问题；操控学派则指出："从目的语文学的角度看，所有的翻译都意味着对源语进行一定程度的操控，旨在达到一定的目的。"（侯晶晶，2001:46）
  汉诗英译的成功取决于正确的翻译决策。译者在进行选择和决策的时候，必须兼顾原作内容、形式、读者及社会文化需求等各种因素。
  基于上文所述的审度，编者所确定的翻译指导原则是，预期翻译文本应反映和体现楚辞研究和译学研究的最新成果，最大限度地迁移或再现原作的形式美、音韵美、节奏美、情感美、意境美和风格美，使译作与原作臻于形神兼似。为此必须：
  1) 进行严谨的文本分析和考据，使译作成为原作在目前最为权威的解读。
  2) 充分发挥理论的解释功能、预见功能、检验功能和指导功能，运用有关汉诗英译中的标准、原则、审度、诗化、移情、炼词、模糊化译法、借形传神、风格重

构、译作评价和诗歌美学价值等理论、理念,采用韵体译法,以诗译诗。

3) 注意中英语言、文化的异同,把作品放在文化翻译观的大语境下进行观照,妥当处理、再现文化信息。移植与归化两法相济:为了弘扬中国文化,对具有鲜明民族特色的典故、花草、传说中的神仙等等主要采用移植法,力求保持原作的文化意义。"青虬"、"白螭"者,龙也;"虬龙鸾凤,以托君子"(王逸)。"楚辞"这一著作名称的英译也须斟酌。

4) 参考各种版本的原作和译作,如王逸的《楚辞章句》、朱熹著的《楚辞集注》、马茂元(主编)的《楚辞注释》(湖北人民出版社,1985)、吴广平的《白话楚辞》(岳麓书社,1996)、陈子展的《楚辞直解》(江苏古籍出版社,1988)、许渊冲译的《楚辞》和杨宪益、戴乃迭译的《楚辞选》等。参考现有各种版本、译本,取其精华,弃其糟粕,但应避免人云亦云、照本宣科、鹦鹉学舌、落入俗套;努力探索楚辞翻译的新路径,力求使新译在内容和形式上都有所创新和突破。

5) 把楚辞看作一个大系统,把其中的每首诗作看作一个子系统,在文体等方面保持连贯性;根据楚辞的形式,借鉴英诗诗体,使译作与原诗在行数、诗节等形式因素方面保持近似。将《渔父》整篇作为诗歌来处理。

6) 精益求精,初稿完成后反复斟酌、改进。

第二节 翻译策略所产生的效果

编者根据审度与决策进行实践,取得了预期的效果。

(1) 文本解读具有一定的权威性

经过考辨,得以澄清、纠正的重要问题有 50 个。例如,对于有关少司命是"女神"、《九歌》"各篇不存在对唱而均为独唱"的见解和历代楚辞学者对于"厥严不奉,帝何求"(《天问》)、"怜思心之不可惩兮,证此言之不可聊"(《悲回风》)等的解读,考辨说明是错误的、缺乏根据的,因而英译都未予以采信。对于《天问》"何环穿自闾社,以及丘陵,是淫是荡,爰出子文。吾告堵敖以不长,何试上自予,忠名弥彰"的诗句,编者根据对屈原及其作品的审度、文本内证和语篇分析,弃伪存真,对诗句进行了重新整合,抛弃了与屈原的思想和个性相龃龉的内容,还原了诗人忧国忧民的情思。编者还移情于屈原,对"过夏首而西浮兮,顾龙门而不见"(《哀郢》)作出了正确的解读。(卓振英,2005:66—70)

(2) 根据原诗形式,借鉴英诗的各种诗体,借形传神,使内容、形体、风格达到近似,较全面地保持了原诗的美学价值。

根据英美读者的阅读习惯、审美取向和语篇内容,把长诗划分为诗章

(canto)、诗节(stanza);并通过语篇分析,根据不同角色(神与巫)划分唱段。例如,《礼魂》译为五行诗节(the quintet),韵式为 a b a b b:

> Th' rites perform'd, majestic th' drums sound
> And melodious th' belles chant. To pay
> Homage we dance in turn and pass round
> The posy. Orchids in spring we'll lay
> And asters in fall for e'er and aye.

王国维在《宋元戏曲史》指出,楚辞中的《九歌》包含"后世戏剧之萌芽",因此,不同于平面的抒情诗,而具有戏剧的立体性。

根据不同角色划分唱段产生的效应,首先是有助于文本的解读。例如,《少司命》里"夫人自有兮美子,荪何以兮愁苦?"是迎神的女巫所提出的问题,照理说,扮演少司命的巫应该有答词。但答词在哪里?对此,历代注家都没找到解答。其实,下两句"秋兰兮青青,绿叶兮紫茎"就是少司命的答词:"你看那青青秋兰:要有人为绿叶配上紫茎才好看哪!"意思是总要有人掌握因缘才行。再下面两句"满堂兮美人,忽独与余兮目成"是迎神的女巫所唱,意思是:"(原来是这样啊?)难怪您在满堂美人中偏偏对我眉目传情!"这样,诗歌的脉络才清楚,意义才连贯,我们也才能领悟迎神歌舞的诙谐多趣。

其次是,有助于重构楚辞崇高亮丽的意境、恢弘磅礴的气势和灵活多变的艺术风格。例如,《国殇》第二节译为六行诗节(the sestet),韵式为 a b a b c c:

> (Sing Warrior Incarnate:)
> Our lines broken through, our ranks are now in disarray,
> One horse is kill'd, and wounded another has become.
> The reins are entangl'd, and bogged down two wheels stay;
> I raise the stick of jade, though, and beat the signal drum.
> Fierce battles over, litter'd with corpses is the plain;
> It seems th' Heavens were falling because of wrath and pain;

下面是《少司命》(*Fate the Minor*)前10行英译:

> (Sing Fate the Minor:)
> Rosemary and autumn orchids bright
> Grow side by side underneath the hall.
> Their leaves deep green, their blooms lily-white,

Their flooding fragrance does me enthrall!
(Sing the Witch as Usherette:)
People may anyhow have their own pairs.
Why shouldn't you free yourself from th' cares?
(Sing Fate the Minor:)
The answer the autumn orchids now tells:
Green leaves match the stems of a purple hue.
(Sing the Witch as Usherette:)
No wonder that among a hall of belles
I alone come into Your Grace's view!

按照同样的思路,编者确定《国殇》前四句是写两军交战时"士争先"的场面,应是众将士齐唱共舞;后续六行是特写,刻画一位驾驭战车的勇士在"左骖殪兮右刃伤,霾两轮兮絷四"的情况下顽强奋战的情形及战后惨烈的结局,是独唱独舞;接下来四句写战士们"身首离兮心不惩"的豪气,参加歌舞的应是勇士和众士兵;最后四句"诚既勇兮又以武,终刚强兮不可凌!身既死兮神以灵,子魂魄兮为鬼雄"是颂词,歌颂为国死难的将士,故歌舞者应是迎神或领祭的巫。这就恢复了九歌本来的艺术特色与艺术高度。

(3) 原作的文化语义得以保持

各民族的历史、地理等因素都可能产生文化积淀,形成该民族的文化特质。在楚辞中,枉渚、辰阳、重华、接舆、桑扈、伍子、比干等人名地名有着深刻的文化内涵。在翻译的过程中,编者从文化翻译观出发,详加考证、妥当处理。例如"方林"(地名)译为 Fanglin,其他专有名词也基本以音译译出。"青虬"、"白螭"者,龙也;"虬龙鸾凤,以托君子"(王逸)。考虑到文化语义和中西文化差异的问题,"青虬"、"白螭"译为 dragons green and white。

《楚辞》书名译作 *The Verse of Chu*,不同于其他版本的译法(如 *Elegies of the South*,*The Songs of the South*),在节奏美、音韵美、语言美、情感美、意象美、意境美的再现等方方面面,文库译本和其他译本也有一定差异。这里就不一一进行比较了。

(4) 在文体上保持了连贯性

汉宣帝"征能为楚辞九江被公,召见诵读"(《汉书·王褒传》);朱熹在《楚辞集注》里谈到,楚辞是可以吟唱的,到了唐朝还有个和尚能够这样做。《大中华文库·楚辞》是把《渔父》整篇作为韵文翻译的。这就保持了楚辞文体的系统性、连贯性及和谐性。

第三节 小结

在策略指导下的翻译行为所产生的效果说明,《大中华文库·楚辞》翻译中的总体审度基本上是详尽、准确的,有赖于总体审度的翻译策略也基本上是正确的。

比较一下不同译作,我们可以看到,不同的决策产生不同的翻译文本:或优或劣,或成或败。原因之一,乃在于审度与决策。

思考题

1. 翻译决策应包含哪些内容?如何进行汉诗英译中的决策?
2. 决策与总体审度之间有着什么样的关系?
3. 尝试追溯李煜《虞美人》一词英译的不同决策,并予以评价:

原作:

春花秋月何时了,往事知多少?
小楼昨夜又东风,故国不堪回首月明中。

雕栏玉砌应犹在,只是朱颜改。
问君能有几多愁,恰似一江春水向东流。

译文 1: *Yu the Beauty*

The autumn moon and spring flowers making their unending rounds,
Nostalgia, which is seething in me, seems to know no bounds!
When spring breezes revisited my little building last night,
How sad I felt to see my former kingdom under a moon so bright.
The carv'd railing and jade-like steps must still be there as before,
And yet the hue of my youth, sickli'd o'er, exists no more.
How much distress do I have? Behold — if you should care to know —
The spring waters of the river in their heart-rending eastward flow.
(zzy,1996:201)

译文 2：*Tune: Yumeiren*
Too long the autumn moon and spring flowers last,
Who knows so much things of my past!
Last night the attic was blown by the east wind
I cannot bear sadness when I recall my lost moonlitland.
Carved balustrades and marble steps should be there as before,
Only rosy faces have been changed.
If you ask me how much against I have found,
It is like flowing spring river, eastward bound.
(mxy,1997:43)

练习题

1. 仔细阅读温庭筠《更漏子》一词及其英译，并尝试追溯译者的翻译决策：

  玉炉香，红烛泪，偏照画堂秋思。
  眉翠薄，鬓云残，夜长衾枕寒。
  梧桐树，三更雨，不道离情更苦。
  一叶叶，一声声，空阶滴到明。

译文 1：*The Hydraulic Chronogragh*
The bower's incense and the candle bright
Betray the sadness in her pretty face as if from spite.
Her eyebrow pigment faint, her raven hair does over spill;
Her bedding cold, the autumn night feels longer still
The Chinese paradols and mid-night rain
Do sound unfeeling 'bout her departure-inflicted pain;
The trees send down leaf after leaf, the rain falls drop by drop;
Before daybreak spatting the door-steps they don't stop.
(zzy,1996:185)

第九章 汉诗英译中的决策

译文 2: Tune:"Song of Water Clock at Night"

Incense from a jade censer
And a tearful vermillion candle
Evoked autumnal moods within the painted chamber.
Penciled eyebrows worn,
Cloud-like locks in disarray;
Long is the night, the covers and pillow cold.

Upon the Wu-t'ung trees
Falls a midnight rain,
Indifferent to the persistent pains of separation.
Leaf upon leave,
Drop upon drop,
On empty steps it drips until the dawn.
(W. R. S., from xyz, 1992:302)

译文 3: *Geng-Lou Zi* (*The Water Clock*)

Embers of incense
In the jade brazier
With candle's crimson tears
Conspire
To glow on gilded walls,
Autumnal mood,
Faded make-up, hair awry,
Coverlet and pillow cold,
A long night ahead.
At midnight the rain
On the wu-t'ung tree
Not knowing the pain
Of loneliness
Falls leaf to leaf
Dripping
On the bare steps

Till dawn.

(J. M., from xyz, 1992:302—330)

译文 4: ***Tune: Song of Water clock at Night***
The tearful candle red
And fragrant censer spread
Within the painted bower a gloomy autumn light.
Fad'd eyebrows penciled
And hair dishevelled,
She feels her quilt the colder and longer the night.

The lonely withered trees
And midnight rain and breezes
Don't care about her bitter parting sorrow.
Leaf on leaf without grief,
Drop by drop without stop,
They fall on vacant steps until the morrow.

(xyz,1992:303)

2. 对于词牌名的翻译,你有何看法?

3. 从语义、形式等层面分析译者们的不同决策及其对译作的影响。

第十章　汉诗英译中的考辨

**学习目标**

加深对考辨的必要性的认识,初步掌握考辨的基本方法,提高思辨能力,培养严谨的学风。

第一节　考辨的必要性

与《诗经》一样,《楚辞》是中国诗歌乃至中国文化的源头之一;主要楚辞作家屈原是我国文学之父、骚人墨客百世不祧之祖。把《楚辞》这样的经典著作译为英文,这对于保持华夏民族的文化身份、促进中西交流,显然有着十分重要的意义。不过,两千多年的语言文化变迁,使得其中不少字句意义不明,疑难比比皆是,而历代《楚辞》学者往往各执一说,令人感到无所适从。

这就使得文本诠释成为汉诗英译的首要环节。英译若要作为权威版本来要求,首先就应该力求成为诠释方面的集大成者,切不可率尔为之。因此,编者采用训诂、考据、推理、文化历史观照、文本内证及外证、互文观照以及诗人与文本的互证等方法,对疑难问题多方求证。通过考辨、考据,做到有所鉴别、有所发现,为英译提供了较为坚实可靠的基础。

第二节　若干疑难的考辨

对于楚辞的某些诗章、字句的理解,历代学者或众说纷纭,莫衷一是,或鹦鹉学舌,人云亦云,或凭空臆断,谬误流传。编者经考辨得以纠正、澄清的问题主要有以下五十例。由于引用数量大,除首次引用外,夹注采用简化式。

一、惟草木之零落兮,恐美人之迟暮(《离骚》)

王逸、朱熹等认为"美人"喻君,黄文焕、朱熹冀等认为自喻,马其昶认为泛言贤士,戴震认为喻壮盛之年。刘德重说:"'美'有壮盛的意思,既曰'恐美人之迟暮',自然是指壮年的人;而其具体对象,联系上下文观之,当以自喻近是。"(马茂元:1985:14)编者认为,王逸、朱熹的理解为是。在《楚辞》中,"美人"或喻楚王,或喻美政(诗人的政治理想)。与《九章·思美人》中的"思美人兮,揽涕而伫眙"、《抽思》中的"与美人抽思兮,并日夜而无正"一样,在这里也是喻指楚王。联系上下文,两句的意思应是:"随着时序的变化,繁茂的草木终会凋零;因此我总担心会坐失与美人(楚王)结合、实现美政的时机。"

英译:

> T'is true that wither may the plants, which today thrive;
> To meet th' Beauty in her youth 'tis wise that I strive.

二、余虽好修姱以鞿羁兮,謇朝谇而夕替(《离骚》)

"朝谇夕替"应如何理解?刘德重认为:"'朝谇夕替',是说一群小人朝朝暮暮在排挤他,不是当面打击,就是背后暗算";解释为朝进谏而夕被废"说虽可通,然与屈原初为左徒时甚得怀王信任不合"(马茂元:28)。

编者认为,刘说难以成立。因为写离骚时,屈原已经"信而见疑,忠而被谤",楚怀王也已"怒而疏屈平"(《史记·屈原贾生列传》)。"朝"、"夕"形容楚王翻脸之速。韩愈"一封朝奏九重天,夕贬潮阳路八千"可作互文参照。"谇,让也",有"劝告;谏诤"(《说文》)之义,如:"立而谇语"(《汉书·贾谊传》)。因此两句应理解为:"我爱好美好正直的品质,却让人感到碍手碍脚;我早上进谏,晚上就被贬黜。"

英译:

> My bane has proved to be my sublimity;
> I pleaded in the morn and was remov'd at eve.

三、女媭之婵媛兮,申申其詈予(《离骚》)

"女媭":王逸说是"屈原姊也";郑玄《周易》注:"屈原之妹名女媭";郭沫若以为指称侍女:"今姑译为'女伴',疑是屈原之侍女";周拱辰《离骚拾细》以为指女巫:"媭乃女巫之称";汪瑗:"媭者,贱妾之称,以比党人也";刘德重说:"郭说较为圆通。'媭'的本义为女,……因而'女媭'应当作为广义的女性来解释。"(马茂元:40)

编者认为"女媭"理解为"我姐姐"为是。"女媭"、"詈"有如下解释:

"贾侍中说:楚人谓姊为媭"(《说文》);

"詈,骂也"(《说文》);

"怒不至詈"(《礼记·曲礼》);

"乃使勇士往詈齐王"(《战国策·秦策》)。

在屈原所处的历史时期,侍女、贱妾地位低下。早在春秋时期已有"男女授受不亲"的主张。假若诗人说"我的贱妾(或侍女)一再责备我说……",恐怕就会被人笑话;而如果说"我姐姐出于爱护,一再责备我说……",则是合情合理的。

英译:

My elder sister fair and virtuous, who's fill'd
With anxiety, does repeatedly me chime;

四、路修远以多艰兮,腾众车使径待(《离骚》)

王逸说:"令众车先过,使从邪径以相待也";朱熹说:"由径路先过而相待我"(朱熹,1990:36—37);吴广平说:"我传令众车直接保卫"(吴广平,1996:45);陈子展说:"传话众车使在路旁等待"(陈子展,1988:75)。

编者认为吴广平是对的。"待"者,防备也。例如:"今城郭不完,兵甲不备,不可以待不虞"(《韩非子·外储说左上》)。"路修远以多艰兮"说明了"腾众车使径待"的缘由。

英译:

I instruct the carriages to be on the watch,

For long and rugged and difficult is the way.

五、《九歌》中的多数诗篇到底是不同角色相互唱和,还是由一个巫兼任多种角色?

吴广平引用钱钟书《管锥编·楚辞洪兴祖补注》"巫之一身二任"条所说的话:"《九歌》'灵'为神而亦为巫,一身而二任,所谓'又做师婆又做鬼'。故《九歌》中之'吾'、'予'、'我'或为巫之自称,或为灵之自称,要均出于一人之口。巫与神又或作当局之对语,或为旁观之指目。作者假神或巫之口吻,以抒一己之胸臆。忽合而一,忽分而二,合为吾我,分相尔彼,而隐约参乎神与巫之离坐离立者,又有屈子在,如玉之烟,如剑之气。胥出一口,宛若多身,叙述搬演,杂用并施,其法当类后世之'说话'、'说书'。时而巫语称'灵',时而灵语称'予',交错以出,一身两任,双簧独演。"并根据这个观点,认为:"《九歌》各篇不存在对唱而均为独唱,但独唱者一人而兼神、巫两种角色,时而此人,时而彼者,充分表现了《九歌》抒写手法的灵活性。"(吴广平:49—50)

编者对此不敢苟同。理由如次:

(1)"巫之一身二任"这种单一、原始的文艺形式与楚国当时的音乐发展水平不相称。1978年5月22日在湖北随州城郊出土了曾侯乙墓65个陪葬编钟。检测结果显示:这些2430年前(早于屈原诞生)的编钟,音域跨越5个八度,只比现代钢琴少一个八度,中心音域12个半音齐全。曾国是楚国范围内的小国。可以推而知之,到了屈原生活的时代,楚国的音乐已相当发达。

(2)"一身二任"说也不符合《九歌》的发展史。《九歌》的历史悠久。《山海经·大荒西经》说,"开上三嫔于天,得《九辩》与《九歌》以下"。"开"就是夏后启。《竹书纪年》说"帝启十年舞《九招》于大穆之野",可见这种音乐活动的规模不小。从帝启十年舞《九招》(约公元前21世纪)到屈原生活的时代(约公元前339—公元前278),其间约有1760多年的时间。根据文艺进化的规律,《九歌》必定会不断发展完善,作为与音乐有着紧密联系的舞蹈等表演技巧也会得到同步发展,而不会停留在"一身二任"的水平上。

(3)《九歌》中不同角色的化妆、道具不同,这是"巫之一身二任"的形式难以适应的。扮演山鬼的巫"被薜荔兮带女罗",而迎神的巫则"被石兰兮带杜衡";大司命"灵衣兮被被,玉佩兮陆离",可能还有"飘风"、"冻雨"伴舞;而迎神的巫"折疏麻兮瑶华,将以遗兮离居"。云中君"华采衣兮若英"、"龙驾兮帝服";少司命荷衣蕙带,孔盖翠旌,而迎神的巫与他们的装扮是不同的。

(4) 从歌词的内容看,迎神歌舞涉及不同角色。例如,《大司命》里"君迴翔兮以下"、"导帝之兮九坑"显然是迎神的女巫所唱,而"纷总总兮九州,何寿夭兮在予"则是扮演大司命的男巫所唱。

(5) 楚国巫文化发达,并不缺乏能歌善舞的巫。

不同角色的区分有助于文本解读。例如,《少司命》里"夫人自有兮美子,荪何以兮愁苦?"是迎神的女巫所提出的问题,照理说,扮演少司命的巫应该有答词。但王逸只说"言己事神崇敬,重种芳草,茎叶五色,芳香益畅也";从杨金鼎(马茂元:157—158)、吴广平(71)、陈子展(101)、张愚山(许渊冲,1994:42)的注解中,也找不到回答。其实,下两句"秋兰兮青青,绿叶兮紫茎"就是少司命采用"比"所作出的回答:"你看那青青秋兰:要有人为绿叶配上紫茎才好看哪!"意思是要有人掌握因缘匹配。再下面两句"满堂兮美人,忽独与余兮目成"是迎神的女巫所唱,意思是:"(原来是这样啊?)难怪您在满堂美人中偏偏对我眉目传情!"这样,诗歌的脉络才清楚,意义才连贯,我们也才能领悟娱神歌舞的诙谐多趣。

英译:

(Sing the Witch as Usherette:)
People may anyhow have their own pairs.
Why shouldn't you free yourself from th' cares?
(Sing Wizard as Fate the Minor:)
The answer the autumn orchids now tells:
Green leaves match the stems of a purple hue.
(Sing the Witch as Usherette:)
No wonder that among a hall of belles
I alone come into Your Grace's view!

又如,《国殇》前四句写两军交战时"士争先"的场面,应是众将士齐唱共舞;后续六行是特写,刻画一位驾驭战车的勇士在"左骖殪兮右刃伤,霾两轮兮絷四马茂元"的情况下顽强奋战的情形及战后惨烈的结局,是独唱独舞;接下来四句写战士们"身首离兮心不惩"的豪气,参加歌舞的应是勇士和众士兵;最后四句"诚既勇兮又以武,终刚强兮不可凌!身既死兮神以灵,子魂魄兮为鬼雄"是颂词,歌颂为国死难的战士,故歌舞者应是迎神或领祭的巫。

据此,英译对各段作了分别处理:

Eulogy on the Martyrs of the State

(Sing in Chorus SoldiersIncarnate:)
Clad in rhinoceros hide, dagger-axes we wield,
The chariots clashing, at the enemy we tear.
Th' banners hiding th' sun, the foes surge like clouds in the field,
Yet we charge ahead despite arrows flitting in th' air.
(Sing Warrior Incarnate:)
Our lines broken through, our ranks are now in disarray,
One horse is kill'd, and wounded another has become.
The reins are entangl'd, and bogged down two wheels stay;
I raise the stick of jade, though, and beat the signal drum.
Fierce battles over, litter'd with corpses is the plain;
It seems th' Heavens were falling because of wrath and pain;
(Sing Warrior and Soldiers Incarnate:)
We set out resolved not to return but die
A heroic death on the remote battle ground.
Heads chopped off, without the least regret we lie;
Wearing sabers, th' strong bows of *Qin* we still hold sound.
(Sing Wizards as Ushers:)
Oh, courageous and valiant souls of the state,
Indomitable, a lofty realm you attain!
Your are slain'd, but with glory will glow your deeds great,
And souls of all souls you shall forever remain!

六、关于湘君、湘夫人的性别

陈子展认为《湘君》叙述湘夫人对湘君的思念，《湘夫人》则叙述湘君（指舜）对湘夫人（指娥皇、女英）的爱慕（88—96）；马茂元在《史记索隐》也说："夫人是尧女，则湘君当是舜。"据许渊冲译本（33，37），《湘君》、《湘夫人》各篇俱男（God）、女（Lady）对唱；据杨宪益译本（39，43），湘君、湘夫人俱为女性（Goddess，Lady），单数；据孙大雨译本（241—245），湘君为男性、湘夫人为女性；根据朱熹的解释（42—49），湘君、湘夫人俱为女性（娥皇、女英）。

陈子展的观点比较符合有关舜与娥皇、女英的传说，也与文本内容相合。

舜在九嶷,湘夫人在洞庭;湘夫人设想着湘君"驾飞龙兮北征,邅吾道兮洞庭",是符合他们所处的地理位置的;他们打算送给湘君的是男子用物'玦'和'佩',而湘君为她们准备的礼物是袂和褋。礼物本欲当面馈赠,因未能相遇而委之水滨。王从仁说:"'玦'和'佩'是男子的用物,是湘君送给湘夫人的。最初把它丢在水里,是为了表示决绝之意。"(马茂元:140)编者认为,把"玦"和"佩"理解为湘夫人为湘君准备的礼物更为合适;湘君和湘夫人相爱颇深,一次不遇即要"决绝",不甚合乎情理。还是朱熹说得对:由于"爱慕之心终不能忘",就"委之水滨","以阴寄吾意,而冀其或将取之"(朱熹:45)。

七、关于少司命的性别

王从仁说:"少司命是一位年青美貌、温柔多情的女神。"(马茂元:161)陈子展认为大司命、少司命都是女神:"大司命、少司命实各自登场,同演出人间之喜剧。盖一司人之寿夭,一司人之美子(爱人),同为主宰人生两大命运之神,而为楚人所迷信者也。中国古神话司命运之女神二人,希腊古神话司命运之女神盖三人也。"(103)吴广平也认为"定为女神似更恰当些"(70)。

编者认为,少司命应是男神。理由之一是:1950年山东济宁发现汉石抱子俑,高30.1厘米,正面形象为男子左手抱幼儿。这与应劭《风俗通义·祀典》中记载的汉代司命神像相符,孙作云等专家学者普遍承认那就是少司命的形象;理由之二是:迎神的女巫的唱词中有"满堂兮美人,忽独与余兮目成"。假若少司命为女神,那就是与男子眉目传情,而这是难以被当时的社会所接受的;理由之三:"竦长剑"、"抚彗星"所表现的是阳刚之气。

八、怊荒忽其焉极(《哀郢》)

吴广平的解释是:"我神伤心碎不知要走向何方?"(165);陆侃如、龚克昌的解释是:"忧思慌慌张张地那里是终极"(许渊冲:98);陈子展、吴广平:"我心头恍恍惚惚难辨方向"(187);"国破家亡,前路茫茫,不知何往"(马茂元:334—335)。

编者认为,怊:"怅也"(《字林》);下文"眇不知其所跖"才是不知所之的意思,而这一句意思应是"流浪、忧伤的生活何时才是终极?"

英译:

    The capital Ying I am now to leave,

Not knowing how long I shall tramp and grieve.

九、过夏首而西浮兮,顾龙门而不见(《哀郢》)

"西浮"应如何理解？王逸只是说,"夏首,夏水口也。船独流为浮也",认为是指船的运动；于省吾说："西浮即西背",张家英说是"西负",即背朝西；郭沫若说是"西思",即心思西边的故乡；郭在贻说是"迅浮",即形容船行之疾；吴广平说："其人东行,其心西向,故过夏首时,又回舟而西浮"(166)；杨金鼎认为,从郢都到夏口是屈流亡的第一阶段,由夏口入湖、湘是第二阶段,"第二段的行程,可以说是由东转西,也可以说是由北转南,所以这里说'西浮',下文转'南渡'"(马茂元:335)。

诗人由西东行,若"西浮"即"西背",那就是说了多余的话。"过了夏首就背朝西"——过夏首之前不也背朝西吗？若为"西思",过夏首前后不也是一直"西思"吗？"迅浮"、"迁流"之类的说法也依据不足,且无意义。"回舟西浮"更是有字事理:只要我们确定屈子的头脑是正常的,他就不会因思念故土而回舟西行,因为那就等于是刚从火坑中逃出又往回跳。既然"可以说是由东转西",何以"也可以说是由北转南"？何以就可以说"西浮"？

首先,我们不妨使用"移情法",去感悟诗歌的意象、意蕴和意境。

假设我们自己就是诗人,仓皇离开沦陷了的郢都,乘舟东行。过了夏首,仍然频频回首西望。我们将看到、感受到什么呢？船向东运动,在烟波浩渺中,处于相对静止的夏首就宛若向西漂逝,而郢都的东门是已经望不见了。我们心里该是多么惆怅凄怆啊！

其次,我们可以进行句法分析。"过夏首而西浮兮,顾龙门而不见"是两个排比句,夏首、龙门分别是"西浮"、"不见"的逻辑主语。西浮的是夏首。

这样一来就清楚了："西浮"的是夏首,而不是诗人的心意或船只之类。写夏首西浮,是为了刻画诗人依恋故乡的感情之深切。这两句的意思应是："船过了夏首,回头望去,它就像是朝西边漂流而去；想看看郢的东城门,但它却已经消失在远方。"

英译：

    I pass by Xiashou, which seems to drift west;
    Th' Dragon-Gate out of sight, I feel distress'd.

十、"何芳草之早夭兮？微霜降而不戒"(《惜往日》)

"不戒"原作"下戒",据洪兴祖《楚辞考异》改。王逸的注释说:"贤臣被谗,命不久也","严刑卒至,死有时也";杨金鼎说:"戒:戒备";"微霜初降的时候即须戒备。意指芳草经不起风霜的摧残,用以比喻贞臣受不住小人的谗毁"(马茂元:396)。吴广平说:"因微霜下降没有提防"(205)。

以上解释都认为,芳草早夭是因为本身"不戒"所致。

编者认为,"贞臣受不住小人的谗毁"回答不了上句的问题,也没有揭示什么有意义的道理。从上下文看,诗人并非责怪芳草本身"不戒"、"没有提防",而是哀怨种花或拥有花草的人(用人者)对香花不爱护,因而给风霜(谗佞)以可乘之机。否则不合全篇思想。两句的意思应是:"香花为什么会夭折?那是因为严霜无情,而人们又不加以怜惜保护。"

英译:

> Wherefore do the fragrant wither and die?
> When frost descends they lack intensive care.
> He who lets idle his ears and his sight
> Is poison to th' honest and meat to th' sly.

十一、后皇嘉树,桔徕服兮(《橘颂》)

"后皇",王逸解释说:"后,后土也;皇,皇天也";杨金鼎也认为指"天地"(马茂元:400)。但朱熹说:"后皇指楚王也"(121);郭沫若译为:"辉煌的橘树啊"(许渊冲:128);吴广平译为:"天地间最美的橘树"(208);陈子展译为:"君王有美树"(228)。

编者认为,"嘉树"不属于楚王,"后皇"也没有"辉煌"的意思。王逸、吴广平、杨之说可取。

英译:

> Oh, under th' sky and on the earth
> Your solemn existence you claim.

十二、憍吾以其美好兮,览余以其修姱(《抽思》)

王逸认为这两句指楚王自夸,杨金鼎也认为"言怀王骄矜得意,自以为是"(马茂元:351)。姜亮夫则认为"指怀王信上官子兰以之为美好修姱,杂正与己之见放为对照也"。

编者认为姜言为是。诗人所疾愤者乃楚王之信谗佞与远忠直,而非楚王之不美好、不修姱。可以参考"少歌"中"憍吾以其美好兮,敖朕辞而不听"两句,其中的"其"(他)与"朕"(我)形成对照。

英译:

You admire and brag about his good looks,
And boast of his qualities of a sage.
You're not only perfidious to me,
But you also vent upon me your rage.

十三、怜思心之不可惩兮,证此言之不可聊《悲回风》

有以下不同解释:"履信被害,志不惩也","明己之词,不空设也"(王逸);"可怜思虑的不可制止啊,证明了这些谗言的无聊"(陈子展:236);"可怜我的痴心无法救药,证明以上的话并不可靠"(吴广平:217);"证:明也,在这里是表白的意思","不可聊:谓无聊之极"(马茂元:412)。

编者认为,诗人失望之际说了一些类似遁世的气话。"此言"指上文所假设的生活态度;惩:改变,如:"不惩其心"(《诗·小雅·节南山》),"变律改经,一皆惩革"(陆倕《新刻漏铭》)。两句的意思是:"可惜我的一片忠心改变不了,看来以上所说到的做法只是说说而已"。

英译:

Howe'er, my integrity does disdain
Th' above—presum'd attitude towards life.

十四、穆眇眇之无垠兮,莽芒芒之无仪(《悲回风》)

吴广平译为:"宇宙渺茫茫没有边际,天地莽苍苍无可匹配。"(218—219)陈

子展译为:"风深渺渺的没有边际啊,又是莽茫茫的没有形象。"(238)

编者认为,这里描述的是诗人内心的忧愁困惑,而非宇宙或风。应参考上下文所述的愁思。朱熹的解释"言己之愁思浩然广大幽深,不可为象也"是对的。

英译:

> My deep thoughts are like the universe great,
> And my mind the circumstances obscure:

十五、八柱何当？东南何亏(《天问》)

吴广平译为:"八根擎天柱与哪八座山相当？为何东南地势低陷海水茫茫"(92);陈子展译为:"八根擎天的大柱子对准什么地方？东南的柱子为什么亏短不一样长"(124);黄寿祺、梅桐生译为:"八根擎天柱坐落在何方？地的东南角为什么倾塌"(许渊冲:54)。杨金鼎认为指的是天,"八根大柱撑在什么地方？东南方为什么陷塌了一大块？"(马茂元:204),把指地作为"一说"备考。

编者认为,天柱本身就是山,如不周山;"何当"是"坐落何处"。《淮南子天文训》言共工触不周山,"天倾西北","地不满东南"。第二句应指东南的地势下倾。

英译:

> What sustains th' eight pillars of th' vault?
> Why does th' earth in th' southeast subside?

十六、康回冯怒(《天问》)

王逸认为康回是"共工名",朱熹然之。但吴广平说"但没有文献依据"(99)。汤炳正《楚辞类稿》认为,"'康回'……奸邪之意"。顾颉刚说:"共工氏也就是鲧:'共工'二字是'鲧'字的缓声,'鲧'字是'共工'二字的急音"。

编者认为"共工名"之说可取。(1)扣帽子以指称传说人物的名字,非原风格,再者屈子在他的诗中也无贬抑共工之意;(2)共工与鲧所处的时代不同,故二者非指同一人:共工与颛顼争帝位,颛顼乃黄帝孙,大大早于尧舜禹;"禹之父曰鲧"(《史记》),为舜所殛,其事远在共工之后。

英译：

> How could Kanhui's wrath have caused
> The earth in th' southeast to subside?

十七、黑水玄趾，三危安在（《天问》）

吴广平引《路史·余论》注"黑水染足，涉者其色黝黑人肤"（104）；杨金鼎引用王逸的话："玄趾、三危，皆山名也"；又引用周拱辰《屈辞精义》："玄趾无考，意即所谓玄股之国者也"（马茂元：227）。

从楚辞句法看，吴广平说为是。楚辞中未见名词甲加名词乙为上句、名词丙加谓语为下句的情形。

英译：

> Where's the Black Stream, which dyes th' wader's
> Toes? Where does Mount Three Perils lie?

十八、白蜺婴茀，胡为此堂？安得夫良药，不能固臧（《天问》）

杨金鼎引王逸所言，认为是指崔文子、王子侨故事（马茂元：240—1）；丁晏认为指嫦娥传说，陈子展然之："白霓为裳还有编了珠宝的首饰，她为什么来在这个庙堂。"（137）

编者取丁、陈子展说。按前一种说法，诗人是认为，王子乔应把不死之药好好藏起来留给自己用，而这不符合诗人的思想和诗歌的格调。

英译：

> In her brilliant Rainbow Array
> With what in th' hall would Chunhu deal?
> Why didn't Yi th' Life Remedy
> In a securer place conceal?

十九、撰体协胁，鹿何膺之（《天问》）

"膺"，陈子展作"响应"解（138）；杨金鼎释为"承受"："神鹿骈生着两个上身，是从哪里承受这种奇特的形体的？"（马茂元：242）

陈子展说更能照应上下文。"被赋予鹿形的风神是如何响应雨神的？"英译：

> (Pinghao can at will summon rain,
> But howe'er does he operate?)
> And how does Lord of Wind, the deer
> With a bird's head, coordinate?

二十、汤谋易旅，何以厚之（《天问》）

王逸的解释是："汤欲变易夏众，使之从己，独何以厚待之乎"；杨金鼎解释为"商汤谋划对于师旅有所赏锡，为什么要如此厚待呢"（马茂元：245）；张惠言说"汤疑当作阳"，即"少康阳为田猎，因以袭浇"；朱熹以为汤乃康之误："汤与上句过浇、下句斟寻事不相涉，疑本康字之误。谓少康也。"（77）编者认为朱熹说可取，其余的解释较牵强。

初，编者据吴广平的译文"浇谋划制造甲胄，怎样使它坚厚？浇打翻斟寻的飞舟，取胜用的什么计谋？"（116）译为：

> To design armor strong and firm,
> What approaches did Ao employ?
> What strategy did he adopt
> When his foe's ships he did destroy?

后改译为：

> 'Twas hard to make his army strong:
> How could Shaokang his goal attain
> And how did he restore the Xia,
> Which fell after th' Zhenxun Campaign?

二十一、舜闵在家，父何以鳏（《天问》）

吴广平译为："舜的母亲就在家中，他的父亲怎么会打单身"，认为这反映了"母系社会里母权的显赫"（117）。王逸、朱熹认为是舜忧虑成家之事而父母不为之娶（令其无妻），杨金鼎同意此说："舜在成家问题上忧愁，他父亲为什么让他独身。"(马茂元：248)后者符合传说。"鳏"作动词用。

初据吴广平说译为：

> Why was Shun's father a widower
> When Shun's mother was well and sound?
> Without Shun's mother's consent how
> Comes Yao his daughters and Shun bound?

后改为：

> Unwed, Shun was laden with cares:
> Why did his sire leave him alone?
> Why did Yao decide to marry
> His daughters to Shun on his own?

二十二、吴获迄古，南岳是止；孰期去斯，得两男子(《天问》)

杨金鼎提供两种选择：(1)"吴得到了古公亶父那里来的人，他们到南岳居住；谁料得到他们迁移到吴这个地方，使吴国得到了两个男子汉？"(2)"吴国得以长久存在，在南方立国，谁会料想到出现这种情况？这是由于得到了太伯、仲雍两个男子的缘故"(马茂元：253)。后者与吴广平的解释(120)基本相同。

编者认为，"使吴国得到了两个男子汉"的说法欠妥：据《史记·吴广平太伯世家》，古公亶父欲立季历，太伯、仲雍主动出走至江南，创建了吴国。其时未有吴也。闻一多说："案去当从一本作夫，字之误也。"这样，"孰期夫斯"就是"谁会料想到出现这种情况"的意思。

英译：

> The State of Wu, which lies around
> Nanyue, has surviv'd for ages.
> Where lies the subtlety of th' case?
> Just because it's had two sages?

二十三、缘鹄饰玉，后帝是飨。何承谋夏桀，终以灭丧(《天问》)

王逸认为后帝是指汤；杨金鼎释为："伊尹借助用饰着美玉的鼎做鹄羹献食

的机会接近汤。伊尹又是怎样接受汤图谋夏桀的任务,终于使夏桀灭亡的呢?"(马茂元:253)

编者认为,"后帝"是指夏桀。《竹书纪年》:"……曰琬,曰琰。后爱二人,而弃其元妃于洛,曰末喜氏,以与伊尹交,遂以夏亡";"十七年,商使伊尹来朝"。《吕氏春秋》也记载,汤欲伊尹往观旷夏,恐其不信,乃自射伊尹。伊尹奔夏,三年,听于末喜之言以告汤。伊尹为灭夏而当间谍,实有文献可作依据。伊尹的烹饪技术是可以肯定的,利用它去接近桀,也顺理成章。

英译:

> The taste of goose pleas'd Jie, the goose
> Which Yi Yin dress'd in a jade plate.
> How did Tang rely on Yi Yin
> And topple down Jie's sovereign state?

二十四、何条放致罚,而黎服大说(《天问》)

王逸认为指汤(将夏桀)"放之鸣条之野";陈子展译为:"怎么夏桀放到鸣条受罚,而众多的贱农就大为开心?"(陈子展:142)

编者认为,汤放桀于南巢,此为文献所载,毋庸置疑;鸣条只是战场。译文应是:"汤在鸣条打败桀之后,把他处以流放的刑罚。老百姓为什么对此感到欢天喜地?"

英译:

> When he banish'd Jie from Mingtiao,
> Why did th' folk hail it with delight?

二十五、受赐兹醢,西伯上告(《天问》)

"兹醢",王逸、朱熹认为指梅伯之醢;杨金鼎也说:"醢,肉酱,这里指纣王时诸侯梅伯的肉酱"(马茂元:278)。吴广平引《史记 殷本纪》正义所引用的《帝王世纪》的记载:"囚文王,文王之长子伯邑考,质于殷,为纣御。纣烹为羹,赐文王,曰:'圣人当不食其子羹。'文王食之。纣曰:'谁谓西伯圣者,食其子羹,尚不知也'",认为是指伯邑考之醢(137)。

编者认为吴广平说可取。"兹"意思是"这"或"那",也可能是"子"的转音。

英译：

> When Zhou cook'd his son and serv'd him
> Th' soup, plead to God did Duke of th' West.

二十六、伯林雉经，维其何故？何感天抑地坠，夫何畏惧（《天问》）

王逸认为指晋太子申生事；黄寿祺、梅桐生也认为指"晋献公太子申生的自杀"（许渊冲：76）；陈子展则认为指"管叔在北林上吊自杀"（153）；郭沫若译为："纣王和他的妃嫔为何要吊死？以衣蒙面，怕见天地？"杨金鼎按申生说，把四句解释为："申生上吊自杀，是什么原因？为什么他死了能感天动地？他到底怕的是谁呢？"（马茂元：280—281）朱熹对此解释表示怀疑，说"未知是否"；吴广平译为："将纣王尸体挂在柏树上，那是什么缘故？"（137）

编者认为，"为什么他（申生）死了能感天动地"、"他到底怕的是谁呢"，这些问题问得有些莫名其妙，也缺乏文献依据。还是后者有理，可以使四句的意义连贯。但前两句应理为"纣王的尸体被挂在柏树上，他怎么会落得这种下场"比较妥当，后两句则是："伐纣多么感天动地，当时是谁感到恐惧？"

英译：

> Wherefore did Ji Fa hang King Zhou's
> Corpse on th' cypress when he did die?
> Who was stricken with fear in th' war,
> Which seem'd to shake the Earth and th' Sky?

二十七、中央共牧，后何怒（《天问》）

王逸以为，中央之洲，有蛇争草实，比喻夷狄相争，君王何以怒之？朱熹言"未详"（87）。杨金鼎列出多种解释，皆似前后不洽。姑采用马茂元其昶说：指厉王怒共伯和摄政的故事。

英译：

> Why did King Li rageat it when
> The duke He the regent became?

二十八、厥严不奉，帝何求（《天问》）

王逸以为，"帝何求"是说"虽从天帝求福，神无如之何"。杨金鼎马茂元解释说："楚王的威严已不能保持，我对天帝又有什么可求的呢"(288)。在以上解释中，"求"逻辑主语或是楚人，或是我。吴广平的译文赞同此说(142)。陈子展译为："上帝对我还要求什么"(156)。逻辑主语是上帝，宾语则是我。

编者认为应理解为屈子的失望之叹："楚国连自己的尊严都保持不了，上帝对它还能有何指望啊？"逻辑主语是上帝，宾语是楚国。如此则于语法可通，与诗人的思想也吻合。

英译：

> What is the hurry to return
> When at dusk thunders me besiege?
> Oh, what can God expect of Chu
> Now it hardly holds its prestige?

二十九、释舟陵行，何以迁之（《天问》）

王逸注："使龟释水而陵行，则何能迁徙山乎？"杨金鼎引《列子·汤问》："龙伯之国有大人，……一钓而连六鳌"的传说，介绍了另一种解释："龙伯巨人不用船，而在陆地上走，怎么能把六鳌从大海中弄走呢"（马茂元：243）。吴广平同意闻一多《天问疏证》的观点：寒浞之子浇的动物化身为鳌，有陆地行舟的传说(115)。编者认为，取闻说为妥。"释"，放也，如："有卖油翁释担而立"（欧阳修《归田录》）。两句意思是："浇把船放到陆地上行驶，是靠什么来推动呢？"

英译：

> The Turtles bearing th' mountains stir,
> But how can th' mountains steady stand?
> What impetus propels his ship
> When Han Ao sails on solid land?

三十、伯昌号衰，秉鞭作牧（《天问》）

吴广平译为："文王痛哭着戴孝服丧，仍然执鞭放牧牛羊"（135），并引用萧兵的话，认为服丧期间如此，不但有带头改革旧俗、鼓励生产的作用，而且还有表示"韬晦"的政治意图（136）。

历史上只有武王戴孝征讨商纣的记载，未闻文王服丧放牧之事。鞭乃权力之象征，因此这两句的含义应是"号令于商衰微之际，管辖一方也。"王逸、朱熹、陈子展等学者基本持此见解，可取。

英译：

> When the Shang was on the decline,
> Duke of th' West rose the peers to lead
> How could th' replacement of th' altar
> Of the Shang's have been a real deed?

三十一、何环穿自闾社，以及丘陵，（是淫是荡，）爰出子文。吾告堵敖以不长，何试上自予，忠名弥彰（《天问》）

王逸注："旋穿闾社，通于丘陵，以淫而生子文"；"屈原言我何敢尝试君上，自号忠直之名以显彰后世乎？诚以同姓之故，中心恳恻，义不能已也"。朱熹也以为指斗伯比"淫于䢵子之女"，"他则不可晓矣"（88）。吴广平译为："斗伯比和䢵女怎样穿过社庙，进入陵墓中？他们这样荒淫这样放荡，于是生出了令尹子文。我说堵敖在位不久长，为什么熊恽杀堵敖自立为王，而忠直的名声更加远扬。"（142）陈子展说："怎得穿遍了从闾里乡社以及丘陵，于是寻出一个将来做令尹的子文？我已经告诉过贤者堵敖、以为楚国衰了不能久长！为什么谏议君上、自我称许渊冲，使得忠直的名声愈加彰扬。"（158）黄寿祺、梅桐生译为："为什么在村头丘陵幽会，私通淫乱却能生出子文？我说堵敖在位不能长久，为何成王杀了国君自立，忠名更加显著得到表彰。"（许渊冲：80）杨金鼎认为，前面两句的意思是："为什么子文的母亲环绕闾社，穿越丘陵，和斗伯比淫乱私通，却能生出贤相子文来"；后面三句的意思是："我说堵敖的统治不会长久，为什么杀了君上，把王位给了自己，而忠名更加显著。"（马茂元：292—293）

结尾部分显现出的非逻辑性，疑为窜文、遗漏或错乱所致。译者不可将错就错,而应根据背景、诗人的情思及整个语篇的总意象等因素,重新进行整合。

据《左传·宣公四年》记载,楚之先王若敖娶䢵国之女,生子斗伯比。若敖死,斗伯比跟着母亲生活在䢵国,与䢵国国君的女儿私通,生下了子文。䢵夫人派人把子文扔到云梦泽中,却有一只老虎来给他喂奶。䢵子打猎看到了,就收养了他。楚国人称奶为"穀(谷)",称虎为"於菟(巫图)",因此给予子文取名"斗穀於菟",字子文。子文长大,有贤人之才,做了楚国令尹,辅佐楚成王。《论语》称其忠。成王弑兄囏自立,"布德施惠"(《史记·楚世家》)。二者分别是楚国历史上的良臣、明主。

但根据上文所引各家解说,屈原却似乎对他们出言不逊。而辱前贤、刺圣主,固非屈子之所为。

诗歌上文说到诗人进谏而不被采纳,楚国安全不保。根据全诗内容及屈子忧国忧民的思想,可以推断,屈子言及子文、成王,是想把他们与当时的令尹子兰和顷襄王进行对照。

基于以上推论,这一语段可理解为:"子文安在啊?不论城市或山村,但愿他能再世!成王挽楚于危败,青史流芳。除非有像他那样的明主和子文那样的良相,否则我就可以对王室的亡灵断言,岌岌可危的楚国国运不长啦!"

英译:

> May Ziwen be found of today,
> Were he in th' wilderness or near;
> May Xiong Yun, who did justly slay
> Th' fatuous, in Chu reappear:
> Or else Chu's fall is what I fear!

三十二、惜诵以致愍兮,发愤以抒情(《惜诵》)

陈子展译为:"痛惜进言以招致忧患啊,发愤就来写诗抒情"(169);吴广平译为:"借助诉讼以表达不幸,发泄愤懑来抒写性情"(147);张愚山译为:"陈子展述往事来表达不幸,发泄愤懑来抒写衷情"(许渊冲:86);杨金鼎译为:"以悼惜的心情,称述往事来表达忧苦之思"(马茂元:304)。

编者认为,陈子展译对"发愤以抒情"的缘由有所交代,且符合诗人的遭际。"诵"的义项之一是,以婉言、隐语讽谏。如:诵言(讽劝自己的言语);诵训(古代掌管百工的工师所讽诵的谏言);致:造成;导致,如:"何意致不厚"(《玉台新咏·古诗为焦仲卿妻作》)。"致负诚托"(唐·李朝威《柳毅传》)。取陈子展说。

英译：

> My plea having prov'd to be a despair,
> I hum an elegy to vent my pain.

三十三、知前辙之不遂兮，未改此度。车既复而马茂元颠兮，蹇独怀此异路（《思美人》）

杨金鼎解释说："'前辙未遂'，指怀王时代倍齐合秦政策的错误"，"未改此度：指顷襄王的媚敌忘仇"，"车颠马茂复：指战争的失败"（马茂元：378—9）；朱熹说："知直道之不可行而不能改其度，虽至于车倾马茂元仆而犹独怀其所由之道不肯同于众人也。"（114）张愚山译为："我明知前面的路不会无阻，也决不改我要推行的法度"（许渊冲：118）。吴广平译为："我明知前面车路不通，但也决不改变道路。尽管车以翻马茂元又跌倒，我依然望着前途"，认为表现了屈原虽长期以来一再遇到政治上的挫折，仍然不改变自己的志向（193—194）。

编者认为，朱熹、吴广平的说法可取。下文有"勒骐骥而更驾兮，造父为我操之"，可见是指屈原自己董道不豫的情操。

英译：

> Even if blocked is the road afore,
> I would never alter my way of yore;
> The cart may turn over and the steeds fall,
> I shall take the unique route after all.

三十四、解萹薄与杂菜兮，备以为交佩；佩缤纷以缭转兮，遂萎绝而离异（《思美人》）

朱熹解释说："言解去二物而以上文之茝荪备为交佩也"，"缭，绕也。缤纷缭转，言佩之美。然适佩之而遽已萎绝而离异矣"（115）。吴广平说："采集成丛的萹蓄与恶菜，备置它们来做左右佩带。尽管佩饰繁盛缠绕，但是最终枯死还得丢开"；"这四句各家的理解出入很大，其喻意迄无定论"（195—196）。陈子展说："采下扁竹一丛啊，准备好了以为左右佩带？佩带它很纷繁地来环绕啊，就让它到枯死了而后撒开"；"旧有注说皆误。焉有萹丛杂菜而可谓芳草者乎"（214—215）。杨金鼎引用了王夫之的话："恶草充佩，则芳草委而不用"，又引用蒋骥所说的:"薃菉皆不芳而可食,以喻中才可用之人,然向之佩之者,或忽焉委而去之,盖时俗之流从如是,况能玩此芳草哉",认为前两句指子兰为令尹,下两句指自己遭谗被迁(马茂元:381—382)。张愚山译为:"你采摘丛生的薃蓄和杂菜,把它们编织成左右的佩带。杂菜啊密密麻麻互相缠绕,香草却日渐枯萎被你抛开。"(许渊冲:120)

"解"字,王逸《楚辞章句》释为"解去",蒋骥《山带阁注楚辞》释为"拔取",释义刚好相反。

编者认为,薃、菉都不是香草。萎,通委,丢弃,抛弃。"委,弃也"(《广雅》);"委而去之"(《孟子·公孙丑下》)。"薃薄与杂菜"与被"萎绝而离异"的香花应是不同意象,诗人是以对比手法讽喻楚王近小人而远君子。这四句可以解释为:"难道可以把薃蓄和杂菜当成左右佩带?原先佩带的香花还那么鲜艳夺目,为什么就将其抛弃?"

英译:

  Can th' weeds and grasses take the flower's place
  As ribbons on the left and on the right?
  Wherefore should the fragrant be cast away
  Ere their leaves wither and their petals blight?

三十五、吾且儃佪以娱忧兮,观南人之变态(《思美人》)

朱熹译为:"于是且复优游忘忧以观世变"(115);陈子展译为:"瞧一瞧那南边人的动态"(215);吴广平译为:"观赏一下南蛮的异态"(196);张愚山译为:"我姑且消闲自娱将忧愁排解,静观朝中小人的种种丑态"(许渊冲:120)。杨金鼎解释说:"南人:指楚国的统治集团","变态:一种出乎情理以外不正常的态度",即"楚国君臣只有欢娱逸乐之心,并无雪耻报仇之意"(马茂元:382)。

编者认为,"儃佪以娱忧"的主语是"吾"而非他人。这两句与下文"窃快在中心兮,扬其凭而不竢"都是说诗人在极度失望中采取的超脱态度。若"南人"是指统治集团,或者诗人是想要"观世变"、瞧"动态",那就超脱不了,如何"娱忧"?"观南人之变态"应指领略流放地土著的特殊风俗。

英译:

  To ease my pain I rove about, watching
  Th' southerners' exotic way of life.

My bosom is fill'd with joy and delight,
For I've transcended sorrows and the strife.

三十六、惭光景之诚信兮,身幽隐而备之(《惜往日》)

朱熹解释说:"无罪见尤,惭见光景,故窜身于幽隐,然亦不敢不为之备也"(117);张愚山译为:"光与影之间能够忠诚可信,惭愧啊我被放逐还得小心"(许渊冲:124)。吴广平译为:"有惭于光和影的不可分离,我将隐身深渊来逃避"(201);杨金鼎译为:"阳光真实,无所不照。但自己则将一身收藏在幽隐的地方,感受不到,深觉可惭。意指生意已尽"(马茂元:391)。闻一多《楚辞校补》说"案备字无义,疑当为避,声之误也……避谓避光景,有惭于光景,故欲避之而隐身于玄渊中也。"

编者要问:"无罪见尤",何惭之有?"光和影的不可分离",何以就要"隐身深渊来逃避"?屈原一直梦想能有机会施展才华、实现美政,那么,"自己则将一身收藏在幽隐的地方"、"深觉可惭"从何说起?

这两句的意思应是:"我的诚信有如影之于光,可惜累遭困顿幽闭;虽然到了如此地步,诚信之心犹然不离不弃。"

英译:

Oh, whereat should the innocent and bright
Suffer from slanders and inflicted pain?
Devoted as shadows are to the light
Am I still, though devotion is my bane.

三十七、物有微而陨性兮,声有隐而先倡(《悲回风》)

吴广平译为:"微弱的东西损伤性命,隐约的声西咆哮猖狂"(212);陈子展译为:"香物是微小的就丧失了生机啊,风声是无形的而气流为它先倡"(232);杨金鼎译为:"在回风震荡之中,凋陨了蕙草的微弱生机","这回风的初起,是有隐微的声音倡之于先的"(马茂元:407);张愚山译为:"美好的蕙草被旋风伤害了生机,别看那风啊,开始时不声不响"(许渊冲:132)。

联系上文"心冤结而内伤",下文所提及的"志介"、"虚伪",以及全篇的内容,编者认为,诗人是借回风摇蕙这一自然现象,抒发感慨,讽刺社会之怪异:群小虽无德无能,却为害不浅;他们生性隐蔽诡秘,却往往占据上风,先声夺人,伤害美好。

英译:

> Lo, th' whirlwind is shaking the orchids fair,
> At the sight of which I can not but sigh.
> To harm the solid the shapeless should dare,
> And th' inaudible should sound loud and high!

三十八、折若木以蔽光兮,随飘风之所仍(《悲回风》)

吴广平说,上句"喻意为韬光养晦",下句"喻意为随遇而安"(215—216);译为:"攀折若木来遮蔽阳光,听凭那狂风把我吹荡。"杨金鼎也认为,上句"是用以象征自己力求韬光养晦",下句"意指心情的空虚"(马茂元:411)。张愚山译为:"折下若木的枝条来遮蔽日光,任凭那狂风将我吹向哪里"(许渊冲:134)。

编者认为,这是诗人的愤激之言,是他在无可奈何的情况下所假设的愤世嫉俗的做法之一。可以参考下文"证此言之不可聊"。"仍"通"扔"。两句的意思应为:"如果我能折若木来遮挡阳光,那我就可以(不顾良知,)任凭风去把我飘荡了。"

英译:

> With twigs from th' Fairy Tree the sun I'd hide
> So that I'd move in light of how th' wind blows.

三十九、心鞿羁而不解兮,思蹇产而不释(《悲回风》)

郭沫若认为,包括这两行在内,诗的最后六行系别处窜入的文字,应删去(马茂元:420);闻一多认为这两句是后人误加于此(吴广平:224);杨金鼎引用蒋骥所说的:"子胥申徒,皆其同类。而忽感二子之死,不能救商与吴广平之亡。故踌躇徘徊,卒不忍遽死;而其愁思萦回而不能解释也",认为"所论深得原意"(马茂元:420)。张愚山译为:"我忧伤郁结得不到排解,绵绵思绪啊将我牢牢缚住"(许渊冲:140)。

编者认为,"释"是消除的意思;这两句是对前面所提的问题"任重石之何益"所作的回答:"这是因为申徒'心鞿羁而不解兮,思蹇产而不释'。"(而随着他的自沉,所有愁思一了百了,他自己也得到解脱)因此这两句并非窜入文字,也非后人所误加,不应删去。

英译:

('Bout his pleads not a pin did th' king care,
Thus he drown'd himself. And of what avail
Was it?) From th' conflicts it did extricate
The sage, who had been driven to despair!

四十、鸟兽犹知怀德兮,何云贤士之不处

朱熹、陈子展、吴广平版本皆作"何云",马茂元版本作"云何"。杨金鼎:"怀德:怀念有德者。这里有责怪的意思";"鸟兽还知道怀念有才德的人呢,为什么贤士反而不留在朝廷呢?"(马茂元,599);吴广平:"鸟兽尚知道怀恩报德,怎怪贤士不肯留在朝廷?"(264)。

编者要问:"责怪"何人何事?上文所说"骐骥伏匿"、"凤凰高飞",指的就是贤士得不到任用。吴广平译较准确。两句可以解释为:"鸟兽都知道怀德,贤士就更不必说了。君王无德,怎么能怪贤士留不住呢?"

英译:

Even birds and beasts are conscious of love and hate,
Let alone talent, who on th' throne dread to attend.

四十一、祝融戒而还衡兮,腾告鸾鸟迎宓妃(《远游》)

吴广平译为:"祝融劝告我立即回车,我传令鸾鸟迎接宓妃"(240);黄寿祺、梅桐生译为:"祝融告诫我要停止前行,我传令鸾鸟把宓妃迎上"(许渊冲:152);陈子展译为:"火神祝融警告就得还辕啊,并通告鸾鸟去迎洛神宓妃"(265);杨金鼎解释:"戒:蒋骥说:'前戒也。'在前面清道警卫"(马茂元:455)。吴广平译为:"祝融劝告我立即回来,我传令鸞鸟迎接宓妃"(吴广平:240)。

编者认为:"戒"在这里是"告请"的意思。这一用法见于《礼仪 聘礼》:"既图事,戒上介亦如之";《礼仪 士冠礼》:"(主人)戒宾曰:'某有子某,将加布于其首,愿吾子之教之'"。前句意思是"因祝融告请而还衡"。告请何事?将以歌舞款待之也。下句的传令者当为祝融,如此则有诗人受到礼遇的意思。前句"戒"若

如杨所说,是"在前面清道警卫",则诗人正在行进中,与"迎宓妃"相龃龉;若诗人自己"腾告鸾鸟迎宓妃",那么,后来乐未尽便"逝以徘徊",则颇不近情理。

英译:

> For Lady of th' Luo the Phoenix is sent
> By the God of Fire, who requests my stay.

四十二、心摇悦而日幸兮,然怊怅而无冀(《九辩》)

这两句有很多解说。吴广平:"心怀喜悦常存有侥幸,最终惆怅而没有希望"(268);陈子展:"心里转乐就觉自幸啊,但遗恨而没有什么希冀"(318);张愚山:"动摇和喜悦伴随着我天天希望,惆怅啊却又打消了我的念头"(许渊冲:178)。以上解释或失去转折,或逻辑不通。朱熹说:"冀,望也。心谓既老将有所遇也,故摇悦而日幸。然卒自知其无望也。"(159)朱熹说:"心谓既老将有所遇,故摇悦而日幸,然卒自知其无所望也。"(608)

编者认为朱熹说可取。这两句是表现由希望到绝望的心理变化过程。

英译:

> Hoping against hope less and less I tend to grieve,
> Though about the fact that hope is slim I am clear.

四十三、事亹亹而觊进兮,蹇淹留而踌躇(《九辩》)

吴广平译为:"国事在变我希望进取,久留此地我徘徊犹豫"(269);张愚山译为:"国事在不停地变化前进,而我却在荒原上徘徊久留"(许渊冲,178);陈子展译为:"事业要勉勉进取就指望进用啊,硬被停滞久了而独自进退踌躇"(318)。

编者认为,"觊进"即"等待进用的机会"。上句吴广平译较为可取。下句的意思则应是:"却被耽搁在此,一筹莫展。"

英译:

> Th' state of affairs changing, I wish to forge ahead,
> But lo, stranded in th' wasteland I can find no way!

四十四、罔流涕以聊虑兮,惟著意而得之(《九辩》)

王逸有两处注释:"怆然深思而悲泣也","知天生贤不空出也";吴广平:"我惆怅哭泣深深思索,君王用心才能得贤才"(274);张愚山:"在惆怅中你姑且想一想吧,只有用心才能得到贤者辅助"(许渊冲:182);杨金鼎:"在失意悲愁中,且来想一想,只有用心求贤的君主,才能得到贤臣"(马茂元:619);朱熹没有作解释。

编者认为,"罔"有表示禁止或劝阻的意思,相当于"别"、"不要"。例如:"罔失法度,罔游于逸,罔淫于乐","罔违道以干百姓之誉"(《书·大禹谟》);"事罔隆而不杀"(《汉书 杨雄传》);"君罔谓汝何之"(《惜颂》);"罔罪尔众"(《书 盘庚下》)。"聊":且。"罔流涕"(抑制住眼泪)是为了"聊虑"。"罔流涕以聊虑"的应是"我"而非君王。"止住眼泪聊且思考一下",于是悟出了"惟著意而得之"(即真心求贤的君主才能得到贤者)的道理。

英译:

> I stop weeping to brood, awakening to th' truth
> That wisdom's visible only to those sincere.

四十五、何曾华之无实兮,从风雨而飞飏(《九辩》)

王逸:"外貌若忠,内心佞也";"风动而草木摇,雨降而万物殖。故以风雨论君,言政令德惠所由出也"。错误地理解了"蕙"这一意象。从下文"以为君独服此蕙兮,羌无以异于众芳"判断,诗人是自比于蕙。

如何理解"无实",也十分重要。"实,荣也"(《墨子经上》)。故"实"应理解为"发荣滋长",但各家却往往解释为"结果",例如,陈子展:"没有结实"(309);吴广平:"不结果"(261);杨金鼎:"怎么重重叠叠的花朵却不结果实,让它随着风雨飘散"(马茂元:592);张愚山译为:"为什么光开花不结果,随着风雨的袭击飘落飞扬"(许渊冲,1994:172)。

编者认为,蕙无实是十分自然的。如果诗人问的是"为什么蕙只开花不结果",那就太滑稽可笑了。诗人所怨的是,为君者对蕙不加以爱护,任凭风吹雨打,没有给它以发荣滋长的机会。

英译：

Why isn't it allow'd to thrive, as their bloom's loud?
And whyshould it be shatter'd by th' rain out of th' way?

四十六、华容备些《招魂》

朱熹注："华容谓美人也"(172)；吴广平译："美女等候在两旁"(289)。陈子展则说："华贵的装饰"(344)。吴广平注："华容：华美的容貌，指美女。备：齐备"(290)。

编者认为，"容"，假借为"用"。如："兵无所容其刃"(《老子·五十章》)(作动词)。在这里作名词，指"用品"。这句所在的四行描述室内陈子展设，下句"二八侍宿"才是指美女。"华容备些"如指美女齐备，岂不与下文"九侯淑女，多迅众些"相互为赘？

英译：

The bedrooms offer a varied sight,
Being adorn'd with treasures rare.
Lamps of orchid oil burning bright,
The furniture is nice and fare.

四十七、步及骤处兮，诱骋先(《招魂》)

对此各家的解说都有些问题。

吴广平说："走到车马奔驰处，狩猎向导在前奔"(301)。何人"走"？向导是步行还是骑马？

陈子展说："步行以及跑马和休息啊，都在诱使人驰骋争先"(356)。"步行以及跑马和休息"怎么能"诱使"人驰骋争先？

吴广平明贤说："步步驰马进复停，诱出野兽争追寻"(许渊冲：204)。何人"诱出"？

朱熹说："步行而及骤马所至之处，言走之疾也，诱盖为前导"(179)。所言既为导猎者，何以既"步"且"骋"？人走再疾，焉能追及骤马？

殷光熹说："步行的从猎者追及驰马所至之处，向导一马当先，跑在前面"(马茂元：523)。狩猎当有其固有队形秩序，何须等待步者"追"？难道原先队伍是混乱的?再说,向导不等于导猎;那么大型的狩猎活动,导猎也往往不止一人。

"处"当为动词,"止"也。《易 系辞上》"或出或处"的"处"就是这种用法。两句的意思是:"步行、骑马的狩猎者停止前进,而导猎者则奔驰向前(去把野兽驱赶出来)。"

英译:

> When foot and horse slow down, the guides
> Charge ahead the game to out scare.
> At rest or in chaste, men are flush'd
> With th' hunt. Turning right we backfare.

四十八、娱人乱只(《大招》)

殷光熹解释说:"乱:音乐的末章,尾声"(马茂元:548)。编者要问:怎么乐人一上场就奏起尾声来?应是乐人的演奏严整得体。《尔雅·释诂》解释说:"乱,治也";《书·顾命》中"眇眇予末小子,其能而乱四方以敬忌天威"中的"乱"即具有这种意义。朱熹(185)、吴广平(312)、陈子展(374)皆言"乱"即"理"(有条理),这是对的。

英译:

> The bells and the chime stones
> Struck in great harmony.

四十九、接径千里,出若云只(《大招》)

吴广平译为:"道路相连通千里,巡行车马多如云"(319);陈子展(382)释义基本相同;殷光熹译为:"土地相连,道路万千,人口众多,遍布如云"(马茂元:558)。

编者认为,"巡行"一词不甚妥当;与道路相关的是行人车马,两句并没有说到人口,殷的释义似与下文"人阜昌只"重复。译为"大道千里,出行的车马如云(描写繁荣景象)"也许渊冲可以避免牵强附会。

英译:

> Along the thoroughfares

Men and carriages stream.

五十、三圭重侯,听类神只。

吴广平:"各路英雄来执政,处理政务象神明"(319);陈子展:"三圭公侯伯、同侯有子男,听从类祭天神啦"(381)。殷光熹的解释是:"公执恒圭,侯执信圭,伯执躬圭";"公、侯、伯三种贵族""受理案件,精审如同神明"(马茂元:559)。编者认为,"各路英雄"不甚准确;把子、男两种贵族包括进去也不太妥当。还是殷说较可取。

英译:

In handling state affairs
Wise as gods the peers seem.

第三节 小结

当某种诠释与作者的思想、个性、创作意图以及整个语篇的总意象相龃龉的时候,译者就必须提出怀疑,并寻求合理的解释以取代之。第31例可以说明这一点。否则就可能采信错误的诠释,产生错误的理解和翻译。例如,"过夏首而西浮兮,顾龙门而不见"的两种译文:Passing Summer Head, westward we float, oh! /The Dragon Gate can't be seen from my boat(许渊冲,1994:99),以及:East moves the Boat, I dream of West, /Far from the Country I love best(杨宪益、戴乃迭,2001:83),就是分别依照对于"西浮"的错误解释翻译出来的(参考例9)。总结起来,本章涉及的考辨方法有训诂、移情、考据、推理、文化历史观照、文本内证及外证、互文观照以及诗人与文本的互证等。

思考题

1. 训诂、移情、考据、推理、文化历史观照、文本内证及外证、互文观照以及诗人与文本的互证等诸多方法之中,哪些是你以前就会了的?

2. 解决疑难问题需要运用思辨能力。本章考辨的过程和所用的思维方法中,哪一过程、哪种方法对于提高你的思辨能力有何启发?

3. 找出杜牧《山行》不同英译中因没有考辨或考辨失当而造成的错误。

原作：

远上寒山石径斜，白云生处有人家。

停车坐爱枫林晚，霜叶红于二月花。

译文 1: A Mountain Scene

A stony path's meandering high up the chilly mount,
Where homes are silhouetted' gainst the white clouds' very fount.
Attracted by th' maples my carriage to a halt I bring;
Th' frost-redden'd leaves at dusk are brighter than the bloom of spring.
(zzy, 1996:181)

译文 2: Travelling in the Mountains

After I climb the chill mountain's steep stone paths,
Deep in the white clouds there are homes of men.
I stop my carriage, and I sit to admire the maple grove at nightfall,
Here I pull up my carriage, entranced.
For the twilight mountainside is ablaze with crimson maples.
(R. K. & N. S., from gzz, 1994:227)

译文 3: Autumn Glory

Off the main road runs a narrow stone path, winding, climbing, vanishing into the cloudy heights where perch a few tiny cottages.
Here I pull up my carriage, entranced. For the twilight mountainside is ablaze with crimson maples more vivid than spring flowers.
(wxl, 1985:57)

译文 4: Travelling in the Mountains

A flag-stone path winds up into the chilly hills,
Where houses are just discernible amid the thick white cloud.
I stop my carriage for I love the maple trees in the twilight,
The leaves after frst are as crimson as spring flowers.
(yxy & gy, 2001:274)

译文 5: Going Uphill

I go by slanting stony path to the cold hill;

Where rise white clouds, there a sequestered cottage towers.
I stop my cab in maple woods to gaze my fill;
Frost-bitten leaves look redder than early spring flowers.
(xyz,2000:121)

 练习题

1. 若翻译白居易《鹦鹉》(见第三章练习题)一诗,你将作出什么样的决策?决策的依据何在?

2. 根据所学的新知识,对你所译的唐诗(第三章练习)进行第三次修改、润色,同时保留初稿、二稿和三稿。

第十一章 汉诗英译中的逻辑调适

学习目标

更系统地了解东西方在思维方式方面存在的差异,树立逻辑调适意识,并掌握逻辑调适的方法。

第一节 逻辑调适的必要性

典籍英译文本必须具有可读性(readability)以及对于目的语读者的逻辑可接受性(logical acceptability),这是毋庸赘言的。然而,中西方思维方式是存在差异的,作为华夏文化载体的典籍所体现的必然是中国的思维特征;再者,由于错简、文字缺失、翻译文本的特定要求等原因,有的典籍本身存在逻辑问题。因此,在典籍英译的过程中,译者就有必要对原文逻辑的结构进行观照、加以思考,并在必要时介入且加以调适(adaptation)。本章根据实践经验,从三个层面总结典籍英译中可能遇到的涉及译者介入与调适的若干问题,即"基于东西方思维差异而进行的介入与调适"、"基于原版本某些因素而进行的介入与调适"、"基于目的语文本要求而进行的介入与调适",并通过个案的分析研究,阐述这些问题的八种解决方法。

第二节 基于东西方思维差异而进行的介入与调适

对于东西方的思维方式,很多学者进行过深入的研究,发表过颇有见地的文章。其中连淑能教授把东西方的思维差异归结为十项。东西方的思维方式存在差异,已是毋庸置疑的事实。在典籍英译中,对这一差异的处理可有两种方法,归化和异化。一般来说,为了让西方读者了解东方和中国的思想、思维方式,可采用异化译法,保留原文的思维特征和逻辑结构;然而,若对于某些字句

胶柱鼓瑟,照搬原作的逻辑建构,便会令西方读者难以接受和理解。在这种情况下,只要不扭曲原作的内容和意境,不伤害原作风格之大雅,译者就可以在逻辑上介入(logical intervention),采用归化法,对原有的逻辑结构酌情作些调适。

一、整体性与分析性及其调适

东方在思维上较注重从整体上把握事物,把握事物的相互联系;西方则倾向于把整体分解为各部分,分门别类地考察各部分、各细节的性质、结构和功能。两种思维方式的差异之一在于"整体性与分析性"(连淑能,2002:42)。

在《鸡鸣赋》中,李渔描述歌颂的是雄鸡,即鸡类中的雄禽,但其中一部分却谈起了整个鸡的群体,包括小鸡和母鸡:

> 有功无誉,谁克当之?
> 惟鸡为然,百无一疵。
> 智能烛夜,信不失时。
> 一唱百唱,义无参差。
> 恋母惟孝,哺卵惟慈。
> 克正夫纲,戒鸣伏雌。

"惟鸡为然,百无一疵",说到了所有的鸡;"恋母惟孝,哺卵惟慈"又分别说到了小鸡和母鸡。在我们注重整体性与求同性的中国读者看来,这并无大碍,但对于一般偏向于分析性、存异性的西方读者就可能觉得离题或概念混淆。为了理顺逻辑关系,《李渔诗赋楹联赏析》一书中采用了:

(1)"概念厘清法"

即采用某些手段,使概念明晰,拨正话语方向,锁定谈论范畴,避免产生"节外生枝"、"混淆不清"之感。编者将上述部分译为:

> Who then, are meritorious
> But have never been given praise?
> 'Tis th' modest cock, who is flawless
> Ev'n if assess'd in all the ways;
> Smartly conscious of night's elapse,
> The cock announces th' break of day
> In a sonorant voice, which is

To be echo'd without delay.
Touched by his husbandly way,
*Th' refrain'd hen remains soft and tame.*①
She hatches eggs with care and love;
Th' offspring return her with the same.

"*Touched by his husbandly way*"用以说明雄鸡对母鸡的良好影响,这就在文学形象方面调整了主次,强化了雄鸡而弱化了母鸡,从而使话语中心始终不偏离雄鸡。

二、模糊性与精确性及其调适

东西思维存在"模糊性与精确性"的差异(连淑能,2002:45)。不少汉诗使用的是白描手法。惯于"观物取象"的中国读者一般都能感受到王之涣的《登鹳雀楼》中"白日"的壮丽、"黄河"的雄浑,白居易的《草》中"野火"的酷烈、草的顽强生命力,杜甫"窗含西岭千秋雪"的雅致,叶绍翁《游园不值》里"一枝红杏"的妖娆,但西方读者则未必如此。考虑到读者的审美取向,可采用:

(2) 景物具象法

即采用下义词(specific words)、辞格或适当增加描写性的话语,对景物加以描绘,使读者得到如临其境、如闻其声的美学感受。为此,编者将"白日依山尽,黄河入海流"译为"*Ling'ring* is the setting sun about the mountain height,/*Surging* is the Yellow River eastward to the sea",使用了下义词Lingering(徘徊)和Surging(奔腾);将"窗含西岭千秋雪"译为"My window does *enframe* the West Ridge clad in thousand-year snows clean",使用了由名词派生而来的"enframe(为画配框)";将"野火烧不尽,春风吹又生"译为"The prairie fires may burn and *lick*",使用了下义词"lick(火焰吞噬)";将"一枝红杏出墙来"译为"A twig of apricot flowers is *flaming* out o'er th' wall",使用了由名词转化而来的"flaming(像火焰般跳跃)"(卓振英,1996:256)。

《鸡鸣赋》里还有这样的内容:

岂不爱眠,虑难辞咎。
未醒其躯,先寤乃味。

---

① 斜体是本文写作时加以改变的,下同。

振羽待鸣兮若惊,试音待发兮如啾。
尔乃形同鹄立,貌似鹰扬。
一声初起,万吻齐张。
不军令以严肃,无国法而纪纲。
初鸣忌促,利在悠扬;
再鸣忌缓,韵短声长;
三唱则无烦律吕,乱鸣而人始彷徨。

该赋歌颂的主要是雄鸡的优良品质,特别是其报晓之功。原作作者对雄鸡的鸣叫作了初鸣、二鸣、三鸣的交代。编者的译文是这样的:

Not that he declines th' benefit of sleep,
But that his sense of duty is strong.
Although not yet fully awake, he tries
His tongue and flaps his wings for th' morning song.
No sooner has he made the starting note
Than his companions in chorus roar.
Lo, he assumes a posture near to that of th' crane
And th' air of an eagle that is ready to soar!
Caw— cuckoo — coo!
Caw— cuckoo — coo!
The world entire becomes active all at once
As soon as he utters the very first caw!
Discipline is carried out without orders,
And peace accomplish'd without a statute law.
As the first movement is slow in nature,
He's never found hasty in any case;.
Aware that the second movement is quick,
After th' transition he picks up his pace;
And at last, unconstrained in his style,
He stimulates with an easy grace.

为了提高可读性,编者把鸣译为 song(歌),二鸣采用音乐用语 movement,同时在译文中使用了下义词 roar,flap 和拟声辞格"Caw — cuckoo — coo! / Caw — cuckoo — coo!",以产生如闻其声、如睹其状的审美效果。

三、句法差异及其调适

思维的差异也反映在语言上。从句法上讲,汉语重意合(parataxis),以意义连贯上下文,连接成分用得少,英语重形合(hypo-taxis),若无连接成分,句子各部分关系就会散乱不清;从章法上讲,英语语篇标志(discourse marker)使用频率高,而汉语则偏低。《鸡鸣赋》里还有如下内容:

是此一禽者,
为羲和氏之功臣,
神农氏之良吏。
暗司日月之光,而人不知;
明归造物之功,而身不与者也。
奈何怒之如贼,叱之若奴;
偕豕作队,与犬同呼;
既利其生而致其死,
复食其卵而断其雏也哉!

根据英语行文习惯,"奈何怒之如贼"与上文之间以使用过渡性词语为妥。因此编者在翻译中采用了:

(3) 空缺补足法

即加上过渡性语篇标志语,以衔接上下文,使过渡自然。以下译文中的斜体部分就是为此而加上的。

And thus, it goes without saying that, as wise Minister like Xihe
And sagacious Magistrate to God of Agriculture,
The cock unnoticeablymeasures the elapse of night and day,
And devotes himself to creation without asking for any pay!
I would at this point venture to question:
What right do we have against him to rave
As if he were a thief? Howe'er can we
Hush him, as if he were merely a slave?

四、伦理型与认知型及其调适

各民族的历史、地理、思维方式等因素都可能产生文化积淀,形成该民族的文化特质。中国人偏于情感,重"义",亲属称谓划分细微;西方人偏于理智,重利,亲情相对淡泊,亲属称谓划分粗略。中国的叔叔、舅舅,在西方通称为 uncle(s),堂兄弟姊妹、表兄弟姊妹一律称为 cousin(s)。在中国人眼里,群体(集体、国家)高于个人,而在西方人心中,个人的生命价值才是最重要的。这一思维差异可概括为"伦理型与认知型"。(连淑能,2002:41)

李渔《避兵行》有这么两句:"先刃山妻后刃妾,衔须伏剑名犹烈。"

诗句描述的这种"壮烈"行为在西方是不会得到崇尚的,但所含内容不能不译。那就采用委婉的手法译为:

I shall first *extricate* my wife and concubines
From th' pain, then with my own sword I shall myself slay.

To extricate somebody from pain(使人从痛苦中得到解脱)虽然也可隐含"结束某人生命"之意,但显得比"手刃"委婉。这种方法就是:

(4) 模糊替代法

即使用模糊语或委婉语,淡化有关内容。这一方法适用于过于直白的话语的翻译。

李清照《夏日绝句》"生当作人杰,死亦为鬼雄"两句有不同译法:

A.
Be a man of men with mettle while alive,
And a soul of souls even if doom'd to die.
(zzy,1996:232)

B.
In the world, being a hero in the crowd,
In the hell, being the same among ghosts.
(tr. wlw, from dxy, 2000:186)

从文化意义的可接受性考虑,A 译采用了概念的模糊替代法,利用 soul 一词的多义性,又以 even if doom'd to die 加以说明,把"鬼"的语义模糊化,相对于译为 ghosts 要好一些。

李渔《何满子》"欲使妇人不妒,除非阉尽男儿"两句,若是死译,必将失之粗俗。因此,编者将原先的译文"Women won't stop being jealous unless all men were *castrated*"修正为:

> Could women e'er be freed from jealous care?
> Oh no. Unless all men were *desex'd*, ne'er!

这是因为,上义词 desex(去性)比 castrate(阉割)委婉。

五、直觉性与逻辑性及其调适

我们讲究直觉性,而西方讲究逻辑性。这就是"直觉性与逻辑性"(连淑能,2002:43)之别。李渔《归故乡赋》极尽渲染铺陈之能事,描写漂泊之苦、归乡之乐,生动抒发作者对故乡的热爱和依恋。在我们眼里,它是一篇好作品,因为我们倾向于"借助直觉体悟,即通过知觉从总体上模糊而直接地把握认识对象的内在本质和规律"(连淑能,2002:43)。然而西方人,包括以英语为母语的读者,则"崇尚科学和理性,注重思维活动的严格性、明晰性和确定性,注重思维程式的数学化、形式化、公理化、符号化和语言的逻辑性,思维方式也必然带有精确性"。对于他们,以下这些诗句就难以做到无懈可击了:

> "书破蠹肥,花稀棘密。
> 妻颜减红,亲发增白。
> 幸犹归之及今,悔长征之自昔。"

如果寻根究底,那么,既然妻子和双亲在家,家室何以荒凉至此?这是难以解释的。"妻颜减红,亲发增白"无非是要说明,光阴似金,要加以爱惜,不要在漂流中错失。经过思考、斟酌,译者在不伤原作大雅的情况下采用语义重构及语篇整合,对逻辑关系加以调整、重构语篇逻辑系统,把"妻颜减红,亲发增白"的意义转移到劝诫游子的那一部分。原先的译文是:

> The books are damag'd and th' hateful worms grow fat;
> The thorny plants are many and th' flowers few;
> The lovely pink on my wife's cheeks has faded away;
> And to my parents' temple hair is added frost new.

后来改为:

Oh, wandering man! To drift about like aimless arrows why do you incline?
Oh, wandering man! Discard my example, and go back to your native land,
Where you may watch waterfalls while sipping at your wine,
Or make wreaths with th' flowering orchids near at hand!
Oh, go home ere your parents' temple hair becomes gray
And ere the lovely pink on your wife's cheeks fades away!

译文照样给人以"光阴荏苒,时不再来"的启示,传达了热爱故乡的情感。这种方法可界定为:(5) 信息移位法。

第三节 基于原版本某些因素而进行的介入与调适

非逻辑现象的原因还存在于原版本的错简、文字缺失等等。

《楚辞·天问》有如下诗句:"何环穿自闾社,以及丘陵,(是淫是荡,)爰出子文。吾告堵敖以不长,何试上自予,忠名弥彰?"各家解说基本没有摆脱王逸所注"旋穿闾社,通于丘陵,以淫而生子文"的藩篱。结尾部分的这种非逻辑性,就应是衍文、遗漏或错简所致。译者根据背景、诗人的情思及整个语篇的总意象等因素,重新进行整合。其英译为:

May Ziwen be found of today,
Were he in th' wilderness or near;
May Xiong Yun, who did justly slay
Th' fatuous, in Chu reappear:
Or else Chu's fall is what I fear!

这就是(6)逻辑重构法,即纠正错误,剔除非逻辑话语,重新整合和建构译文的逻辑体系。李渔的《鸡鸣赋》中,有这么两句:

既利其生而致其死,
复食其卵而断其雏也哉!

若照本宣科地将"其卵"译作 his eggs,就可能产生"公鸡会下蛋"的歧义。因此编者采用逻辑重构法,将这两句译作:

And above all, how can we bear to consume

The eggs, which are his offspring in th' direct line?

第四节　基于目的语的文本要求而进行的介入与调适

翻译文本在内容、形式各方面有各自的要求。若原版本排序有误，译者就可以采用：

(7) 篇章调序法

即将原有篇章的逻辑顺序加以调整。例如，《盘庚》中篇开头"盘庚作，惟涉河以迁"，是介绍盘庚的迁都计划的，时间在前；上篇是针对"盘庚迁于殷，民不适有居"而发表的，时间在后。因此，编写中的《古今汉英演讲赏析》按照演讲发表的时间顺序，将中、下、上排序为1、2、3。

典籍中的某些文字，若并不适合需要，也可以采用：

(8) 赘余删除法

即删除既定范畴之外及多余的词、句或段。例如，盘庚演讲中诸如"盘庚迁于殷，民不适有居"、"盘庚作，惟涉河以迁"，以及《甘誓》中"大战于甘，乃召六卿。王曰"等话语，并不属于演讲词的逻辑范畴，编者便将其作为注释或赏评文字来处理。

第五节　小结

译者必须具备东西方思维方式比较研究的意识。基于这种意识，在翻译之先为翻译文本预设一个合适的逻辑体系，是有必要的。翻译研究是交叉学科，其研究涉及诸多学科门类。中西比较思维的理论成果理应成为我们的研究工具。然而，检索结果说明，有关翻译与逻辑思维的研究领域尚鲜有学者涉足。

思考题

1. 从话语的总体倾向看，东方人会把表达结论等重要信息的词语置于句首还是句末？西方人呢？能否从民族性格角度解释这一差异？

2. 为什么必须为翻译文本预设一个逻辑体系？

3. 定义法是科研常用的方法之一，本章对于调适的方法就一一加以了界定。定义法是通过揭示人、物或事件的特征和基本属性,来描述或规定一个词或一个概念的意义。被定义的人、物或事件叫做被定义项,其定义叫做定义项。一般来说,定义项越多,概念就越清晰。定义有不同的方法,如词法定义、情境定义、内涵定义、外延定义、列举定义、实物定义(又称直观释义或实指定义)、理论定义、本义狭义定义、递归定义(又称归纳定义)、循环定义、规定性定义(又称规创定义或约定定义)、厘定性定义、劝导性定义等。搜索并浏览以上诸法。

4. 试用英文为"马"这种动物下个定义,然后对照词典所给的定义,加以比较。

练习题

1. 把以下句子翻译成汉语:

I'm very much delighted that you have been successful since then.

It'd be wrong to think that money is almighty.

2. 你觉得"A desk is a piece of furniture with a flat or sloped surface and typically with drawers, at which one can read or write."这个定义怎么样?你能否通过增加定义项而使概念更加完整清晰?

第十二章 汉诗英译中的移情

学习目标

理解翻译方法论研究中的"移情"这一概念,提高对其可行性、必要性和科学性的认识,并学会用之于实践。

第一节 何谓汉诗英译中的"移情"?

移情(Empathy)原是个美学—心理学概念。在美学的范畴里,它是指审美活动中主体的感情移入对象,使对象仿佛有了人的情感,其汉译为"移情作用";而从心理学的角度看,它是指想象自己处于他人的境地,去理解其感情、欲望、思想、动机和行为,汉语往往译为"神入"。本章将其推衍至译学方法论研究,笼而统之地以"移情"概括"神入"与"移情作用"两个概念,既指译者想象自己处于诗人或诗中之"我"(例如金昌绪《春怨》一诗中的"妾")的境地,去感悟其思想感情,又指译者在进入诗人的心理状态或模拟其审美定势之后,把感情"外化"而移入诗歌形象,使诗歌形象心灵化和人格化,从而与诗人的审美感受产生共鸣。

第二节 移情的理论依据

在汉诗英译中运用移情是可行的、科学的、重要的。对此,下文将逐一加以探讨。

一、移情的可行性

康德指出:"一个鉴赏判断所要求的必然性的条件是共通感的观念。"(康德,1964:76)所谓共通感,"就是将个人感受事物时所享受的愉快、崇高传达给

他人的必然性心理规律"(林同华,1987:106)。这就意味着,诗人所创造的艺术形象是具有可感受性的。"春色满园关不住,一枝红杏出墙来"等诗句流传至今,依然脍炙人口,其原因正在于此。康德以后的心理学家经过研究,发现人们普遍都有根据外物与人的心理的直观相似性而将其加以归类的心理体验,并把这种心理规律称为审美相似律。例如,我们会把大海与博大、寒冷与悲惨、登高与奋发联系起来,因此,当"东临碣石,以观东海"(曹操:《步出夏门行·观沧海》)、"今我来思,雨雪霏霏"(《诗经·采薇》)或"欲穷千里目,更上一层楼"(王之涣:《登鹳雀楼》)的意象在我们的脑海浮现的时候,我们就能联想到胸怀博大、悲苦哀愁或是积极向上,感同身受地领会诗歌的意蕴。

人的思维具有超时间、超空间的特点。所谓"寂然凝虑,思接千载;悄然动容,视通万里;吟咏之间,吐珠玉之声;眉睫之前,卷风云之色:其思例之致乎"(刘勰:《文心雕龙·神思》),阐明的正是形象思维的超时空性。即使诗人生活在千年之前,诗中的景物生发于万里之外,我们依然可以运用意象、联想和想象,做到"神与物游"(刘勰,《文心雕龙·神思》),去追溯诗人的审美感受和审美创造。共通感的观念、审美相似律和思维的超时空特性为移情法的可行性提供了美学、心理学和思维科学的依据。译者是能够发挥想象力,模拟诗人的审美定势,去重现、观照和感受诗歌形象的,是能够获得诸如"蛙声十里出山泉"(查慎行《次实君溪边步月韵》句)的直觉(Intuition)、诸如"霜叶红于二月花"(杜牧《山行》句)的知觉(Perception)、诸如"日出江花红胜火"(白居易《忆江南》句)的联觉(Synesthesia)和诸如"留得残荷听雨声"(李商隐《宿骆氏亭寄怀崔雍崔兖》句)的统觉(Aperception)的。

二、移情的科学性

王国维在《人间诗话》中把诗歌的艺术境界划分为"有我之境"和"无我之境"。前者指"以我观物,故物皆着我之色彩","我"的感情强烈、外露;后者指"以物观物,故不知何者为我,何者为物",诗人的情感融化于客观景物之中,似乎被隐蔽或淡化,实则意与境浑,物我一体。"以我观物"也好,"以物观物"也好,二者都有情感的移入。由此可见,移情是汉诗创作的规律之一。把移情作为汉诗英译中的审度方法是符合这一规律的,是对本源的模仿或回归。

接受美学揭示,审美过程是能动的再创造过程:一方面是主体的审美能力的外化,另一方面是客体的审美特征的心灵化。这种双重双向建构也符合诗歌的阅读欣赏。读者受到诗歌的刺激,产生审美反应、感知和接纳,在心目中形成诗歌意象，并对其进行审美观照，做出审美判断。例如，在我们把李商隐的"春蚕到死丝方尽，蜡炬成灰泪始干"这一客观存在变为主观心意中的物象之后，我们会把"无私奉献"这一人格特征投射到"蜡炬"和"春蚕"身上，而蜡炬和春蚕也似乎具备某一类人的特征，令我们感到其崇高之美。这说明，诗歌欣赏的过程包含着移情的过程。译者必须经历这一过程，这是毋庸赘言的。和一般读者不同的是，由于肩负翻译的使命，其阅读欣赏多少带有功利性。

诗歌翻译的过程也符合"将客观存在变为主观存在，再由主观存在上升为新的客观存在的心理规律"（童庆炳，1993:346）。由于诗歌翻译是一种审美创造，它必然有想象力的加入，而所谓想象，就是在联想的基础上对原有意象进行加工，以"创造出新的意象的理性形象思维过程"（曾杰、张树相，1996:111）。译者或是内模仿诗人的情感，并把它灌注给想象中的诗歌形象，然后运用目的语（Target Language）去物化审美创造的成果；或是基于诗人的情感，"把自己富于个性、民族性和时代性的审美体验"赋予诗作和原有意象，"对其作出特殊的解释，创造出更加生动丰满的艺术形象和更加深邃广博的意蕴意境"（卓振英，1997[3]:45），两者之中都有移情。原有意象的加工与新意象的创造过程同时也就是移情的过程。因为所谓意象，就是心与物的和谐统一，二者缺一不可。

对于诗歌创作、欣赏和翻译的考察说明，汉诗英译运用移情是符合文艺美学、审美心理学和思维科学的规律的。

三、移情的重要性

根据总体审度（Overall Survey）的理念，透彻理解原作是汉诗英译做到形神兼似的先决条件，而理解有赖于"对全诗总意象（Total Concept）的把握"（卓振英，1997:44）。而以移情作为总体审度的方法，去观照诗人与诗作，这对于把握诗歌的总意象有着十分重大的意义。

语言的使用者是确定语符含义的重要因素。译者调动自己的审美感知与审美意识，通过移入诗人的思想感情，"化我为他"，可以消减自己与诗人之间的心理距离，实现"审美主体之间的情感交流"（曾杰、张树相，1996:152），从而透彻地感悟诗人的人生观、价值观和审美态度，而这对于正确理解诗作是十分有意义的。诗人的审美感知、审美情感和审美意志等信息进入译者的大脑之后，会自动地去耦合、接通、激活译者的审美心理结构，使之重组和强化。这种移情就等于"邀请"诗人参与对于诗作的解读。正如演员只有进入角色才能把人物扮演得惟妙惟肖一样，译者只有设身处地，才能将诗歌翻译得形神兼似。

译者与诗歌意象之间也应是一种审美移情关系。它体现了审美活动的"情感交流性"(曾杰、张树相,1996:152)。这种移情具有两个方面的意义。首先,它有助于感悟诗歌的意蕴、意境和把握诗歌的总意象。译者融诗人之情感与自己的审美体验于一体,置诗中的景物于眼前,进行审美观照,创造出来的意想将是完满而不是残缺的;其心目中的总意象也将是意象经过完形、整合之后作为一个有机整体的全方位、多维度展现。这就有可能使译作的义值涵盖诗歌的原义和诗歌在流传中被赋予的增殖义。其次,它有助于生成能够准确地物化诗歌意象的目的语。恩格斯说过,"一切差异都在中间阶段融合",这"中间阶段"使"差异互相过渡……并且使对立互为中介"。在诗歌翻译中,什么是能使源语(Source Language)和目的语得以"互相过渡"的中介呢?是意象和总意象。翻译的心理过程就说明了这一点。译者先以源语作为思维的工具,对诗作及其意象进行解读和观照,在心目中形成新的意象及总意象;新的意象及总意象刺激译者的目的语生成机制,并为其使用目的语的恰当语符去重构和物化意象及总意想提供一个认知图式(Cognitive Map)。对此,编者在汉诗英译的实践中是深有体会的。

第三节 移情的实践依据

汉诗英译是否运用移情,这往往关系到译作的成败优劣。正反两个方面的译例俯拾皆是。兹列举若干,并加以剖析。

【例1】独怜幽草涧边生,上有黄鹂深树鸣,
　　　　春潮带雨晚来急,野渡无人舟自横。

———— 韦应物:《滁州西涧》

A 译:
These I love: hidden plants that grow by the river's edge;
above, yellow warblers in the deep trees singing;
spring tides robed in rain, swifter by evening;
the ferry landing deserted where a boat swings by itself.
(tr. B. W., from gzz,1994:135)

B 译:
I keenly love the brookside grass obscure and yet serene,
Above which orioles warble high up in th' woods so green.

The spring tide, hasten'd by the rains, occurr'd last night so swift
That th' ferry boat, unmann'd, is left midst th' wilderness adrift.
(zzy,1996:97)

韦应物洁身自好,关心民生;欲改革而无力,思归隐而不能,只好任其自然。他曾说"扁舟不系与心同"(《自巩洛舟行入黄河即事寄府县僚友》)。此诗融汇着他的恬淡与忧伤,是有所寄托的。幽草安贫守节,黄鹂居高媚时,诗人爱的是前者;春潮带雨,气势汹汹,野渡无人,不得其用,诗人怜的是后者。

有人认为,A译"用一句译全诗,句法安排很巧妙"。"These I love=I love these,其中 these 代表后面的四个宾语 hidden plants, yellow warblers, spring tides 和 the ferry landing…"(gzz,1994:135)。殊不知这样一来,风格浅露,韵味淡薄,与原诗意蕴相去深远。B译"the grass obscure and serene"融诗人的恬淡于"幽草","…is left midst the wilderness adrift"寄诗人之无奈乎"野渡",基本上做到意与境浑,形神兼似。译者是经过一个"化我为他"及对意象进行审美观照和审美创造的过程的,总意想的形成对译文的产生也确实起了刺激和导向的作用。

【例2】红豆生南国,春来发几枝。劝君多采撷,此物最相思。
——王维:《相思》

A译:
Red beans are grown in a southern clime.
A few branches burgeon in spring time.
On your lap, try to gather as many as you can;
The best reminder of love between woman and man.
(xzj,1990:77)

B译
The love peas flourish in a southern clime.
In spring, with tender twigs, they reach their prime.
'Tis wish'd thou'll gather plenty of their seed
The token best of love sincere indeed!
(zzy,1996:107)

诗人于江上赋此诗以赠别其友李龟年,"红豆"是友情的象征。B译赋予"红豆"以原义及"广义的爱"这一增殖义,所创造出来的意象是比较准确而圆满的;A 译以"红豆"象征男女之爱,则有悖诗人心意。移情与否,结果不同。

【例 3】白日依山尽,黄河入海流。欲穷千里目,更上一层楼。
——王之涣:《登鹳雀楼》

A 译:
The sun behind the western hills glows,
And toward the sea the Yellow River flows.
Wish you an endless view to cheer your eyes?
Then one more storey mount and higher rise.
(tr. ctg, from gzz,1994:17)

B 译:
The setting sun behind the mountains glows,
The muddy Yellow River seawards flows.
If more distant views are what you desire,
You simply climb up a storey higher.
(xzj,1990:32)

C 译:
Ling'ring is the setting sun about the mountain height,
Surging is the Yellow River towards the vast sea.
Aim higher and up the tower take another flight
To acquire a vision broader than one thousand *li*.
(zzy,1996:139)

编者移诗人热爱祖国河山及奋发向上之情怀于己身,并运用想象,把"黄河"、"白日"等景物置于"眉睫之前",去追溯诗人的审美体验:登高临远,江山如画。黄河的浑浊和狂暴不见了,余下的是壮阔与百折不回;白日的炎热和刺眼舍弃了,显现的是雄浑与绚丽多彩。千里之外的景色隐喻新的领域和境界,等待着人们去探索与成就。积极进取之心油然而生,激励性的"更上一层楼"不禁夺腔而出……

基于这种溯本追源的心路历程,编者在 C 译一、二行采用了倒装句式,选用了富于表现力的"lingering"、"surging"等词。三、四行使用祈使句,其内容对人对己都能适用;其中"aim higher"既有"立志更高远"之意,又与登楼的原义相合;"vision"及"another flight"有较强的兼义性和象征性。

A 译三、四行意为"你想一睹无限风光、一饱眼福吗?那就再登一层楼、再爬高些吧!"似乎出自导游之口,未能再现原诗高格及诗人的主体意识。B译中的"muddy Yellow River"("浑浊的黄河")显然是在诗人没有"参与"的情况下译出的;三、四行意为"如果你想看得更远些,只要再爬高一些就行",与译有类似的缺陷。究其原因,乃在于翻译过程中缺乏诗人与译者的情感介入。

【例四】儿童相见不相识,笑问客从何处来。

——贺知章:《回乡偶书》

A 译:
My children do not know my face,
But smiling ask, "O stranger, whence art thou?"
(tr. H. A. G., from xyz, 1992:182)

B 译:
And my children, meeting me, do not know me,
They smile and say: "Stranger, where do you come from?"
(tr. W. B., from xyz, 1992:182)

C 译:
The native children, in whose eyes I am a stranger entire,
Politely smile on meeting me: "Where comest thou?" they inquire.
(zzy, 1996:90)

编者设想自己是年已 86 岁的诗人,辞官回到阔别 50 多年的家乡。想到自己乡音未改,鬓毛已衰,不禁感慨系之。家乡的小孩子们见了面笑着问我:"请问客人是从那儿来的呀?"他们不认得我这个家乡人,以主为宾,情有可原;但他们那富于戏剧性的问话对于我却是不小的震撼。真是人生易老啊!

基于这种心理体验,编者把"儿童"译为"native children",比较忠实;A、B译分别译做"my very children"和"my children",则显然是在没有诗人"参与对于诗作的解读"的情况下对"儿童"这一形象的扭曲。

【例5】纤云弄巧,飞星传恨。

——秦观:《鹊桥仙》

A 译:
Clouds have their peculiar flair and skill;
They can change their size and shape, as they will.
Stars have qualities more wonderful still;

The hopes of their fellows, they can fufil…
(tr. xzj, from xyz, 1992:384)

B译：

Clouds float like works of art;
Stars shoot with grieve at heart.
(xyz,1992:384—385)

C译：

Her yearning in th' clouds the Girl weaver subtly weaves,
While the shooting stars display how th' Cowherd grieves.
(zzy,1996:222)

词人移情于牛织，通过描写"七夕"之会，颂扬了纯真专一的爱情和对这种爱情的执著追求，从而寄托词人对爱情的态度和理想。译者只要"内模仿诗人的审美感知、审美情感和审美意志"，就不难领会弄巧的不是纤云，而是善织云锦的织女；飞星所传的是牛织对于造成他们天各一方的势力的怨愤；"纤云"与"飞星"这两个意象是牛织的情感——也可以说是词人的情感——的载体。A译把云与星当作了颂扬的对象，B译赞美了云，又把星当作生恨的主体，这些情感误置的情况应归因于没有词人的"参与"。C译之所以较为忠实，是因为编者经历了移情的过程，领悟到了词人的知、情、意，并以之观照"飞星"与"纤云"，较准确地把握住了它们的意蕴。

以上个例分析进一步说明，汉诗英译运用移情法是可行的、科学的。它有助于使译作达到形神兼似的境界。

思考题

1. 试举例说明文学翻译中移情的重要性。
2. 为什么说汉诗英译中的移情是科学、可行的？你今后会不会践行？
3. 本章所举译例中有哪些误译给你留下深刻的印象？

练习题

1. 陆游《鹧鸪天》一词及其英译如下：

懒向青门学种瓜，只将渔钓送年华。
双双新燕飞春岸，片片轻鸥落晚沙，

歌缥缈，橹呕哑，酒如清露鲊如花。
逢人问道归何处，笑指船儿是我家。

Partridges in the Sky
The melon grower of the Green Gate who cares
To copy? In fishing I shall find delight.
The swallows dart about the spring banks in pairs,
And hosts of gulls on the evening sand alight.
The oars creaking, songs are resounding in th' air,
Th' dishes seem to bloom, and as dew th' wine's as clear.
Smiling and pointing to the boat, when ask'd where
I shall return, I'll reply: "My home's right here!"

请追溯译者移情的心理过程。

2. 将本章涉及的翻译方法作一归纳。

第十三章 汉诗英译中的"借形传神"及变通

学习目标

认清诗歌内容与形式的紧密辩证关系,增进有关汉诗和英诗的学识,提高对于"借形传神"及变通的必要性和可行性的认识。

第一节 "借形传神"及变通的必要性

借用英诗的形式翻译汉诗,以再现或重构原诗的神韵,这就是所谓"借形传神"。由于英汉两种诗歌不存在雷同的形式,翻译时就须加以变通。

借形与变通是必要的。这是因为,诗歌是形式与内容结合最为紧密的一种文学样式。一首诗就是一个符号系统。它是由各种声音符号、文字符号、句法符号、格律符号和意象符号等子系统有机结合而成的、用以表达思想感情的统一体。一旦任何一个子系统发生衰变、瓦解或被卸除,整个系统就会跟着嬗变、瓦解和消亡。这就是说,诗歌的形式因素是诗歌信息即内容的载体,离开特定的形式,特定的内容就无所依附。正如叶芝所说的:"一种感情在找到它的表现形式—颜色、声音、形状或某种兼而有之之物—之前,是并不存在的,或者说,它是不可感知的,也是没有生气的。"(胡经之、王岳川,1994:81)

符号学家苏珊·朗格说过,"整个作品的情感就是符号的'含义'","诗歌总是要创造某种情感的符号",这种创造"不是依靠复现能引起这种情感的事物,而是依靠组织的词语—负载有意义及文学联想的词语,使其结构贴合这种情感的变化"。(朗格,1986:207,267)

所谓"结构",即是语言形式。

象征主义文艺理论家瓦雷里(1871—1945)认为,形式具有引发性(即形式本身也有意义,可以产生思想)和整体的暗示性。"这意义是不能脱离那芳馥的外形的。因为它并不是牵强地附在外形的上面,像寓言式的文学一样;而是完全濡浸

和溶解在外形里面,如太阳的光和热之不能分离。"(胡经之、王岳川,1994:81)

形式主义文艺理论家日尔蒙斯基也指出,形式成分与艺术内容一起进入诗作的整体之中,参与了审美意想的创造。"如果说形式成分意味着审美成分,那么,艺术中的所有内容事实也都成为形式的现象。"①(胡经之、王岳川,1994:181—182)

根据布克洛斯基的"反常化"理论,诗歌语言是使用"反常化"程序,对实用语言进行"扭曲"、"变形"、"施加暴力"等艺术加工以使之变得异乎寻常地突出和显赫的语言。这种程序贯穿于语音选择、词汇构成和搭配、句法安排等各个层面。"我们将把那种被特殊程序创造出来的事物称为艺术作品,而所谓特殊程序的目的在于,要使这些事物尽可能地被人们作为艺术品来感受。"(胡经之、王岳川,1994:177)

以上理论阐明了诗歌形神一统的道理。

为了更为具体地说明这个道理,我们可以试用解构的方法,对王之涣《登鹳雀楼》一诗加以分析。原诗是:

> 白日依山尽,黄河入海流。
> 欲穷千里目,更上一层楼。

这首诗情景交融,寄托了诗人对山河的热爱,隐喻了积极进取的精神和站得高、看得远的哲理。然而,在卸除了节奏、韵律等格律要素,把诗歌语言改换为实用语言之后,就成了:

> 太阳就要下山了,黄河向大海的方向流去。如果你想望见千里以外的景色,那就再爬上一层楼去吧。

其结果是:

1. 诗歌的音乐美、形式美、对称美等审美特征消失,不再具有朗朗上口、可以配乐吟唱、便于记忆的特点;

2. 语言形式的变化引起了语义的变化,含蓄蕴藉的模糊美消失。原诗首联日、山、河、海诸意象所负载和隐含的对于山河之爱被淡化,末联"楼"和"千里目"的联想意义及象征性、"更上一层楼"的多义性消失,所言唯景色与上楼而已。诗歌的意境瓦解,味道全无。

---

① 日尔蒙斯基. 文学理论. 诗学. 修辞学[M]. 1977 年俄文版 16—17 页. 转引自胡经之、王岳川(主编). 文艺学美学方法论[M]. 北京:北京大学出版社. 1994. 181—182.

如果以类似这样的译品作为传播媒介,就难以为受众(读者)所接受,就难以达到文化传播的效果。

由此可以得出这样的启示:汉诗英译不可置形式于不顾。形之不存,神将焉附?散文化翻译方法、非韵体翻译方法是译不出汉诗的神韵的。只有采用以诗译诗的方法,才能做到形神兼似,最大限度地迁移或再现原诗的形式美、音韵美、节奏美、情感美、意境美和风格美。

第二节 "借形传神"及变通的可行性

"借形传神"及变通的理论依据是文艺美学及汉英比较诗学的研究成果。人类对于诗歌的审美思维具有共性,例如,诗歌的音韵、节奏、意象、意境能够普遍引起美的愉悦。英汉两种诗歌在形式上具有近似性。汉诗有一句至八句乃至多于八句的诗、词、曲,而英诗则有双行、三行、四行……十四行等诸多诗体;两种诗歌都讲究诗歌语言的使用;英诗的节奏体现在重读、非重读音节的规律性交替,汉诗的节奏则通过平仄声的规律性交替来实现;英诗有韵脚(rhyme proper)这种与汉诗类似的押韵方式。这就使得汉诗英译与原诗的形似成为可能。

诗歌的内容和形式本来就不是一成不变的。例如,源于意大利的十四行诗(the sonnet),16 世纪由 Thomas Wyatt 和 Henry Howard 引入英国之后,其题材和形式都产生了变化:莎士比亚以之表达人文主义新思想,弥尔顿、拜伦以之抒发政治理想与热情,使之摆脱了以歌咏爱情为主的旧传统;弥尔顿在 To Mr. Cyriack Skinner Upon His Blindness 一诗中,"八行组"(octave)之后的内容未作停顿便跨入"六行组"(sestet),华兹华斯、拜伦分别在他们的诗歌 The Subjugation of Switzerland 和 Sonnet on Chillon 中,在"八行组"用了三个韵(韵式为 abba acca),打破了只用两个韵(韵式为 abba abba)的限制。(吴翔林,1991:85—88)另外,即使是格律诗,也是可以有变格的,汉诗、英诗皆然,而人们绝不会因此而对诗人或诗作吹毛求疵。在诗歌创作中可以推陈出新,在诗歌翻译中,对形式酌情加以变通,这应是顺理成章的事情。

以下译例为可行性提供了事实依据。

【例 1】上邪! 我欲与君相知,长命无绝衰。山无陵,江水为竭,冬雷震震,夏雨雪,天地合,乃敢与君绝!

——汉乐府民歌《上邪》

英诗三行套韵体(the terza rima)采用的是抑扬格五音步,每节三行,押韵

格式为 a b a , b c b , c d c ...雪莱的《西风颂》即依此写成:

> O wild West Wind, thou breath of Autumn's being,
> Thou, from whose unseen presence the leaves dead
> Are driven, like ghosts from an enchanter fleeing,
> Yellow, and black, and pale, and hectic red,
> Pestilence-striken multitudes: O thou,
> Who chariotestto their dark wintry bed
>
> The winged seeds, where they lie cold and low,
> Each like a corpse within its grave, until
> Thine azure sister of the spring shall blow

参照该诗体,编者将《上邪》译为:

Oh Providence

> Oh Providence! I pledge myself for e'er
> To being with my lover closely bound.
> Our keen and deep affections shall wane ne'er!
>
> Unless the mountains might collapse to th' ground,
> Unless the streams and rivers all go dry,
> Unless the thunders should in winter pound;
>
> Unless snowflakes should fall from th' summer sky,
> Unless the earth should merge with heaven's volt,
> We'll never never break our silken tie!
>
> (zzy,1996:39)

英译为抑扬格五音步(iambic pentameter),韵式为 a b a , b c b , c d c ...,基本上以英诗的形式重构和再现了原诗丰富多彩的形式美、起伏跌宕的音韵美、质朴有力的风格美和对爱情坚贞不渝的情感美。

【例 2】应怜屐齿印苍苔,小扣柴扉久不开。
春色满园关不住,一枝红杏出墙来。

——叶绍翁:《游园不值》

英诗四行诗节(quatrain)通常指押韵格式为套韵(alternate rhyme) a b a b 的四行诗节,例如 Tennyson 的 *The Palace of Art*:

> For there was Milton like a seraph strong,
> Beside him Shakespeare bland and mild;
> And there the world-worn Dante grasped his song,
> And somewhat grimly smiled.

编者仿此体将绝句《游园不值》译为:

Shut Without the Garden
My clog-prints on the greenish moss must have incurr'd the spite;
I knock at th' wooden gate but there's no answer after all.
A gardenful of spring can't be shut up, though. Within sight
A twig of apricot flowers is flaming out o'er th' wall.
(zzy,1996:256)

英译为抑扬格。七个音步嫌多,但由于一行汉诗的信息载量往往大于一行英诗,要保持行数相同就只能采用变通的办法。译作基本上重构了音韵美,再现了探头墙外的红杏所代表的盎然春色。

四行诗节的形式可广泛用于童谣、民歌、顺口溜的翻译:

【例3】枯鱼过河泣,何时悔复及!作书与鲂鱮,相教慎出入。
——汉乐府民歌《枯鱼过河泣》

A Dri'd Fish Is Being Carri'd across a Stream
A dri'd fish is being carri'd across a stream.
"It is too late to regret!" blubbers he.
Hence he writes a letter to the carp and the bream,
Reminding them that prudent they should be.
(zzy,1996:48)

四行诗节的韵式还有联韵(couplet rhyme,a a b b)、间韵(intermittent rhyme,a b c b)和抱韵(enclosing rhyme,a b b a),翻译时可酌情借用:

【例四】直如弦,死道边;曲如钩,反封侯。
——汉乐府民歌《京都童谣》

A Folk Rhyme Circulated in the Capital
Those straight like the string of a bow
Are condemn'd to a life of woe;
While those as sly as a crook
Oft manage marquisate to hook!
(zzy,1996:50)

【例5】林则徐曾在他的诗中引用如下典故:宋神宗召见隐士杨朴,问近日是否有人赠诗于他。杨答道,临行时其妻吟诗云:"更休落魄耽杯酒,且莫猖狂爱吟诗。今日捉将官里去,这回断送老头皮。"这首诗的英译原先用的是间韵(intermittent rhyme):

You won't be able to indulge in wine,
And your fascination with verse will lull;
Now that you are arrested by the crown,
You will for certain forfeit your old skull.

编者经过修改,便把它译为:

Frustration in wine you can no longer drown;
Your crazy fascination with verse will lull.
Today you have been arrested by the crown,
This time you will for certain lose your old skull!
(zzy,1996:319)

这就成了套韵。

有的律诗可用两个四行诗节来翻译:

【例6】手握乾坤杀伐权,斩邪留正解民悬。
　　　眼通西北江山外,声振东南日月边。
　　　展爪似嫌云路小,腾身何怕汉程偏。
　　　风雷鼓舞三千浪,《易》象飞龙定在天!

——洪秀全:《述志诗》

My Aspiration
Hong Xiuquan
Predominating power once I hold over the state,

I'll cherish virtue, purge vice and change people's adverse fate.
Thenorthwest beyond mounts and streams cannot escape my eyes;
My roar will shake the southeast where the sun and th' moon arise.
The sky'll seem narrow when I bring my limbs into full play,
When soaring I'll defy the twists and turns of th' Milky Way.
The dragon, as foretold by *Th' Book of Changes*, will in th' vault
Of heaven appear, calling forth storms, waves and thunderbolt!
(zzy,1996:327)

【例7】空山新雨后,天气晚来秋。
　　　 明月松间照,清泉石上流。
　　　 竹喧归浣女,莲动下渔舟。
　　　 随意春芳歇,王孙自可留。

——王维:《山居秋暝》

英诗十行诗节(ten-line stanza)韵式之一为 a b a b c d e c d e,例子是 Keats 的 Ode to a Nightingale:

　　Forlorn! The very word is like a bell
　　To toll me back from thee to my sole self!
　　Adieu! The fancy cannot cheat so well
　　As she is famed to do, deceiving elf.
　　Adieu, adieu! Thy plaintive anthem fades
　　Past the near meadows, over the still stream,
　　Up the hill-side; and now 'tis buried deep
　　In the next valley-glades:
　　Was it a vision, or a waking dream?
　　Fled is that music:Do I wake or sleep?

《山居秋暝》就是仿照该体译出的:

An Autumn Eve During My Stay in the Mounts
　　The rain has lent a new charm tothe heights,
　　And autumn's so real in the eve of day.
　　A serene moon through tall pines sifts its light;
　　A limpid spring on rough rocks winds its way.

A bustle from the bamboos does announce
The girls' return from bleaching, and the leaves
Of lotus for a fishing boat make way,
Which seems to slide and bounce.
Though flowers may wither, and fall the leaves,
Princes would yearn to hither stay.

(zzy,1996:104)

译作以英诗的形式描绘了山野景色和劳动场面，表达了诗人对大自然和劳动人民的热爱，再现了原诗的美学特征，符合英美人的阅读心理和审美取向。与此类似的例子还有：

【例8】隋大业长白山谣《长白山头知世郎》

长白山头知世郎，纯著红罗锦背裆。
横稍侵天半，抡刀耀日光。
上山食獐鹿，下山食牛羊。
忽闻官军至，提刀向前荡。
譬如辽东死，斩头何所伤！

The Seer of the World—A Ballad Circulated in the Area
of Mount Ever-White in the Reign of Daye of the Sui Dynasty

In red robes of silk and red waistcoat of brocade
The seer is operating in Mount Ever-White.
His lance, held sideways, hides half the sky in the shade;
His sword, when wielded, forms a sun-like sphere of light.
In mountains deep he feeds on wild game: bucks and deer;
Downhill he is provided with goats and cattle.
He swoops ahead on the Royal Troops, sword in hand,
Whene'er news arrives that they're near—
He'd rather die beheaded in such a battle
Than perish east to Liao in a strange land!

(zzy,1996:81)

【例9】玉炉香，红烛泪，偏照画堂秋思。眉翠薄，鬓云残，夜长衾枕寒。

第十三章 汉诗英译中的"借形传神"及变通

梧桐树,三更雨,不道离情正苦。一叶叶,一声声,空阶滴到明。

——温庭筠:《更漏子》

中国的词、曲都是诗歌特殊体裁,这些体裁为英诗所无,但翻译时同样可参照形式上最为近似的英诗诗体,并酌情加以变通。

英诗有四行诗节的联韵体(couplet rhyme),其韵式为 a a b b。例如雪莱的 *The Sensitive Plant*:

> A sensitive plant in a garden grew,
> And the young winds fed it with silver dew,
> And it opened its fan-like leaves to the light,
> And closed them beneath the kisses of night.

仿此诗体,编者将《更漏子》这首词译为:

> **To the Tune of the Hydraulic Chronograph**
> **The bower's incense and the candle bright**
> Betray the sadness in her pretty face as if from spite.
> Her eyebrow pigment faint, her raven hair does over spill;
> Her bedding cold, the autumn night feels longer still.
>
> **The Chinese parasols and mid-night rain**
> Do sound unfeeling 'bout her departure-inflicted pain;
> The trees send down leaf after leaf, the rain falls drop by drop;
> Before daybreak spatting the door-steps they don't stop.
> (zzy,1996:185)

英译基本节奏为抑扬格;每一诗节各行的音步数都是 5,7,7,6。在对英诗形式加以变通之后,既能适合英美人士的阅读习惯,又可以兼顾原诗作为"长短句"的特点。

【例 10】可笑严介溪,金银如山积,刀锯信手施。尝将冷眼观螃蟹,看你横行得几时!

——明代民歌:《可笑严介溪》

编者译为:

> **Ludicrous Is Yan Jiexi**
> With gold and silver pil'd up like a hill,

Ludicrous Yan Jiexi is in our view:

His knife and saw he brandishes at will.
We coldly watch the crab which crawls askew
And ask: "Can there be much time left for you ?"
(zzy,1996:298)

本译为抑扬格五音步,押运方式为 a b a b b。参照的是英诗的五行诗节(the quintet)。William Jones 的 *Sons of Poverty* 即属于这种诗体:

Must ye faint—ah! How much longer?
Better by the sword to die
Than to die of want and hunger;
They heed not your feeble cry,
Lift your voice to the sky!

汉诗中的古诗(古风)、民谣、曲赋、吟体诗、顺口溜等的翻译可酌情参照当代英诗的"半格律半自由诗"的形式。请看 Robert Graves 的 *The Enlisted Man*:

Yelled Corporal Punishment at Private Reasons:
'Rebels like you have no right to enlist—
Or to exist!'
Major Considerations leered approval,
Clenching his fist,
And gave his fierce moustache a fiercer twist.
So no appeal, even to General Conscience,
Kept Private Reasons' name off the defaulter-list.

这首小诗基本节奏为抑扬格,但有多处变格。八行之中有五行用了韵。"半格律半自由诗"是自由诗与格律诗相互渗透形成的,它"填补了两者之间的鸿沟,形成了'连续光谱'"。这种诗体"在英诗的园地里已经扎下了深厚的根子,枝繁叶茂了。"(吴翔林,1991:290—291)编者在翻译《红楼梦》的一首诗时就借助了这种诗体:

【例 11】陋室空堂,当年笏满床!
衰草枯杨,曾为歌舞场。
蛛丝儿结满雕梁,绿纱今又在蓬窗上。
说甚么脂正浓,粉正香,如何两鬓又成霜?

昨日黄土陇头埋白骨,今宵红绡帐底卧鸳鸯。
金满箱,银满箱,转眼乞丐人皆谤。
正叹他人命不长,那知自己归来丧?
训有方,保不定日后作强梁;
择膏粱,谁承望流落在烟花巷!
因嫌纱帽小,致使枷锁扛;昨怜破袄寒,今嫌紫蟒长。
乱哄哄你方唱罢我登场,反认他乡是故乡。
甚荒唐,到头来都是为他人做嫁衣裳!

——曹雪芹:《好了歌》解注

Explication to The Song of Rise and Fall
Incredibly, the hurnble rooms and shabby hall
Had once been fill'd with audience tablets and all!
And where poplars wither and grasses rankly grow'
There had been held many a pompous show.
Cover'd with spider's webs the painted beams are now seen;
But what us'd to be a shabby window is hung with curtains green.
Didn't she of t boast of her rosy face and buoyant youth with delight?
Alas, her temple hair has so soon turn'd frost-white!
When he buri'd the dead yesterday, what sorrowful tears he shed
And yet tonight he's embracing his bride in the luxurious bed.
'His suitcases have been cramm'd with silver and gold,
Why! In a twinkling he becomes a beggar people scold.
O'er the other's untimely death he had sigh'd,
Who could imagine that, when he got home, he himself died?
Many a good father finds himself stricken with grief
O'er his well—bred son's turning a thief;
And one who chooses to mary his daughter above
Ne'er anticipates that she is to be reduc'd to a soil'd dove.
Listen, there are still those officials who have spar'd no pains
To seek higher ranks and who are now in chains.
Yesterday you loathed your ragged coat for its lack of strength,
Today you dislike your purple python robes for their length.

In chaotic contention you crazily yourselves engage;
Hardly has one play'd his part when the other steps onto the stage.
How absurd 'tis that others should, in the final analysis, use and wear
The trousseaux which you have exerted yourself to prepare!
(zzy,1996:310—311)

英译各行音节数相近但不相同,参照变格的规律,抑扬格、抑抑扬格等节奏形式交替使用,并采用了英雄双行诗体的押运方式。译法较灵活,译文较生动活泼,有助于再现原诗俏皮的风格和表述丰富的哲学蕴涵。下面一首词也是以"半自由半格律诗"的形式译出的:

【例12】纤云弄巧,飞星传恨,银汉迢迢暗度。
金风玉露一相逢,便胜却人间无数。
柔情似水,佳期如梦,忍顾鹊桥归路?
两情若是长久时,又岂在朝朝暮暮!

——秦观:《鹊桥仙》

Celestral Beings on the Magpie Bridge
Her yearning in th' clouds th' Girl Weaver subtly weaves,
While the shooting stars display how th' Cowboy grieves.
Across the Milky Way they meet
But once out of a year's so many eves!
Howe'er, no secular love can e'er compare
With th' holy sentiments they for a time share..
Their tender feeling is like a long long stream;
Their rendezvous is like a transient dream.
Their hearts may bleed now that they part
At th' Magpie Bridge—men are inclin'd to deem.
But nay, so long as undying love will stay,
Whereat should they be bound up each night and day?
(zzy,1996:227—228)

该译两个诗节(stanza)各对应行的音节数相同,基本节奏形式为抑扬格,韵式为aabacc/ddedff,格律成分占主导地位。英译再现了七夕之会的情景,表现了牛织高尚纯真的爱情,表达了诗人对于爱情的理想和价值观。

读者若想继续探究,可参考以下各例,其中的翻译中的构思就不再一一说明了。

【例13】阿芙蓉,阿芙蓉,产海西,来海东。
　　　　不知何国香风过,醉我士女如醇醲。
　　　　夜不见月与星兮,昼不见白日,
　　　　自成长夜逍遥国。长夜国,莫愁湖,
　　　　销金锅里乾坤无。涵六合,迷九有,
　　　　上朱邸,下黔首,彼昏自痼何足言,
　　　　藩决膏殚付谁守?语君勿咎阿芙蓉,
　　　　有形无形瘾则同:边臣之瘾曰养痈,
　　　　枢臣之瘾曰中庸,儒臣鹦鹉巧学舌,
　　　　库臣阳虎能窃弓。中朝但断大官瘾,
　　　　阿芙蓉烟可立尽。

　　　　　　　　　　　　——魏源:《江南吟十章(其八)》

Ten Poems on South China Events,
Composed in the Style of Bai Xiangshan(No. 8)

Wei Yuan

Opium, opium! What a product of th' west!
Across the ocean to the east it comes;
Like an intoxicating wind sweeping across
The land, our men—and women alike—it benumbs.
Indulging in th' kingdom of hallucination,
For nothing at all indeed will the addicts care.
Their eyes bedimm'd cannot see the constellations
At night; by day e'en of the sun they aren't aware.
During their dawnless night,
On th' shore of th' Care-Free Lake.
O'er th' gold-consuming pot
The whole world they'll forsake!
All o'er the Nine Domains, within the country's bounds,
From red mansion residents down to th' common men.
Victims of the incurable habit are to be found;

Moreo'er, when state treasury runs out, who'll th' nation defend?
However, opium's by no means the only thing to blame,
For there are still invisible drugs whose effect is th' same;
Influential officials' faith in th' doctrine of the mean,
Frontier commanders' tolerance towards the evil foe,
Pedantic subjects' practice of repeating others' words,
And treasurers' likeness to Yang Hu, who stole th' state-own'd bow.
Provided those "addictions" of th' bureaucracy are relinquish'd,
Immediately andeasily will opium be extinguish'd!
(zzy,1996:322)

【例 14】老天爷,你年纪大,耳又聋来眼又花。你看不见人,也听不见话。吃斋念佛的活活饿死,杀人放火的享受荣华。老天爷,你不会做天,你塌了吧!

——清代民歌《老天爷你年纪大》

To the Senile Heaven

You are dim-sighted, my poor Heaven,
And deaf, being in senile decay.
You can neither see what men do,
Nor can you hear what people say.
Devout Buddhists are starv'd to death,
While arsonists and homicides prosper day by day.
Since you are so incompetent,
Poor Heaven, collapse you may!
(zzy,1996:341)

以上论证和译例分析足以说明,借形传神及变通的方法在理论上是有据可依的,在实践上是切实可行的。

思考题

1. 本章是如何论述"借形传神"的可行性的?
2. 有的学者主张,译者心中要有读者。试从接受美学角度阐述这一见解。

练习题

1. 根据所学的新知识,对你所译的唐诗(第三章练习 3)进行第五次修改、润色,同时保留所有译稿。注意你的译作的形式。

2. 陆游《示儿》一诗及不同英译如下:

原作:

　　死去元知万事空,但悲不见九州同。
　　王师北定中原日,家祭毋忘告乃翁。

译文 1: *To My Sons*

All will be over, to be sure, when run out have the sands;
Unable to seethe land unified, I'll still be sad.
When the righteous forces sweep north and capture the lost lands,
Forget not, while off'ring sacrifices, to tell your dad.
(zzy,1996:240)

译文 2: *To My Son*

After death I know all things will be void.
I only regret I do not live to see my country reunited.
If one day the royal army, marching northward, should conquer Zhong-Yuan again,
Do not forget to tell your father at the family sacrifice.
(lzw,1982:126)

译文 3: *Tell My Son*

I know all things are empty after death,
But the sorrow is I can't see the unification of China.
Until the day of king's armies recover the Central Plains,
At home, inform your father on the memorial ceremony.
(wlw,2000:184)

试从总体审度及借形传神等角度评价各种译作。

第十四章 汉诗英译中的风格重构及变通

学习目标

深化对于诗歌风格体系的认识,学习风格重构和变通的基本方法。

第一节 风格的可知性和可译性

"文如其人"——这句话可以加以引申,用来描述作品风格与作家之间的密切关系。文学风格是作家个性在旨趣、题材、样式的选择以及语言文字的使用等方面的体现。就汉诗而言,遣词、造句、语法、修辞、语体、语气、音韵、节奏、形体、篇章结构、语言文采、时代特征等等有关语言及其使用的各个方面的特色构成诗歌的显性风格体系,而格调、韵致、神思、本色、虚实、立意、意象、意境及艺术感染力等特质则构成隐性风格体系。风格体现诗人的个性,是构成诗歌意境的要素之一。正因为如此,风格的翻译与再现这一课题历来备受关注。严复"信、达、雅"三字原则中的"雅",刘重德教授提出的"信、达、切"中的"'切'——切合原文风格"(刘重德,1994:11),指的都是翻译中的风格问题。Savory 所说的译者必须解决的三个问题,即"(1) What does the author say? (2) What does he mean? (3) How does he say it?"(刘重德,1994:18),其中的(3)也是指风格。正如王宗炎教授所指出的:"能否译出原文风格是衡量译本的最高标准,尤其是在翻译文学作品或用文学笔调写历史书的时候。"(王宗炎,1980:1)

关于文学风格的可译性与不可译性,很多学者做了有益的探讨,其中刘重德教授所写的 *The Translatability of Literary Style* 和刘宓庆教授所写的"翻译的风格论",洋洋万言,旁征博引,论证有力,令人信服。根据他们的论证,诗歌的风格意义是具有可知性的;汉英两种语言存在共同的风格标记,都具有表感功能(emotive function),即能使读者(听者)产生情感反应的功能,而由表感功能产生的风格感应力也大同小异。(杨自俭、刘学云,1995:99—600)人类在

思维、审美取向方面存在着很多共性。所有这些都足以从理论上说明,风格是可译的。诸多形神兼似的译品已经为可译性提供了例证,即事实依据。试看文天祥《过零丁洋》中"惶恐滩头说惶恐,零丁洋里叹零丁"这两句诗的英译:

A 译:
On the Panic Shoal, remarks on being panic I forth sent;
Crossing the Lonely Bay, over loneliness I now lament.
(zzy,1996:258)

B 译:
For perils on Perilous Beach I heaved sighs;
On lonely Ocean now I feel dreary and lonely.
(xyz,1994:272)

译者在翻译"零丁洋"和"惶恐滩"时,不是采用直译译为 lingding Bay 和 huangkong Shaol,而是利用意译的方法,分别译为 Panic Shoal, Lonely Bay 和 Perilous Beach, lonely Ocean,从修辞的角度看,译文使用了重复(panic, panic; lonely, lonely)和双关(Panic Shoal, Lonely Bay; Perilous Beach, Lonely Ocean),从音韵的角度看,使用了作为行内韵的同源词(lonely—loneliness; perils—perilous),A 译又用了尾韵(sent—lament),基本上再现了原诗句中惋叹的语气和双关的手法。

再看另外一个例子:

待月西厢下,迎风户半开。隔墙花影动,疑是玉人来。

——王实甫:《西厢记》

A 译:
The moon in expectancy rises o'er the west—wing room;
To let in breezes th' door is left half open in the gloom.
A rustle through the flowers is heard from beyond the wall;
Could it signify that th' soul of my heart has come to call?
(zzy,1996:276)

B 译:
Wait for moonrise in Western Bower,
Where the breeze opens half the door.
The wall is shad'd by dancing flowers,

Then comes the one whom I adore.

(xyz,1992:455)

这是崔莺莺约张生前来幽会的书简,使用的是暗示的手法,风格含蓄。A 译 The moon in expectancy, th' door is left half open, th' soul of my heart 等译文较为委婉。B 译使用的祈使句所传达的似乎是,以不太客气的口吻要求对方等待,而实际上"待月"、"迎风"的是莺莺自己;令"户半开"的也不是风而是莺莺;"花影动"是暗示隔墙的张生前来赴会,并不是花本身在舞动(The wall is shad'd by dancing flowers),相对而言,A 译 A rustle through the flowers is heard from beyond the wall 具有暗示作用,更为可取;由于 B 译在用词、句式、语义方面与诗的整体风格和意境不太相符,容易造成语用失误(pragmatic failure),难以实现原诗应有的表感功能与交际功能。

以上例子足以说明,汉诗英译中的风格再现是重要的,也是可能的。本章所要讨论的是诗词英译中风格变通的理据和方法。所谓风格变通,是指在英语缺乏与汉语对应的风格符号,或者由于思维、语言、文化差异等原因,照搬原文语言风格形式会妨碍诗歌意境的重构或影响诗歌语用功能的实现等情况下,寻求近似的风格手段,以便最大限度地保持原诗意境与整体风格特征的创造性翻译行为。

第二节 变通的理据和方法

如果说,有关中英两种文化(包括审美取向和思维特征等)和两种语言的共核(common core)或共性的研究成果为风格的再现提供了依据,那么,汉英两种文化的差异性(cultural diversities)、汉语(源语)和中国文化的流变性(cultural drift)则在理论上为汉诗英译中的风格变通提供依托。

下文将对变通的若干情形及策略逐一进行探讨。

一、语义上的变通

(1) 文化意义的动态性所要求的变通

"文变染乎世情,兴废系乎时序。"(刘勰:《文心雕龙·时序》)这就是说,文学的演变、兴衰是受到社会文化发展的影响和制约的。文化是动态的,任何一个民族的价值观、道德观、天人观都处在变化之中。政治、经济制度的沿革,生产、生活方式的改变,文化、种族的交流融合,等等,等等,所有这些都会促成这种变化。

关于文化意义的动态性,刘宓庆教授曾作过如下描述:"使用中的语言的意义永远是动态的,因为话语是一种行为(act,Wittgenstein,1958),它伴随意向,因而获得一种语势(force),奥斯丁(J. L. Austin)称之为意向性语势(illocutionary force)";"这种意义动态性必定处在某种人文环境中,我们就称之为文化语势"。文化语势可以由"转变或转换机制"及"推进或发展机制"产生,后者指的是"话语(篇章)铺叙或陈敷过程中词语意义获得了新的文化意义动势"(刘宓庆,1999:104—105)。

一首经世不衰的诗歌就是一个开放的系统,它的意义同样具有动态性。诗歌在流传中可能会被赋予新的意义,即增殖义。"历代无数的审美主体(读者、译者或评论家等)把自己富于个性、民族性和时代性的审美体验赋予了诗作,对其作出特殊的解释,创造出更加生动丰满的艺术形象和更加深邃广博的意蕴意境。这些赋予和阐释积淀下来,被后代所继承并获得艺术生命力。"(卓振英,1997:45)这是在汉诗英译的过程中进行文化解码(cultural decoding)和重新编码(recoding)时不可忽略的,必要时应在风格方面予以变通。

【例1】壮志饥餐胡虏肉,笑谈渴饮匈奴血。

——岳飞:《满江红》

A译:
I could feed on the Hun's flesh, forsooth,
In hunger—in the spirit of youth,
We would drink their blood with laughing and talking.
(mxy,1997:143)

B译:
To break through our relentless foe,
Valiantly we'd cut off each head;
Laughing, we'd drink the blood they shed.
(xyz,1992:412)

C译:
We are pledg'd to hungrily feed on the northern invaders,
And, as if thirsty, with the blood of the Huns we'd go on sprees.
(zzy,1996:236)

古代称西、北各民族为胡、匈奴。岳飞词中的"胡虏"、"匈奴"所指的是来自西、北的入侵者。一者,"壮志饥餐胡虏肉,笑谈渴饮匈奴血"表达的是歼灭、击败入侵者的决心,而并非真的要食其肉、饮其血;二者,时代变迁了,上述各族已部分地融入中华民族的大家庭,民族感情、译文的文化可接受度是应当加以考虑的。因此,翻译这两句诗时就必须首先考虑翻译的策略。C 译作了变通处理:"feed on the northern invaders"明确地点明打击的对象是入侵者,"feed on"在这里有歼灭之意;"with the blood of the Huns we'd go on sprees"比较含蓄,而原作所包含的痛恨侵略者的情感和克敌制胜的英雄气概又得到了表达。

相对而言,A 译"feed on the Hun's flesh"(吃匈奴的肉)、"drink their blood"(喝他们的血)以及 B 译"drink the blood they shed"(喝他们所流出的血),读起来过于直露,反抗侵略的英雄的形象也似乎被涂抹上了野蛮、残忍的色调,对于当今的读者来说较难接受。

【例 2】春蚕到死丝方尽,蜡炬成灰泪始干。

——李商隐:《无题》

A 译:

The silkworm ceases not to spin her thread before she's dead;
Unless burnt to ashes endless tears a candle'll shed.
(zzy,1996:188)

B 译:

The silkworm dies in spring

when her thread is spun;

The candle dries its tears only

when burnt to the end.

(tr. I. H. ,from xyz,1992:312)

C 译:

Spring silkworm till its death spins silk from lovesick heart;
A candle but when burned up has no tears to shed.
(xyz,2000:287)

这两行诗句原来寓指爱情坚贞、至死方休,由于在流传中被赋予了增殖义,现在也可用以表达为人民和正义的事业鞠躬尽瘁,死而后已的高尚情怀。A 译以人称代词指蚕,且显化了"蚕"与"烛"的主观意识:"cease not"表达了"蚕"的志向;"Unless burnt to ashes"表达了"烛"的决心,使之包容了诗句的原义和增殖义。B 译 The silkworm dies in spring/when her thread is spun;/The candle dries its tears only/When burnt to the end. 仅描述了蚕的生命及烛的燃烧过程;C 译 Spring silkworm till its death spins silk from lovesick heart;/ A candle but when burned up has no tears to shed 则仅按狭义(爱)去阐释诗句中的春蚕。

【例 3】离离原上草,一岁一枯荣。野火烧不尽,春风吹又生。

——白居易:《草》

A 译:
Behold the grasses green and thick,
Which wither every year and thrive.
The prairie fires may burn and lick;
When breezes blow they'll yet revive.
(zzy,1996:161)

B 译:
Tall and hanging down, the grasses on the wide plain
Flourish and wither once in every year.
Wild fire could not burn them up to extirpate;
Springtide zephyrs blow and they come to life again.
(sdy,1997:417)

C 译:
Grass on the plain spreads higher and higher;
Year after year it fades and grows.
It can't be burned up by wild fire,
But revives when the spring wind blows.
(xyz,2000:247)

在流传中,诗句里"草"这一意象已产生"进步事物不可战胜"的增殖义。"离离"是迭声,三种译文分别用反复(repetition)或同义反复(tautology)green and thick, tall and hanging down 和 higher and higher 来翻译,与原文形式上近似,语义上基本等效;"野火烧不尽"用的是白描手法,A 译译文 The prairie fires may burn and lick 改换为隐喻(动词 lick 把火喻作有生命的东西),更加生动。

(2) 联想意义所要求的变通

同一个概念,不同的民族会有不同的联想意义,这种差异也是变通的理据之一。

【例4】昔我往矣,杨柳依依。今我来思,雨雪霏霏。

——《诗经·采薇》

A 译:
My native willows green and gay
Did wave me farewell in the past;
Now that I'm on my homebound way,
The sleet is falling thick and fast.
(zzy,1996:17)

B 译:
Long ago we set out
When willows were rich and green.
Now we come back
Through thickly falling snow.
(tr. B. W.,from xyz,1992:56)

C 译:
When I left here,
Willows shed tear,
I come back now,
Snow bends the bough.
(xyz,1992:56)

D 译:
Long ago, when we started,
The willows spread their shade.
Now that we turn back
The snowflakes fly.
(tr. A. W.,from web et al,1994:79)

"杨柳"在中国诗词中有"送别"的联想意义,但在英美文学中则没有。为此,A 译采用显化的手法(wave me farewell),使杨柳的双重意义得以再现。B 译缺失了"离别"的联想意义。C 译虽然也把杨柳人格化,但意义不明确,因为"垂泪"的原因可以是喜、怒、哀或者乐;Snow 在东西方都未必象征凄苦:"瑞雪兆丰年",而 a white Christmas 是人们求之不得的。sleet 可就不同了,它带来寒冷,造成泥泞,打湿衣衫。"雨雪"还是译为 sleet 比较妥当。其他各种译法也未能表现出杨柳和雨雪的象征及联想意义。

【例5】望门投止思张俭,忍死须臾待杜根。
我自横刀向天笑,去留肝胆两昆仑。

——谭嗣同:《狱中题壁》

A 译:
An Inscription on the Wall of the Jail
Some seek asylum like Zhang Jian within many a friendly gate;
While others stay to bear th' ordeal like Du Gen and for a chance wait.
Holding my sword crosswise I heartily laugh to th' skies, inspir'd that,
Like th' Kunlun Mountains, the two types of comrades are equally great.
(zzy,1996:335)

B 译:
Written on the Wall of the Prison
You may seek refuge to preserve our nation's strength;
I will die soon to awake our people at length.
I brave the sword o'erhead and laugh towards the sky;
Stay or leave, live or die, our minds stand mountain-high.
(xyz,2000:215)

各民族的历史、地理等因素都可能产生文化积淀,形成该民族的文化特质。中国读者可以很自然地由"昆仑"联想到"崇高",外国读者(除了中国通)就不一定能够做到如此,其原因正是文化的异质性。据此,两种译法都作了变通:A 译把隐喻改换为明喻,并以 great 填补语义缺项;B 译仍保留隐喻手法,但同样采取补缺措施,以 mountain-high 挑明了联想意义。

【例6】生当作人杰,死亦为鬼雄。至今思项羽,不肯过江东。

——李清照:《夏日绝句》

A 译:
Be a man of men with mettle while alive,
And a soul of souls even if doom'd to die!
Xiang Yu, who would rather perish than survive
By crossing th' River, is held in esteem high.
(zzy,1996:232)

B 译：
Be man of men while you're alive;
Be soul of souls e'en if you're dead!
Think of Xiang Yu who'd not survive
His men whose blood for him was shed!
(xyz,2000：183)
C 译：
In the world, being a hero in the crowd,
In the hell, being the same among ghosts.
Still Xiang Yu is missed,
He will not take his defeat lying down.
(tr. Wlw,from dxy,2000：186)

原诗写得很有气概，给人以阳刚之美的艺术感受。乌江这一地理名词具有其历史、文化意义，宜保持，但只有 A 译用 th' River 加以再现。对于来世及人死后成鬼的观念，现代人比古人淡薄，中外皆然。从文化意义的可接受性考虑，有关诗句的翻译必须加以变通。A 译利用 soul 一词的多义性，把"鬼"的语义模糊化，又以 even if doom'd to die 加以说明，译文内容、风格与原诗近似，避免了因文化流变而可能造成的语用失误，翻译策略较可取；B 译基本上译出了原作的气势，不足的是，在语义方面，e'en if you're dead 所言为死后之事，"至今思项羽……"两行的英译也尚可斟酌。C 译 In the hell, being the same among ghosts 则似未考虑译语的可接受度及言语的语用功能，描写起鬼世界来；后两行散文风格特征明显，拖沓、欠严整，与原作声韵铿锵、气势磅礴的风格相去较远。

二、句法修辞上的变通

中国与西方的文艺审美定势是存在差异的。杨振宁博士说过："中国的文化是向模糊、朦胧及总体的方向走，而西方的文化则是向准确而具体的方向走。"(刘重德，VII:1994)这种倾向也会体现在诗歌的创作及阅读的审美取向方面。所谓"不着一字，尽得风流"(钟嵘:《二十四诗品》)，"深文隐蔚，余味曲包"(刘勰:《文心雕龙》)，"羚羊挂角，无迹可求"(严羽:《沧浪诗话》)，就是讲的对于含蓄美和模糊美的追求。相对而言，英诗注重意象(imagery)，汉诗注重意境

(artistic conception)。在谈及中国的悼亡诗时,茅于美先生指出,其艺术形式"重含蓄不多外露,喜词尽而意无穷……无须铺陈,有时只是清白如话的素描,便感人肺腑。"(茅于美,1987:85)实际上,中国其他类别的诗歌也具有这些特点。

杨自俭教授指出,"重视读者,研究读者的视野是文学与翻译上的一个重要发展。讲话要看对象,写书译书应想到读者,这样才能有针对性,才能发挥其作用。这是功能论。"(杨自俭、刘学云,1994:767)对于语言、文化差异(包括修辞、句法、表达法和习惯用法的差异)以及思维的方式、特征和风格的差异,译者应加以审度,必要时对修辞等创作手法作适当的变通。

【例7】山河破碎风飘絮,身世浮沉雨打萍。

——文天祥:《过零丁洋》

A 译:
Like the catkin in the wind land's being lost, which gives me pain;
While my life suggests the duckweed being spatter'd by the rain.
(zzy,1996:258)

B 译:
Like willow down the war-torn land looks desolate;
I sink or swim as duckweed in the rain appears.
(xyz,1994:272)

两种译法都把隐喻改换为明喻;在译文中,诗人对国运和个人命运的惋叹口吻一如原作。

【例8】春色满园光不住,一枝红杏出墙来。

——叶绍翁:《游园不值》

A 译:
A gardenful of spring can't be shut up, though. Within sight
A twig of apricot flowers is flaming out o'er th' wall!
(zzy,1996:256)

B 译:
The ravishing beauties of the garden could not be contained;
A bough of glowing apricot blooms stretched out of the wall.
(sdy,1997:459)

C 译:

The garden cannot shut up the full blooming spring;
An apricot stretches out a branch o'er the wall.
(xyz,2000:183)

假若"一枝红杏出墙来"以白描手法平白译出,也许适合中国读者的审美取向和阅读心理,但未必能使英美人得到"与观原文无异"的艺术效果。

A 译用了隐喻(动词 flaming 以火喻花),生动地描绘出红杏的动态美和色彩美,基本上使译文与原文达到功能对等。"工致而不流动,则神气索然。"(谢榛,1997:1132)B 译及 C 译也都对描写的手法作了适当的改换,不足的是,B 译用了过去时,没有现在时生动;原诗以"特写"的手法描绘"一枝红杏",特写镜头下的"红杏"既是主要的审美对象,又被赋予了主体性,而 C 译犹如改换了镜头,使之成了附庸。

【例 9】两个黄鹂鸣翠柳,一行白鹭上青天。
窗含西岭千秋雪,门泊东吴万里船。

——杜甫:绝句四首(其三)

A 译:

A pair of yellow orioles twittering in the willows green,
A line of silv'ry egrets soaring up the dome of th' sky so blue;
My window does enframe the West Ridge clad in thousand-year snows clean;
My door enjoys the anchor'd ships prepar'd to sail to distant Wu.
(zzy,1996:133)

B 译:

A pair of orioles sing amid the willows green.
And up the sky a flock of herons white now soar.
Westward the snow-capped peaks are through my windows seen,
While junks from far-off Dongu lie beyond my door.
(tr. ttk,from gzz et al,1994:93)

C 译:

Two golden oriotes sing amid the willows green;
A row of white egrets flies into the blue sky.
My window frames the snow-crowned western mountain scene;

My door oft says to eastward-going ships "Goodbye!"
(xyz,2000:103)
D 译:
From vivid green willows
Comes the call of two orioles;
A file of white water birds
Rises into the clear blue heavens; as if
Held in the mouth of my window
Are the mountain ranges with
Their snows of many autumns;
Anchored by our gate are
The long distance boats of Wu.
(R. A. ,2001:257)

这是一首写景诗,原诗使用的是白描手法。A 译进行了改换,使用了拟声(twittering)、隐喻(enframe)、拟人(enjoys),基本上再现了如画的景色;B 译基本上照搬原诗的手法,读来不够生动;C 译采用了隐喻(frames),这是可取的,不过其拟人 My door oft says to eastward-going ships "Goodbye!"与 D 译的 in the mouth of my window 听起来有些怪诞:门竟然会对船说"再见",这就有点儿像是神话中的情节了;英语有 river-mouth 这种搭配,但没有 mouth of the window 之说。有无变通,变通是否妥当,这直接影响到译文的质量。

【例 10】驿外断桥边,寂寞开无主。
已是黄昏独自愁,更着风和雨。
无意苦争春,一任群芳妒。
零落成泥碾作尘,只有香如故。

——陆游:《卜算子》

A 译:
The Diviner—Ode to the Plum Flower
By the broken bridge beyond the post thou bloom'st
In solitude, expecting none to flatter.
At dusk the rains spatter, when thou suffer'st lonely cares,
And the blasting winds do boom and thee shatter.
As thou hast ne'er vi'd with the favour'd in spring,

What matters if they should thee envy and blame?
Thou may'st wither, fall and be ground to dust, thy fragrance,
However, will remain as before the same!
(zzy,1996:241)

B 译：

Pu Suan Zi—To the Mei Flowers

Beyond the post and by the broken bridge
In solitude you blow and unloved.
The deepening dusk has only brought you sadness,
Which to increase the winds and rains
Are lashing you so merciless!
You have no heart to vie with spring hues:
Their envying you affects you not.
Anon ground to dust
You shall vanish in the earth,
Yet your wonted scent forever lives.
(hhq,2001:221)

C 译：

Ode to the Mume Blossom — Tune: "Song of Divination"

Beside the broken bridge and outside the post hall
A flower is blooming forlorn.
Saddened by her solitude at nightfall,
By wind and rain she's further torn.
Let other flowers their envy pour.
To spring she lays no claim.
Fallen in mud and ground to dust, she seems no more,
But her fragrance is still the same.
(xyz,1990,327)

三种英译都使用了拟人格（personification），把梅花心灵化、人格化，这在风格上与原诗是一致的，属于重构。A 译还根据中外阅读审美和汉英两种文字的差异，把白描改换为拟声（onomatopoeia），使用了 spatter, shatter, boom 等词，对风雨之狂烈描绘得更加生动，这是风格上的变通。

【例 11】力微任重久神疲,再竭衰庸定不支。
苟利国家生死以,岂因祸福避趋之!
谪居正是君恩厚,养拙刚于戍卒宜。
戏与山妻谈故事,试吟断送老头皮。
——林则徐:赴戍登程口占示家人(其二)

A 译:

Oral Compositions to My Family upon Leaving for the Frontier (*No.2*)
I couldn't have been able any longer to sustain
The vital post, which has tir'd this unworthy person out.
Whate'er's in th' interest of the state I'll do with might and main,
And personal weal or woe is not to be car'd about.
Demotion only shows His Majesty's favour, and life
In the' frontier will perfectly suit my mortal dim and dull.
Let me, on leaving, retell a story to my dear wife
And read aloud the poem therein 'bout "forfeiting th' old skull".
(zzy,1996:317)

B 译:

Before Going into Exile

Weary for long with feeble strength and duty great,
Mediocrity exhausted, could I not sink low?
I'd risk life and brave death to do good to the state.
Could I but for myself seek weal and avoid woe?
The banishment just show the royal favor high;
My border service is good to do what I can.
I tease my wife with a story of days gone by:
Why not try to chant verse to see off your old man?
(xyz,2000:295)

原诗旨在安慰家人,也体现了诗人重国事、轻名利的高尚品质和豁达乐观的精神。风格诙谐、含蓄,引用了有关隐士杨朴的笑话(用典 allusion)。诗中的"戏"是逗笑之意,并非戏弄;"试吟"者是诗人自己。A 译对原诗旨趣、意境、风格是经过一番研究的,词语、句式、口吻与原诗基本吻合。B 译 tease 一词及末行 Why not try to chant verse to see off your old man? 这一句式的使用,会使人理解为,诗人取笑妻子,并希望妻子给自己吟诗送行;诗人虽有故意自贬之词,但并没有认为自己 sink low(沉沦);"断送老头皮"的语义在译文中的缺失,又破坏了原作所具有的幽默的再现。所有这些是与原诗的整体风格系统相违背的。

【例12】烟笼寒水月笼沙,夜泊秦淮近酒家。
　　　　商女不知亡国恨,隔江犹唱后庭花。

——杜牧:《泊秦淮》

A 译:

The mist shrouding cold waters, th' moon dimly showing the shore,
I moor near wine shops on the Qinhuai River after dark.
On the opposite bank a songstress, who knows not the sore
Over lost sovereignty, is singing "Flowers in th' Back Park".
(zzy,1996:179)

B 译:

The chilly water is shrouded in mist and the sand bathed in moonlight,
As I moor at night on the Qinhuai River near the taverns.
The singsong girls are ignorant of the tragedy of a lost regime,
They are still singing the Backyard Flowers beyond the river!
(yxy & gy,2001:270)

Shroud 意为"为……盖裹尸布"、"覆盖",在这里是一种隐喻用法,是对"笼"的变通,既生动又得体(即符合原诗忧患国运的总意象)。

三、语体语气上的变通

古诗文中,人物话语的语体色彩往往是隐性的,而不是一目了然的。为了取得应有的"文化适应性及审美有效性"(刘宓庆,1999:275),一般来说,译者须根据人物社会地位、身份及其他语境因素,运用自己的认知能力和创造力,加以显化。

【例14】使君从南来,五马立踟蹰。使君遣吏往,问是谁家姝?"秦氏有好女,自名为罗敷。""罗敷年几何?""二十尚不足,十五颇有余。"使君谢罗敷:"宁可共载不?"罗敷前置辞:"使君一何愚!使君自有妇,罗敷自有夫。"

——汉乐府:《陌上桑》

A 译：

The prefect, coming from the south, takes fire;
Halting his carriage and five suddenly,
He sends an officer o'er to inquire
About the pretty girl's identity.
"She's designated by the name of Luofu,
Being the worthy daughter of the Qins."
"Impart to me: what's the age of Luofu?"
"She's 'tween fifteen and twenty," the man grins.
The prefect brightens up, and his eyes shine.
He asks in person: "Why not come away
With me and get on this carriage of mine?"
Luofu, taking a step forward, does say:
"From what you have just said, my lord, Luofu
Have realiz'd how thick-headed you can be.
Just as you're marri'd on the part of you,
So I have an ideal husband to me."
(zzy,1996:41—44)

B 译：

The Lord Governor drives his coach from the south;
His five horses suddenly slow their ace.
He's sent his sheriff: "Quickly bring me word
Of what house may this lovely lady be?"
"In the house of Ch'in the fair lady dwells;
She calls herself the Lady Lo-fu."
"Oh tell me, sheriff, tell me how old she may be!"
"A score of years she has not yet filled;
To fifteen she has added somewhat more."
The Lord Governor calls to Lo-fu:
"Tell me, lady, will you ride by me or no?"
She stands before him, she giveshim answer straight:
My Lord Governor has not ready wits.
Has he not guessed that just as he has a wife

So I too have my husband dear?
(tr. A. W. ,from lsx,1980:58—59)
C 译:
From the south comes a lordling
In carriage with five horses;
Surprised, halts and sends one
To make an inquiry,
"Who is that beauty,
and who are her kin?"
"She is one of the Qins,
and her name is Luofu."
"And what may her age be?"
"Her summers not twenty,
yet more than fifteen."
Then he, condescending,
Says,"Luofu, will 't please you
To enter my carriage?"
She faces him boldly,
And thus makes reply:
"What nonsense you talk, sir!
You have your own wife,
And I my own husband.
....
(yxy&gy,2001:346)

  原作与目的语存在着很大的时空差。刘宓庆教授说过:"由于时序变迁,原作的风格早已演变蜕化,这时如果按对应方式转换将目的语以模仿原语风格方式复制就很难为当代的读者所接受。"(杨自俭、刘学云,1994:603)

  A,B,C 各译从语域、语气、语体入手,作了变通。其译文中,使君及其所遣之吏使用的是官腔官调(officialese),而罗敷语气直率、语言质朴。A 译又根据语境,显化了潜隐信息,对使君及其所遣之吏的表情作了描述,如 the man grins, The prefect brightens up, and his eyes shine,表现力、感染力较强,实现了原作言语的语用功能。

【例14】耕犁千亩实千箱,力尽筋疲谁复伤?
但得众生皆得饱,不辞羸病卧残阳。

——李纲:《病牛》

A 译:

The Farm Cattle

I've plough'd a thousand mu of land and fill'd the barns with grain;
When tir'd out whose commiseration can I hope to gain?
I lie at ease, though sick and feeble when the sun is set:
As long as common folk are well provided, why should I regret?
(zzy,1996:230)

B 译:

To a Sick Baffalo

You've ploughed field on field and reaped crop on crop of grain.
Who would pity you when you are tired out and done?
If old and young could eat their fill, then you would fain
Exhaust yourself and lie in the setting sun.
(xyz,2000:147)

风格与诗人的气质是密切相关的。李纲是北宋政治家,其诗多写报国愤时之慨,感情激昂,真实感人。诗人以牛自喻,表达了以民生为重、置个人得失于度外的高尚情怀,格调颇高。诗人并未明确道出"牛"是黄牛还是水牛,英译为 cattle(较笼统)比 baffalo(水牛——较具体)更合适。原诗为无主句,根据其旨趣、意境及英语句法,应补上主语,而主语人称代词用第一人称比用第二人称更为合适。

【例15】老农家贫在山住,耕种山田三四亩。
苗蔬税多不得食,输入官仓化为土。
岁暮锄犁傍空室,呼儿登山收橡实。
西江贾客珠百斛,船中养犬长食肉。

——张籍:《野老歌》

A 译:

Song to the Poor Farmer

The farmer lives in poverty and deep deep in the mount,
The hillside fields he tills below four mu by actual count.

The crops are sparse, the taxes high; what's left to be din'd?
And yet his grain decays in state-own'd barns as rent in kind.
In winter when his shabby hut presents tools but no hope,
His sons will have to gather acorns on the mountain slope.
In striking contrast merchants on the West River are worth
One hundred hu of pearls, their dogs assur'd of meat from birth.
（zzy,1996:149）

B译：

The Old Peasant

In the hills lives a poor old peasant
Farming a few patches of hilly land;
Sparse his crops, many the taxes, and he goes hungry
While grain in the state granaries turns to dust;
At the year's end his home is bare but for plough and hoe,
He takes his son up the mountain to gather acorns;
But the West River merchant has hundreds of bushels of pearls
And the dog on his boat gorges every day on meat.
（yxy&gy,2001:171）

原诗押韵,有很强的节奏感,通过贫富对比,产生极大的震撼力。从音韵、格律、语体等角度看,A译基本上以步代顿,节奏感较强；改变原诗一韵到底的韵式,而采用英雄双行诗体的押韵方式,声韵铿锵；修辞上也进行了变通,用了异叙(syllepsis) lives in poverty and deep deep in the mount 及 presents tools but no hope,语言生动活泼；语言上属于书面语体。B译各行音节数不等,无一定节奏形式；不押韵；语言风格方面较随便、呆板,未能重构原作总体风格,因而感染力不如A译强。

四、意象、意境方面的变通

意象、意境是诗歌的格调和诗人的精神气质及思想感情的体现与依托,其再现与变通是诗歌风格翻译中的最高层次。

【例16】寥落古行宫,宫花寂寞红。白头宫女在,闲坐说玄宗。

——元稹:《行宫》

A 译：

The Imperial Resort

The ancient palaces present a rueful sight;

'Tis vainly that are blooming flowers red and bright.

Those white-hair'd ladies, who've surviv'd their mental pain,

Now sit at ease recalling Xuanzong and his reign.

(zzy,1996:172)

B 译：

At an Old Palace

Deserted now the Imperial bowers

Save by some few poor lonely flowers...

One white-haired dame,

An Emperor's flame,

Sits down and tells of bygone hours.

(tr. H. A. G., from xyz,1992:289)

C 译：

The Ancient Travelling Palace

Empty and falling down is the ancient traveling palace.

The palace flowers put forth their red blooms in silent neglect.

Inside a white-haired palace woman

Idly mumbles of the glorious days of Hsuan Tsung.

(tr. S. J., from xyz,1992:289)

D 译：

At an Old Palace

Deserted now imperial bowers.

For whom still redden palace flowers?

Some white-haired chambermaids at leisure

Talk of the late Emperor's pleasure.

(xyz,1992:289)

该诗有何特色？行宫、宫花、宫女等意象如何处理？"宫女"是何等人？是单数还是复数？她们"说"玄宗何事？为了意境及整体风格的再现，这些问题是翻译时必须探究明白的。

元稹这首格律严整的五绝可与白居易的《上阳白发人》进行互文观照。被选入宫的十六七岁少女"脸似芙蓉胸似玉",然而,"未容君王得见面,已被杨妃遥侧目",天宝末年便被"潜配"到上阳宫。"绿衣监使守宫门",她们一生的自由、幸福都被剥夺了。冷宫的寂寞令她们红消绿减,白发频添。四十多年后,这些"少亦苦,老亦苦"(以上诗句引自《上阳白发人》)的宫女们只能闲坐着"说"起玄宗遗事来。此诗以乐景写悲,"语少意足"(洪迈:《容斋随笔》),意境深邃,诗味隽永:寥寥二十个字,宫女们凄凉的身世、哀怨的情思,以及诗人对于宫女们深切的同情、对于世事盛衰的感慨和对于践踏人性的统治者的谴责,便跃然纸上。

几种译文对宫花、行宫两个形象的再现都比较准确,在其他方面则有较大差异:

A 译把宫女译为 ladies,是不够准确的,严格说来应是 the emperor's concubines,但考虑到 ladies 的广义性和音节数目的限制,只好采取内容让步于形式的译法;who've surviv'd their mental pain 这一非限制性定语从句显化了宫女们的悲苦,与原诗的含蓄是不一致的,但对于英美读者来说,这等于在原诗意境与"读者期待视野"之间架起一座桥梁;... recalling Xuanzong and his reign 语义宽泛,与原诗较接近。总的说来,对意境和整体风格的重构还算差强人意。

B 译押韵,但口语语体明显;One white-haired dame 为单数,不足以形容统治者践踏人性的罪孽之深;dame 是美国俚语;An Emperor's flame,未指明哪位皇帝,而这又关系到诗歌的题材和所涉及的史实;flame 意为"老相好",是非正式英语,其语义(内容)也与史实不符;tells of bygone hours 模糊了话题与玄宗的关联。

C 译 palace woman 为单数,不妥,以之指称"宫女",也欠贴切(palace woman 是宫中做事的妇女);说她独自 mumbles(含混不清地说) of the glorious days of Hsuan Tsung,这对宫女形象有所扭曲;glorious days 只言"辉煌",直白且语义褊狭,而原诗"说玄宗"的语义模糊,即具有多义性,可容纳或褒或贬的谈论。

D 译误译了宫女的身世:chambermaids 是指 a female servant employed to clean and tidy rooms and make beds(引自 Longman Dictionary of Contemporary English);pleasure 则把"说"的话题庸俗化。

【例 17】春眠不觉晓,处处闻啼鸟。夜来风雨声,花落知多少?

——孟浩然:《春晓》

A译：

Spring Morn

Awakening from slumber to a morn of spring,
I hear the birds everywhere beautifully sing.
The winds shatter'd and the rains splatter'd yesternight:
How many flowers have dropp'd in a wretched plight?
(zzy,1996:99)

B译：

A Spring Morning

I awake light-hearted this morning of spring,
Everywhere round me the singing of birds—
But now I remember the night, the storm,
And I wonder how many blossoms were broken.
(tr. W. B.,from gzz,1994:23)

C译：

Spring Dawn

I slept in spring not conscious of the dawn,
But heard the gay birds chattering all around,
I remember, there was a storm at night.
Pray, how many blossoms have fallen down?
(tr. R. P.,from xyz,1992:197)

D译：

Spring Morning

This morn of spring in bed I'm lying,
Not to awake till birds are crying.
After one night of wind and showers,
How many are the fallen flowers!
(xyz,2000:27)

（分析文字并入下例）

【例18】朝辞白帝彩云间,千里江陵一日还。
两岸猿声啼不住,轻舟已过万重山。

——李白:《早发白帝城》

A 译：

Embarkation at Baidi Early in the Morning

I left Baidi nestling in rosy clouds at break of day,

And in the eve I'll reach Jiangling a thousand li away;

The jabbering of apes along the banks still seems to last,

Oho, ten thousand sweeps of mounts my swift boat has flash'd past!

(zzy,1996:115)

B 译：

Quitting Poti at Dawn

Poti amid its rainbow clouds we quitted with the dawn,

A thousand li in one day's space to Kiang-ling are borne.

Ere yet the gibbon's howling along the banks was still

All through the cragged Gorge our skiff had fleeted with the morn.

(tr. W. J. B. F. ,from xyz,1992:218)

C 译：

Leaving the White Emperor Town at Dawn

Leaving the White Emperor crowned with cloud,

I've sailed a thousand li through canyons in a day.

With monkeys' sad adieus the riverbanks are loud,

My skiff has left ten thousand mountains far away.

(xyz,1992:218)

D 译：

The River Journey from White King City

At dawn I left the walled city of White King,

Towering among the many-coloured clouds;

And came down stream in a day

One thousand li to Jiangling.

The screams of monkeys on either bank

Had scarcely ceased echoing in my ear

When my skiff had left behind it

Ten thousand ranges of hills.

(tr. S. O. ,from gzz et al,1994:68)

有学者认为,把"猿声"译作 The jabbering of apes,正像把孟浩然《春晓》中的"夜来风雨声"译做 The winds shatter'd and the rains splatter'd yesternight 一样,"猿声"、"风雨"的意象过于强烈、渲染,不符合唐诗的温柔敦厚;而译为 With monkeys' sad adieus the riverbanks are loud 就比较合适,这是因为,猿是神仙的伴侣,见李白走了,依依不舍。

关于这个问题,读者可参看第六章("诗歌的模糊性及翻译的标准和方法")例5、例6的分析文字。这里还要补充一点,那就是,假、恶、丑的反面形象适当强烈一些,可以更好地反衬出正面形象的真、善、美,强化译作的艺术感染力。

上面两首诗的诸多译法由于用词、句式、修辞、形体、音韵等方面有明显差异,因而,韵致、格调和艺术感染力也不尽相同。

第三节 小结

以上译例及其分析只是用以说明,汉诗英译中的风格变通是必要的,也是可能的。至于哪些方面需要变通以及如何变通,那就取决于译者的个性、功力和创造力了。

除了以上所探讨的内容,东西方思维的差异也要求我们在某些方面作些变通。关于这一点,读者可以看看第十章("汉诗英译中的逻辑调适")。

有关调适、变通的理念是符合《周易》"唯变所适"的可变规律的。我们有理由吸取《周易》的精华,在文化上以变求存,在典籍翻译实践上以变求通,在翻译理论研究上以变求新。

思考题

1. 为什么风格翻译备受关注?
2. 讨论卢纶《塞下曲》(其二)一诗的显性风格体系和隐性风格体系,并加以总结:

   林暗草惊风,将军夜引弓。
   平明寻白羽,没在石棱中。

3. 评价上面这首诗的不同英译在风格重构与变通方面的成败得失。

译文 1: *A Frontier Melody（No.2）*

The woods obscur'd, the grass seeming to moan,
In th'dark his bow the general adeptly bent.
He found his arrow deep inserted in a stone
At dawn when he was tracking where the feathers went.
(zzy,1996:141)

译文 2: *Border Songs*

The woods are black and a wind assails the grasses,
Yet the general tries night archery—
And next morning he finds his white-plumed arrow
Pointed deep in the hard rock.
(W. B. , from lsx, 1980:54)

译文 3: *Warriors True*

Sinister whispers in the gloom of the forest. It's the wind in the grass—or? The warrior lets fly at a threatening shape. Next morning the arrow is found sunk in a rock right up to the snowy vanes.
(wxl,1985:36—37)

练习题

1. 评价李白《望庐山瀑布》不同英译的译文风格。
原作：
　　日照香炉生紫烟,遥看瀑布挂前川。
　　飞流直下三千尺,疑是银河落九天。

译文 1: *Watching the Waterfall in the Lushan Mountains*

Around the sunlit Incense Burner glows a purplish haze;
The waterfall afore the stream afar attracts my gaze;
With torrents plunging down three thousand feet, it flies and flies
As if it were the Milky Way descending from the skies!
(zzy,1996:117)

译文 2: *Sighting the Cataract of Mount Lu*
The sun shining on the Incense-burner Peak
Issueth purple smoke to wreathe round,
Seen afar the cataract seemeth hung from the cliff top
To the water front of the Mount.
The flying torrent for three thousand feet
Ceaselessly dashing down headlong.
Is taken to be the Silvery Stream falling from
The ninth heaven to the ground.
(sdy,1997:235)

译文 3: *Watching the Waterfall at Lushan*
In sunshine Censer Peak breathes purple vapor,
Far off hangs the cataract, a stream upended;
Down it cascades a sheer three thousand feet —
As if the Silver River were falling from Heaven!
(yxy & gy,2001:100)

译文 4: *Viewing the Waterfall at Mount Lu*
Sunlight streaming on Incense Stone kindles a violet smoke;
Far off I watch the waterfall plunge to the long river,
Flying waters descending straight three thousand feet,
Till I think the Milky Way has tumbled from the ninth height of Heaven.
(Burton Watson, from gzz, 1994:64)

2. 从互联网(如"知网")搜索浏览有关"风格翻译"的讨论,选读你认为水平较高的 1—3 篇。

3. 从互联网(如"知网")搜索浏览你所喜爱的某一诗词的不同英译,并从风格层面予以评论。

第十五章　汉诗英译中的"炼词"

学习目标

掌握"炼词"的基本方法,培养、提高自身的严谨精神和精品意识。

第一节　何谓汉诗英译中的"炼词"?

汉诗有"诗眼"一说。所谓"诗眼",指的是一首诗中最为关键和精彩的词句。它或能表现客观事物的精微,或能勾画人物的韵致;或能创造鲜明的意象,或能蕴含深刻的哲理。一首好诗往往工在一字、一句。为了追求这种词句,诗人便对众多的词汇和语句加以反复琢磨,从中挑选出最为恰当者。这种写诗方法,诗学上称为"炼字"。贾岛"僧敲月下门"一句中,"敲"比"推"好;王安石"春风又绿江南岸"一句中,"绿"字比"到"、"过"、"入"或"满"都要好,这些都是"炼字"的典范。

针对汉诗诗学的这一特点,我们在汉诗英译的过程中就必须词斟句酌,相应地在译文语言的词句上反复锤炼、推敲,以求保持和再现原诗的意象、意境、音韵和节奏等诗歌美学价值,再创造出形神兼备的译品。这就是"炼词"。

本章将从诗学、词汇学、修辞学的角度,探讨汉诗英译过程中"炼词"的若干方法。

第二节　利用英语构词法炼词

恰当地利用转化、派生、合成等构词法,或能使译语生动形象,以取得"传神"的艺术效果,或能使文辞简约,解决一句汉诗的信息载量往往大于一行英诗的矛盾,以臻于"形似"。

【例1】满园春色关不住,一枝红杏出墙来。

——叶绍翁:《游园不值》

A 译:

A gardenful of spring can't be shut up, though.

Within sight a twig of apricot flowers is flaming out o'er th' wall.

(zzy,1996:296)

B 译:

But full of spring beauty it can't be shut wholly.

A red apricot branch stretches o'er the fence fully.

(tr. czd, from gzz,1992:50)

词汇学认为,词类转化能使语言简洁、形象。A 译"flaming"(像火焰般闪烁)一词就是由名词转化而来的,它比 B 译的"stretches"更生动地再现了红杏的光彩和动态。

【例2】窗含西岭千秋雪,门泊东吴万里船。

——杜甫:《绝句》

A 译:

My window does enframe the West Ridge clad in thousand-year snows clean;

My door enjoys the anchor'd ships prepar'd to sail to distant Wu.

(zzy,1996:133)

B 译:

My window frames the snow-crowned western mountain scene;

My door oft says to eastward-going ships "Goodbye!"

(xyz,2000:103)

派生,即通过加词缀进行构词的方法,也可借以炼词,使行文简洁、形象。A 译"enframe"一词是由"frame"(名词)派生而来的,有"为画配框"或"置画于框中"之意,比 B 译更生动地烘托出了窗外如画的景致。

【例3】霜叶红于二月花。

——杜牧:《山行》

A 译:

Attracted by th' maples my carriage to a halt I bring:
Th' frost-redden'd leaves at dusk are brighter than the bloom of spring.

(zzy,1996:133)

B 译：
I stop my cart, only cause
I love the beautiful sight—
Of a maple grove, all red,
Before the approach of night.
Maple leaves after a frost
Are more beautiful in tone
Than flowers in February
With their colors better known.

(xzj,1991:329)

A 译以冒号连贯上下文，使之起到语篇标志（discourse marker）"because"的作用；并用合成法构成"frost-redden'd"一词，使之负载了"因经霜而变红的"这一信息，行文简洁，因而有可能做到以两行英文再现原诗句的意旨；而 B 译则不得不花费八行的笔墨，难以做到形似，也有违原作流畅简洁的风格。

第三节　从语义、语体和搭配关系等角度炼词

一、词语的雅与俗

从语体的角度看，词语有雅俗之分。诗歌，尤其是古典诗歌，往往使用高雅的用语或专门的诗歌用语，因此，我们在翻译的过程中就必须注意诗歌语言的这一取向。

【例 4】佳期如梦。

——《鹊桥仙》

A 译：
Their rendezvous is like a transient dream.
(zzy,1996:227)

B译：
Their happy date seems but a dream.
（xyz1992:385）

A译"rendezvous"属雅语；而B译"date"作"约会"解是美语的一种非正规用法，不符合原作蕴藉隽永的境界。

二、上义词与下义词

在同一个语义同义场中，主导同义词（Synonymic Dominant）比较笼统，其他同义词则比较具体。例如，"cry"是笼统的，"sob"、"wail"、"weep"和"howl"则是具体的。具体词生动简洁，富于描写性，相当于笼统的词加上修饰成分，例如"sob"相当于"cry"加上"with short, quick breaths"；笼统的词则可用以指称较抽象模糊的事物或理念，概括力较强。译者应视具体情况作出选择。请看下例：

【例5】两岸猿声啼不住，轻舟已过万重山。
——李白：《早发白帝城》

A译：
The jabbering of apes along the banks still seems to last,
Oho, ten thousand sweeps of mounts my swift boat has flash'd past!
（zzy,1996:115）

B译：
With monkeys' sad adieus the riverbanks are loud,
My skiff has left ten thousand mountains far away.
（xyz1992:218）

A译"jabbering"笼统，与原文"猿声"对应；"flash'd"具体，生动地描写出舟行之疾。B译"sad adieus"过于具体，与"猿声"不对等，而"left"一词又过于抽象，缺乏描写性。

有时，同义或近义词的选用可避免重复单调，使文体生动活泼：

【例6】春江潮水连海平，海上明月共潮生。
——张若虚：《春江花月夜》

A译：
In spring the brimming river melts into the sea,
O'er which the moon serene arises with the tide.
(zzy,1996:92)
B译：
In spring the river rises as high as the sea,
And with the river's rise the moon uprises bright.
(xyz1992:190)

A译使用"brimming"，"melts"及"arises"，避免了重复，而B译用同一词根的"rises"，"rise"及"uprises"则有单调之嫌。

三、词语选择限制原则

词语的搭配是受选择限制原则制约的。我们可以说"thick soup"，"strong coffee"，却不可用"thick"和"strong"先后修饰"coffee"和"soup"，否则就是犯了搭配不当的错误。例如：

【例7】离离原上草，一岁一枯荣。

——白居易:《草》

A译：
Behold the grasses green and thick
Which wither every year and thrive.
(zzy,1996:161)
B译：
O'er the plain is a stretch of fragrant grass.
Once a year, it wax and is on the wane.
(xyz,2000:268)

A译以"wither"和"thrive"译"枯荣"比较恰当，因其本义及转义可兼提草木与人事；而根据语义特征，B译的"wax"与"wane"二词一般用以指月亮的盈亏、时事的兴衰、潮水的涨落和气力的旺竭，却不能用以形容草木的荣枯。

【例8】梧桐树，三更雨，不道离情更苦。一叶叶，一声声，空阶滴到明。

——温庭筠:《更漏子》

A 译：
The Chinese parasols and mid-night rain
Do sound unfeeling 'bout her departure-inflicted pain;
The trees send down leaf after leaf, the rain falls drop by drop;
Before day-break spatting the door-steps they don't stop.
(zzy,1996:185)

B 译：
Upon the Wu-t'ung trees
Falls a midnight rain,
In different to the persistent pains of separation.
Leaf upon leaf,
Drop upon drop,
On empty steps it drips until the dawn.
(tr. W. R. S., from xyz,1992:302)

C 译：
At midnight the rain
On the Wu-t'ung tree
Not knowing the pain
Of loneliness
Falls leaf to leave
Dripping
On the bare steps
Till dawn.
(tr. J. M., from xyz,1992:302)

"滴"的施动者既是雨点，又是落叶。A 译对"一叶叶，一声声"分而述之，并以"they"指称二者，而与之搭配的"spatting"又可兼指雨或像雨一样落下的物体的"拍打"，这是较妥当的。B、C 译说雨"drips""Leaf upon leaf"（"一叶接一叶地滴"）及"Falls leaf to leaf"（"一叶又一叶地下"），则属于搭配不当。

四、词语的感情色彩

词语的感情色彩也不可忽略，例如：

【例9】白日依山尽,黄河入海流。

———王之涣:《登鹳雀楼》

A 译
Ling'ring is the setting sun about the mountain height,,
Surging is the Yellow River towards the vast sea.
(zzy,1996:97)

B 译
The setting sun below the mountains glows,
The muddy Yellow River seawards flows.
(xzj,1991:32)

A 译的"Surging"表现了黄河的雄浑;B 译"muddy"一词则有伤原诗意象美和热爱山河的情感美。可见,翻译中有必要对词义的褒贬加以斟酌。

第四节 从修辞的角度炼词(句)

为了再现原诗的意象、意境,译者有时必须摆脱原文的语言形式。就修辞而言,原文没有用修辞格的,译文可酌情使用之;如果原文用了辞格,译文有时可以酌情改换之。这里仅举数例:

【例10】月落乌啼霜满天,江枫渔火对愁眠。
姑苏城外寒山寺,夜半钟声到客船。

———张继:《枫桥夜泊》

A 译
The moon is set, the crows decrying dark and frosty skies;
The maples vague, the fishing lamps are blinking ere mine eyes.
The ringing bells from Hanshan Temple outside Gusu float
Afar at midnight to the sad and troubl'd napper's boat.
(zzy,1996:137)

B 译
Moon setting, crows cawing, frost filling the sky,
Through river maples, fishermen's flares confront my uneasy eyes.
Outside Gusu City, Cold Mountain Temple—

Late at night the sound of its bell reaches a traveler's boat.
(tr. B. W,from web et al,1993:64)

A译采用拟人格"decrying"(大声反对)翻译乌鸦的"啼",在融情于景、渲染气氛方面比B译"cawing"更具表现力;以隐喻"float…to"翻译原文的"到",也要比B译"reaches"生动。

【例11】夜来风雨声,花落知多少?

—— 孟浩然:《春晓》

A译
The winds shatter'd and the rains splatter'd yesternight;
How many flowers have dropp'd in a wretched plight?
(zzy,1996:99)

B译
I remember, there was a storm last night.
Pray, how many blossoms have fallen down?
(tr. R. P. ,from xyz,1992:197)

C译
After one night of wind and showers,
How many are the fallen flowers?
(xyz,1992:198)

A译采用拟声词"shatter'd"(哗啦啦地响)和"splatter'd"(淅沥作响)译"风雨声",比B译、C译只说"storm","wind and showers"要生动些。

【例12】飞流直下三千尺,疑是银河落九天。

—— 李白:《望庐山瀑布》

A译
With torrents plunging down three thousand feet, it flies and flies
As if it were the Milky Way descending from the skies!
(zzy,1996:117)

B译
These "rapids", thrown, it seems, from nowhere
Plunge 390 feet down the steep,
As if the Milky Way in frenzy

Into the lower Ninth Heaven, leap.

(xzj,1991:97)

原文"飞流"不宜机械地译为"flying stream",因此 A、B 译都对原文的比拟作了改换,译为隐喻。A 译谓语动词"flies and flies"既是隐喻,又是反复,比 B 译"plunge"更生动地再现出飞流的气势。

【例 13】山不厌高,海不厌深。周公吐哺,天下归心。

——曹操:《短歌行》

A 译

For their love of earth mounts attain their height;
The seas deep and vast ne'er of water make light.
To one like th'Duke of Zhou, who broke off thrice
A meal, mass support is th'keenest delight!

(zzy,1996:55)

B 译

What if the mountain is high,
Or how deep the sea?
When the Duke of Zhou greeted a guest,
In his service all wished to be.

(yxy & gy,1986:41)

原诗"山不厌高,……"二句借喻诗人思贤如渴。A 译把山和海人格化(拟人),沟通了对于这种比喻关系的联想;B 译的设问意为"山高海深又怎么样?"背离了原作的隐含意义。"周公吐哺,天下归心"表达了诗人的政治理想,其中"周公吐哺"既是借代,即以周公代替礼贤下士的人,又是暗引。A、B 译都用了引喻。A 译明喻"To one like th' Duke of Zhou…"及判断句式比 B 译(使用的是陈述句式)更好地明确了周公与诗人间的关联。

【例 14】隔墙花影动,疑是玉人来。

——王实甫:《西厢记》

A rustle through the flowers is heard from beyond the wall,
Could it signify that th'soul of my heart has come to call?

(zzy,1996:276)

比喻形象（即作为喻体的人或事物）反映了各民族的文化渊源、思维习惯和审美取向。在汉诗英译中，原诗的比喻形象如果不符合英美人的概念，译者就应将它改换。本例中的"玉人"要是照字面直译为"jade figure"，英美人就很难悟出原作所蕴含的意义，因此改换喻体而译为"th'soul of my heart"（＝lover）。

第五节 小结

以上分析、比较说明，炼词对于保持和再现原诗的诗歌美学价值有着不容低估的意义。由于对炼词（句）重视的程度不同，或者在这方面的功夫深浅不同，译作就有成败优劣之别。

炼词与炼句（行）是紧密相关的。炼词是炼行的基础，炼行（句）是炼词的归附。当然，炼句（行）也有其自身的规律，对此，编者在"汉诗英译的总体审度与诗化"一章中已有所讨论。炼词炼句（行）的目的是译好全诗，因此译者必须做到全局在胸，切不可只见树木而不见森林。

思考题

1. 本章所总结的炼词方法有哪些？
2. 你能否对炼词的方法作出补充？
3. Anthony Appiah 于 1993 年所提出"厚翻译"（thick translation, i. e., translation that seeks with its annotations and accompanying glosses to locate the text in rich cultural and linguistic context）的理念。不少人对"厚翻译"颇为赞赏。你认为"厚翻译"是否适用于诗歌翻译？
4. 从炼词角度评判张继《枫桥夜泊》的不同英译，并提出改进的意见。

原作：

　　月落乌啼霜满天，江枫渔火对愁眠。
　　姑苏城外寒山寺，夜半歌声到客船。

译文 1：*Mooring at the Maple Bridge for the Night*

The moon is set, the crows decrying dark and frosty skies;
The maples vague, the fishing lamps are blinking ere mine eyes.
The ringing bells from Hanshan Temple outside Gusu float

Afar at mid-night to the sad and troubl'd napper's boat.
(zzy,1996:137)

译文 2:*Night Mooring at Fengqiao Village*
The moon is sinking; a crow croaks a-dreaming;
'Neath the night sky the frost casts a haze;
Few fishing-boat lights of th' river side village
Are dozing off in their mutual sad gaze.
From the Cold Hill Bonzary outside
The city wall of Gusu town,
The resounding bell is tolling its clangour
At midnight to the passenger ship down.
(sdy,1997:124)

译文 3:*Moring by Maple Bridge at Night*
At moonset cry the crows, streaking the frosty sky;
Dimly lit fishing boats 'neath maples sadly lie.
Beyond the city walls, from Temple of Cold Hill
Bells break the ship-borne roamer's dream and midnight still.
(xyz,2000:105)

练习题

1. 根据所学的新知识,对你所译的唐诗(第三章练习)进行修改、润色,同时保留初稿、二稿、三稿和四稿。

2. 从本教程所引用的译诗中选取实例,说明"炼词"的重要性。

3. 贺铸《鹧鸪天》是悼亡诗中的精品。研究其英译的过程稿,并从炼词角度评论各译稿在前稿基础上做了哪些改进。

　　　　重过阊门万事非,同来何事不同归?
　　　　梧桐半死清霜后,头白鸳鸯失伴飞。

　　　　原上草,露初晞,旧栖新垄两依依。
　　　　空床卧听南窗雨,谁复挑灯夜补衣?

Patridges in the Skies
Draft 1:
Reentering the Changmen Gate, I find everything changed;
Since we had shared life, why not death? Why did you go first,
Leaving me as the chinese parasol half dead after hoary frost,
And the white-haired mandarin duck flying alone?
Grass on the plain still wet with dew,
One lying in the grave, the other stays in the old abode, miss each other.
On the bed deprived of my mate I listen to the pelting rain,
Who could turn up the wick in the oil lamp mending my coat ?
Draft 2:
Reentering th' Changmen Gate, everything changed I find;
Since we'd shar'd life, why not death? Why did you leave me behind
Like a Chinese parasol half dead after hoary frost,
Or a lone white-hair'd mandarin duck flapping with th' mate lost?
The grasses on the plain must still be wet with dew at dawn?
I in the old nest for you in the new grave always mourn.
I groan, listening to th' pelting rain on th' half-vacant bed:
Whoever could mend my coat in the lamplight in your stead?
Draft 3:
Reentering th' Changmen Gate, everything changed I find;
Since we'd shar'd life, why not share it through? Why leave me behind
Like a Chinese parasol half dead after hoary frost,
Or a lone white-hair'd mandarin duck flapping with th' mate lost?
The grasses on the plain must still be wet with dew at dawn?
I in the old nest for you in the new grave always mourn.
I groan, listening to th' pelting rain on th' half-vacant bed:
Whoever could mend my coat in the lamplight in your stead?

第十六章　诗、词、曲、赋及楹联的诗化译法

学习目标

深化对于诗词曲赋的了解，掌握诗化译法的各种技巧。

第一节　诗、词、曲的语体色彩

清代的李渔在《窥词管见》中说：

　　词之关键，首在有别于诗固已。但有名则为词，而考其体段，按其声律，则又俨然一诗，觅相去之垠而不得者。如《生查子》前后二段，与两首五言绝句何异。《竹枝》第二体、《柳枝》第一体、《小秦王》、《清平调》、《八拍蛮》、《阿那曲》，与一首七言绝句何异。《玉楼春》、《采莲子》，与两首七言绝句何异。字字双亦与七言绝同，只有每句叠一字之别。《瑞鹧鸪》即七言律，《鹧鸪天》亦即七言律，惟减第五句之一字。凡作此等词，更难下笔，肖诗既不可，欲不肖诗又不能，则将何自而可。曰，不难，有摹腔炼吻之法在。诗有诗之腔调，曲有曲之腔调，诗之腔调宜古雅，曲之腔调宜近俗，词之腔调，则在雅俗相和之间。如畏摹腔炼吻之法难，请从字句入手。取曲中常用之字，习见之句，去其甚俗，而存其稍雅，又不数见于诗者，入于诸调之中，则是俨然一词，而非诗矣。是词皆然，不独以上诸调。人问以上诸调，明明是诗，必欲强命为词者，何故。予曰，此中根据，未尝深考，然以意逆之，当有不出范围者。昔日诗变为词，定由此数调始，取诗之协律便歌者，被诸管弦，得此数首，因其可词而词之，则今日之词名，仍是昔日之诗题耳。

这就是说，诗雅，曲俗，词在语体上则介乎诗与曲之间。词比诗俗，却比散曲雅：散曲的语言以尖新、浅俗、活泼为胜，接近口语。根据这一点，我们在翻译中应采用具有不同语体特征的词语和句法。

第二节 诗、词、曲、赋和楹联的翻译

关于赋的英译,我们若能以诗译诗、以文译文,令诗文各得其所,那么,在形似方面就是比较理想的。因在其他章节对楚辞及李渔的赋的翻译有所涉及,有关赋的英译问题的探讨这里就从简从略。

一、关于词牌的英译

词牌是词的格式的名称,是有其来历的。它是前人作词时加于词前的题目,包含着一定的文化信息。当初,词调与词题基本上是合一的。后来(大约从宋代开始),词的内容逐渐与词调脱离,光有词调不足以表明该词的内容,这才另加词题。

关于词牌的来源,大约有下面的三种情况:

(1)源于乐曲的名称。例如,女蛮国使者梳着高髻,戴着金冠,满身璎珞,看起来很像菩萨,教坊因此谱成《菩萨蛮曲》,词牌《菩萨蛮》便由此而来。《西江月》、《风入松》、《蝶恋花》、《钗头凤》等则是来自民间的曲调。

(2)源于某一首词中的几个字或它们的字义。例如《忆秦娥》,属于这个格式的最初一首词是李白所写的,它的开头两句是"箫声咽,秦娥梦断秦楼月",所以词牌就叫《忆秦娥》,又叫《秦楼月》;《忆江南》本名《望江南》,又名《谢秋娘》,因白居易"江南好"这首词的最后一句是"能不忆江南",故词牌又叫《忆江南》;《如梦令》原名《忆仙姿》,之所以改名《如梦令》,是因为后唐庄宗所写的《忆仙姿》中有"如梦,如梦,残月落花烟重"等句;《念奴娇》之所以又叫《大江东去》,是因为苏轼《念奴娇》的第一句是"大江东去";因为苏轼这首词的最后三个字是"酹江月",该词又叫《酹江月》。

(3)源于词题,这种情况最为普遍。例如,《踏歌词》歌咏的是舞蹈,《舞马词》歌咏的是舞马,《欸乃曲》歌咏的是泛舟,《渔歌子》歌咏的是打鱼。这类词牌下面有时会注明"本意",即是说,词牌同时也是词题。

但是,大多数的词后来都不是用"本意"的,因此,一般是在词牌下面用较小的字注出词题。在这种情况下,词题和词牌在意义上可以不发生任何联系。

学术界对词牌的翻译有过讨论。有的人主张用拼音,如菩萨蛮译为 *Pusaman*,但这样做外国人难以明白其中原有的意义;有的主张根据某首词的主题,确定该词词牌名的英译,这样又会失去词牌原有含义,且容易引起混乱:

若把王观的《卜算子》译为 *Farewell*，把陆游的《卜算子》译为 *Ode to the Plum Flower*，则二者在文学样式上似乎毫无关联。许渊冲教授采用意译，例如菩萨蛮译为 *Buddhist Dancers*，编者认为这是比较可取的。

二、词、曲英译的一致性原则

词、曲的翻译最好能遵循一致性的原则，即对所译某一曲牌或词牌的所有作品在格律、形体方面基本保持一致。若一位译者翻译多首同一曲牌或词牌的作品时在韵式、分阕、行数等方面没有定格，读者会感到变化莫测，很难判定你所译的是哪首词或曲。

三、词、曲翻译中的破格

从诗到曲，在格律要求方面由严趋宽。词、曲的翻译可以在节奏、跨行、押韵等方面采取比较宽松自由的做法。以节奏为例，英诗诗格中的替代法（substitution）就能给译者带来较大的自由度。关于替代的详细方法，读者可以参看吴翔林先生所著《英诗格律及自由诗》(北京：商务印书馆，1993)第 60 至 88 页。

四、楹联的翻译

在翻译李渔的楹联时，编者采用了如下方法：
(1) 参照英诗英雄双行体，上、下联脚押韵，较长的楹联加上行内韵或头韵。例如，对联"庐山简寂观"：

天下名山僧占多，也该留一二奇峰，栖吾道友；
世间好语佛说尽，谁识得五千妙论，出我仙师。

编者将其译为：

The monks having occupi'd most of th' mounts *sound* and *renown'd*, shouldn't there be *found* for my fellow Taoists one or two grotesque peaks as their *ground*?
Buddha having employ'd all of the words *kind* and *refin'd*, who can now *expound* the Great Master's Five-Thousand-Character Scripture[2]

that's *profound*?

上下联都由独立主格结构加疑问句组成,句式相似,修辞问句富于表达力;上联四个黑体单词中,前三个是行内韵,与尾韵呼应;下联前三个行内韵中,第三个与尾韵呼应,能产生回环往复的音乐美。

2) 尽量做到扬抑互协,以再现原文的节奏美。例如,且停亭联:

名乎,利乎? 道路奔波休碌碌;
来者,往者,溪山清净且停停。

编者试译如下:

For fame, or for wealth? Alas, on life's journey how people bustle and rustle in their quest!

Comers and goers: 'Midst serene hills and limpid rills why not savor the sweetness of rest?

(tr. zzy et al, from zzy, 2011:98)

若以符号"—"、"﹡"代表重轻读音节(扬、抑),则上下联的节奏可符号化为:

﹡—﹡—,—﹡﹡——﹡——﹡﹡—﹡﹡—﹡﹡﹡—,
—﹡﹡—﹡,—﹡——﹡—﹡—﹡——﹡﹡—﹡﹡—.

可见,译作是具有一定节奏感的。

3) 词性、句式尽量对应,适当使用辞格,用词语体色彩尽量接近原文,以弥补在翻译过程中,由于目的语缺乏源语所具有的特殊的语言美构建能力(例如对仗)而造成的损失。上例虽非尽善尽美,但 bustle and rustle 以及 serene hills and limpid rills 所包含的行内韵、quest 和 rest 构成的尾韵使之音韵铿锵,辅以连词 or 与 and 的对应、感叹句与修辞问句的对应,修辞上又使用了隐喻(life's journey, the sweetness of rest),用词也算典雅,因而从总体看尚属差强人意。当然,我们还可以使用其他手法,这就难以一一列举了。

下文将对汉诗(诗词曲赋)英译中的诗化方法进行梳理。

第三节 诗化译法的若干技巧

物质产品与精神产品的生产有其相似性:在一般情况下,工序越多,投入的劳动成本越高,所产生的附加值也就越高。对于诗化译法来说,把汉诗译为英语的散文就好比完成了"初级产品"的生产,译者还面临着如何对它进行"深加工"——即把它诗化的问题。诗化所包括的形式的近似化(如分行、调序等)、节奏的实现、韵脚的寻求等步骤可视作整个工艺流程中的工序。诗化使诗歌翻译比其他文体的翻译多了一个需要很好发挥想象力、创造力、翻译能力和才华学识的重要环节。舍此就无法解决如何最大限度地保持或再现原诗的美学价值,以便使译作原诗臻于形神兼似的问题。

诗化是有规律可循的。本书第四章讨论了"诗歌的模糊性及翻译的标准和方法"。这里将对诗的样式、节奏和押韵等问题的解决办法进一步加以讨论。

一、样式的形似

中国有一句至八句乃至多于八句的诗、词、曲、赋,而英诗则有双行、三行、四行至十四行诸多诗体。这就使得英诗与原诗在样式方面的"形似"成为可能。例如,绝句的英译可以参照英诗诗体,译为四行诗(quatrain),律诗则可参照意大利八行体(ottava rima)或八行两韵诗(triolet)而译为八行,等等。

杜牧的绝句《山行》,有一英译共十二行,其中仅"霜叶红于二月花"一句就有四行之多(徐忠杰,1990:328—329),未免有累赘之嫌。非但形不似,且也背离了原诗简洁凝练的风格。而许渊冲教授所译《大风歌》则与英诗中三行同韵的三体近似,可谓得形似之妙:

> A big wind rises, clouds are driven away.
> Home am I now the world is under my sway.
> Where are brave men to guard the four frontiers today!
> (xyz,1992:90)

根据语言形态学分类法,汉语是以分析型为主的语言,而英语则既有分析形式又有综合形式。汉语比英语更简练。一般来说,一句汉诗的信息载量比一行英诗大,而英译每行的音节数量又不能无所限制,这就使得在行数方面保持形似十分困难。因此,译者经常会遇到"山重水复疑无路"的困境。但只要掌握了基本的方法,善于、勤于思索,也会找到合适的方案,到达"柳暗花明又一村"的美好境界。下面是一些常见的方法:

a. 音节缩略,如 ever, amidst, the, we shall 在必要时分别拼写为 e'er, midst, th', we'll 等,以减少音节数量。

b. 以短代长，即以音节少的同义词代替音节多的单词，如 morn 代替 morning，bloom 代替 flower，young 代替 tender。

c. 信息转移：陆龟蒙《新沙》有"渤澥声中涨小堤"句，英译太长，故"渤"字所负载的信息转移至题目，将题目译为 A New Sandbar *in the Bohai Sea*。英诗可有跨行（enjambement），因此前后各行的音节数可通过信息转移予以调整。例如，张继《枫桥夜泊》（"月落乌啼霜满天，江枫渔火对愁眠。姑苏城外寒山寺，夜半钟声到客船。"）可以译为：

> The moon is set, the crow decrying dark and frosty skies;
> The maples vague, the fishing lamps are blinking ere mine eyes.
> The ringing bells from Hanshan Temple outside Gusu float
> Afar at mid-night to the sad and troubl'd napper's boat.
> （zzy，1996:137）

就是把原诗第二句里"愁眠"的信息转移至第四行，而把第四句的"到"转移到第三行。

d. 短语代句：《采薇》"载渴载饥"译为"stricken with such hunger and thirst"，《树旗谣》里的"一日三遍打"译为"With lots of punishments inflicted on us every day"，以及《更漏子》的"衾枕寒"译为"her bedding cold"便是以动词的非谓语形式、介词短语和独立主格结构代替句子。

e. 句型转换：通过句型转换，减少音节数量。例如，《秋词》中"晴空一鹤排云上，便引诗情到碧霄"二句，原先译为"Poetic inspiration, which is render'd to the azure, seems to gleam / When through the fleecy clouds hovers a single crane upon a lovely day"，后译为"Poetic inspiration in the azure seems to gleam / When up into the clouds soars a crane on a sunny day"，通过句型转换和其他方法使每行减少了四个音节。

f. 英语的一些 specific words（与 general words 相对）不但形象生动，而且十分简约，可供选用。例如，在译"行道迟迟"（《采薇》）时，可选用"stagger"（= to move unsteadily on one's feet）一词，译《永遇乐》"烽火扬州路"时选可用"devour"（= to eat up quickly and hungrily）一词。

二、节奏的实现

节奏使诗歌声情并茂，增加表现力和感召力。无节奏不可言诗。汉诗是按平仄互协的规律实现节奏与旋律的,而英诗则根据节奏法(scansion),按音节和重音计算韵律,度量韵律的单位称为音步。汉诗英译可以借鉴常见的几种音律,即抑扬格、扬抑格、抑抑扬格和扬抑抑格,实现诗译的节奏。有的译家不讲究节奏,如卢纶的五绝《和张仆射塞下曲》(其三)

月黑雁飞高,单于夜遁逃。
欲将轻骑逐,大雪满弓刀。

译为:

Geese fly high in the moonless night.
The Kahan runs for his life.
Our cavalrymen ride on his trail,
Snow covers our bows, our swords.
(dzx & B. R. 1992:121)

其各行音节数分别为八、七、九、七,轻重音排列为重重重轻轻重轻轻重,轻轻重重轻轻重,轻重轻轻轻重轻轻重,重重轻轻重轻重,基本上无节奏音韵可言,而原诗却是格律严整,读之铿锵。这就难以取得马建忠所主张的"使阅者所得之益与观原文无异"的读者效应。(孟广龄,1990:12)

我们可使用以下方法实现所确定的音律:

a. 调序法:白居易《轻肥》中的"朱绂皆大夫"一句,如译为"Vermillion parttern'd robes mark'd officials ranking high."则有违扬抑格(trochee),故调整词序,把"vermillion"作为后置定语,改为"Pattern'd robes vermillion..."。

b. 换字法:《山行》中"二月花"一语因译为"the flowers of spring"不符合抑扬格(iambus)的要求,故换词改为"the bloom of spring",使之合乎节奏而又不伤原义之再现。

c. 缩略法:《相思》里"愿君多采撷"一句译为"'Tis wish'd thou'll gather plenty of their seed",便是把"It is wish'd that thou will..."加以缩略,使之合辙。可以作缩略处理的例子还有:

th'=the; ne'er=never; tim'rous=timorous; 'gin=begin; 'bout=about; o'er=over; ta'en=taken; 'thwart=athwart;等等。

顺便提一下,除非紧接在音素[t]、[d]之后,词尾-ed 在散文中并不构成音节,而在诗行中则构成音节,读为[-id],因此在有些书中印为-éd,不构成音节的词尾-ed 则写为-'d。

d. 标点法:和文字一样,标点符号具有负载信息或衔接语篇的功能,恰当使用可以减少音节的数量。在以下各例中,标点符号之后括号内的文字是因该符号的使用而省略的:

原诗:

停车坐爱枫林晚,霜叶红于二月花。

——杜牧:《山行》

英译:

Attracted by th' maples my carriage to a halt I bring:(*Behold*!)
The frost-redden'd leaves are brighter than the bloom of spring.
(zzy,1996:181)

原诗:

应怜屐齿印苍苔,小扣柴扉久不开。

——叶绍翁:《游园不值》

英译:

My clog-prints on the greenish moss must have incurr'd the spite:(*for*)
I knock at th' wooden gate, but there's no answer after all.
(zzy,1996:256)

原诗:

打起黄莺儿,莫教枝上啼。啼时惊妾梦,不得到辽西。

——金昌绪:《春怨》

英译:

I scare the orioles off th' trees, for fear
That they might in due time warble and tweet:(*because*)
I may not have reach'd Liaoxi the frontier
When they disturb me in my dream that's sweet!
(zzy,1996:150)

原诗:

自古逢秋悲寂寥,我言秋日胜春朝。
晴空一鹤排云上,便引诗情到碧霄。

——刘禹锡:《秋词》

英译:

Odes to Autumn (No. 1)
Liu Yuxi
Distress induc'd by autumn has long been a favour'd theme,
But autumn time is lovelier than the morns of spring, I'd say:
(*My reason is that*)
Poetic inspiration in the azure seems to gleam
When up into the clouds soars a crane on a sunny day!
(zzy,1996:157)

原诗:

待月西厢下,迎风户半开。隔墙花影动,疑是玉人来。

英译:

The moon in expectancy rises o'er the west-wing room;
To let in breezes th' door is left half open in the gloom.
A rustle through the flowers is heard from beyond the wall:(*I wonder*,)
Could it signify that th' soul of my heart has come to call?
(zzy,1996:275)

三、韵脚的寻求

押韵和节奏一样,使诗歌富于声乐美。汉诗更重押韵,可谓无韵不成诗。上节所引卢纶五绝的英译无韵,失去了原诗的音韵美,可谓一憾。

英诗押韵方式多种多样,与汉诗较为近似的是韵脚(rhyme proper)。韵脚的要求是,押韵的词的重读音节中元音音素(及其后的辅音音素)必须相同,但其前面若有辅音,则该辅音应当不同。

曹操论兵云:兵无定法。寻韵也是这个道理,译者须据具体情况,发扬创造精神，借鉴或探索出恰当的押韵方法。下面略述数种寻韵方法以供参考。

a. 还原法：有些动词原形合韵，而过去式或充当第三人称单数一般现在式谓语的时候不合韵，在这种情况下可使用助动词令其还原。如陆龟蒙《新沙》("渤澥声中涨小堤，官家知后海鸥知。蓬莱有路教人到，亦应年年税紫芝。")编者译为：

A New Sandbar in the Bohai Sea

After the roaring tides a profitable sandbar did appear,

Officials had got wind of it before the seagulls were in th' know.

The immortals would've been tax'd on the purple ganoderma each year

If the tax-collectors could have found a way to Penglai to go! (zzy, 1996: 195)

为使一、三行押韵，第一行使用了助动词"did"。

b. 调序法：即调整词序，使所需音节落在韵脚的位置上。上例二、四行押韵是在调整了"to go to Penglai"的词序之后获得的。

c. 延伸法：在符合原诗意韵的条件下，某一诗句可加上一些词语，以达到押韵的要求。例如，《游西山村》一诗英译末行须与第六行"The flutes and drums announce that Spring Offering's drawing near"(箫鼓追随春社近)共韵，故译为"Supported by a crane I'd frequent th' doors to me so dear"(拄杖无时夜叩门)，最后四个单词所构成的形容词短语，是在诗人热爱乡村生活的思想感情的基础上所作的形态上的延伸。

d. 换字法：可换用合韵的同义词。如"健儿须快马，快马须健儿"译为"the gallant rider longs to get a horse;/The horse does, likewise, a good rider need"不押韵，而以"steed"代替"horse"，则押韵的问题迎刃而解。

除了上文讨论的完全韵(perfect rhyme)，其他押韵方式也可以酌情使用，以获得翻译中的更大的自由度(参考第二章第二节)。

本章所讨论的各种技巧，都必须以"辞不害义"、"形能传神"为前提。否则便是舍本而求末。

押韵的工具书是同义词词典(*Dictionary of English Thesaurus*)，译者也可以通过网站 http://www.onelook.com/的 OneLook Dictionary Search 获取所需信息。诗、词、曲、赋和楹联翻译的实例，读者可参看书末附录Ⅰ至附录Ⅳ。

思考题

1. 在节奏的实现、音节的缩略和韵脚的寻求方面,你有什么新信息和新思想?

2. 评论李渔芥子园杂联之六《月榭联》的英译。

原作:

　　有月即登台,无论春夏秋冬;

　　是风皆入座,不分南北东西。

译作: *Couplets for the Mustard-seed Garden（No. 6）: The Moon Pavilion* 1

Be it spring, summer, autumn or winter2, the bright moon invites people to ascend;

From the south, the north, the east or th' west, a coziness the winds cordially lend.

练习题

1. 翻译李渔的《龙门联》:

　　变化鱼龙地,飞翔鸾凤天。

2. 评价芥子园杂联(其三)的英译:

　　到门唯有竹,

　　入室似无兰。

Couplets for the Mustard-Seed Garden—*No. 3*

Greeting the eye outside the door are the bamboos green,

Feasting th' sense in the room is th' fragrant orchids unseen[2].

3. 对白居易《草》的英译进行多维度评价。

原作:

　　离离原上草,一岁一枯荣。

　　野火烧不尽,春风吹又生。

　　远芳侵古道,晴翠接荒城。

　　又送王孙去,萋萋满别情。

译文 1: *The Grasses*

Behold the grasses green and thick,
Which wither every year and thrive.
The prairie fires may burn and lick;
When breezes blow they'll yet revive.
Their fragrance floats toth' ancient way,
Their luster tinctures th' ruins of town.
One more scion going away,
'Tis in the blues they themselves drown.
(zzy,1996:161)

译文 2: *Grasses*

Tall and hanging down, the grasses on the wide plain
Flourish and wither once in every year.
Wild fire culd not burn them up to extirpate;
Springtide zephyrs blow and they come to life again.
Distant verdure overcometh ancient highways;
Fair-day emerald stretcheth away to waste cities.
Bidding farewell to wanderers going somewither,
Lush-growing grasses waft in the breeze full of parting cares.
(sdy,1997:417)

译文 3: *Grass on the Ancient Plain*

Farewell to a Friend
Grasson the plain spreads higher and higher;
Year after year it fades and grows.
It can't be burned up by wild fire,
But revives when the springwind blows.
Its fragrance o'erruns the old way;
Its green invades the ruined town.
To see my friend go far away,
O'erladen with grief, it bends down.
(xyz,2000:247)

第十七章 对仗英译研究

学习目标

了解、扩充有关对仗的知识,掌握对仗英译的补偿手段,进而在这方面有所创新。

第一节 关于对仗及其英译

"对仗"是个诗律术语,指诗、赋、词、曲、楹联中所要求的对偶。由于汉语的单音词较多,即使是复音词,其中的词素也有相当的独立性,易于构成对偶,对仗便自然成了汉语所特有的文学修辞手段。对仗可使文学作品在形式和意义上显得整齐匀称,产生和谐、对称、巧妙睿智的审美愉悦,因而得到广泛的运用。对仗包括词语的互为对仗和句式的互为对仗。词语对仗要求词义同属一类,词性基本相同,平仄互协,结构对称;同字相对是应该避免的。而句式的对仗则要求句子的结构相同,如以主谓短语对主谓短语,以动宾短语对动宾短语等。构成对仗的两句中,上句叫做出句,下句叫做对句。按格律要求,律诗中间两联(颔联、颈联)就必须对仗。对于绝句,对仗可用可不用。

格律形式是具有艺术含义的;形神兼似是诗歌翻译的最高境界。然而,英诗并没有对仗这一格律因素。在汉诗英译中,对仗应当如何处理?这是汉诗英译方法研究中的一大难题。检索发现,学术界对此鲜有涉及,更谈不上有深入的研究。本章将就此展开初步的探讨。

第二节 对仗英译方法的探讨

诗歌的翻译应当遵循以诗译诗的原则,兼顾内容与形式,做到形神兼似,最大限度地迁移或再现原诗的形式美、音韵美、节奏美、情感美、意境美和风格美。

古语说,"失之东隅,收之桑榆";俗语说,"一白遮九丑";物理实验证明,在高速旋转的情况下,由赤、橙、黄、绿、青、蓝、紫各种颜色的圆球串成的环状物所呈现的只有白这一种颜色。常识、知识与先人的智慧给了我们以启迪:在一定条件下,失却的东西是能够用它物补偿的;在一定条件下,美学特征是可以相互组合、转换和替代的(例如,皮肤白皙可以弥补长相方面的不足)。我们可以根据这个道理,去寻求对仗英译的途径和方法。

实践说明,对仗英译是有法可依的。下文将通过个案的研究与分析,对有关方法逐一加以讨论。

一、音韵补偿法

虽然中文的对仗并不要求用韵,但是,音韵的合理使用不仅能使译文增添音乐美,而且能发挥韵脚的语篇呼应功能,因而可以部分地补偿因无法对仗而失去的语言美。例如:

a. 李渔"且停亭联"的原文是:名乎,利乎?道路奔波休碌碌;来者,往者,溪山清净且停停。

其英译是:

> For fame, or for wealth? Alas, on life's journey how people *bustle and rustle* in their *quest*!
>
> Comers and goers:'Midst *serene hills and limpid rills* why not savor the sweetness of *rest*?
>
> (tr. zzy et al,from zzy,2011:98—99)

通过使用行内韵 bustle and rustle 与 serene hills and limpid rills,尾韵 quest 与 rest,译文声韵铿锵,所具有的语言美学总价值基本上与原文接近。

类似的例子还有:

b. 白居易《草》"离离原上草,一岁一枯荣。野火烧不尽,春风吹又生"四句诗中,颔联包含对仗。译为:

> Behold the grasses *green and thick*,
> Which wither every year and *thrive*.
> The prairie fires may *burn and lick*;
> When breezes blow they'll yet *revive*.
> (zzy,1996:161)

除了同义反复(tautology)等技巧,译文还使用了音韵补偿法。音韵补偿法还可包括头韵(alliteration)补偿法。例如:

c. 林则徐"苟利国家生死以,岂因祸福避趋之"两句译为:

> Whate'er's in th' interest of the state I'll do with *might and main*,
> And personal *weal or woe* is not to be car'd about.
> (zzy,1996:317)

出句英译中的 might and main 与对句英译中的 weal or woe 都押了头韵。

二、平行结构法

英语平行结构(parallelism)指的是,诗文之中相接续的,在语音、韵律、语义、语法结构等方面相互对应的语言结构。它与对仗具有较大的相似性,因此,利用英语的平行结构,就可以令译文与原文中的对仗臻于异曲同工的艺术效果。例如:

d. 王勃《滕王阁》"画栋朝飞南浦云,珠帘暮卷西山雨"的英译是:

> Its painted ridge-beams fondling the morning clouds from South River-mouth,
> Its beaded curtains flirting with the evening rains brew'd in West Hill.
> (zzy,1996:86)

英译两行都是由逻辑主语与逻辑谓语(现在分词短语)构成的独立主格结构,且都使用了拟人格;行末都是介词加地理名词。这样的例子还有:

e. 王之涣《登鹳雀楼》"白日依山尽,黄河入海流"两句译为:

> Ling'ring is the setting sun about the mountain height,
> Surging is the Yellow River eastwards to the sea.
> (zzy,1996:97)

该联出句、对句的英译结构上都属于"主语+谓语+状语",句式上都属于倒装句,时态上都采用现在进行时,或多或少地具有对仗的工巧、有序。

f. 贾岛"鸟宿池边树,僧敲月下门"两句译为:

> Some birds are resting in the pond-side trees;

A monk is knocking on the moonlit door.
(zzy,1996：174)

译文的句式、时态一致。在结构上，词语一一对应：Some birds 对 A monk，are resting 对 is knocking, in the pond-side trees 对 on the moonlit door。

g. 李渔《龙门联》"变化鱼龙地，飞翔鸾凤天"英译为：

Within, the platform for fishes to turn into dragons lies;
Above, freedom is given for phoenixes to fly in th' skies.
(zzy,2011：101)

也是出于同样的道理，只是比上例多了尾韵。
上述三例的译文都较活泼生动，有助于构建与原文近似的形式美。

三、节奏补偿法

英诗的音步律对于对仗的翻译也具有补偿功能。例如，
h. 李白"举头望明月，低头思故乡"两句译为：

I raise my head: a lonely moon is what I see;
I stoop, and homesickness is crying loud in me!
(zzy,1996：114)

两行的时态都是现在时，其描写都是依照诗人的躯体动作加上他的所见、所思这一程序，且用了尾韵；此外，由于利用了抑扬格（iambus），使英译在语音上轻重相间，音长基本上等值，上下基本上对称，声音基本上和谐。原作对仗之美在译文中分流，由上述技巧共同承载、重新建构。我们还可以看看节奏补偿法的另一例子：

i. 杜荀鹤《山中寡妇》的颔、颈二联是：

桑柘废来犹纳税，田园荒后尚征苗。
时挑野菜和根煮，旋斫生柴带叶烧。

译为：

The mulberry trees untended, silk duties must still be paid;
Her fields uncultivated, under taxes is she laid.
To satisfy her hunger underrooted herbs are stew'd;

>   For lack of ready wood she burns leaf'd branches freshly hew'd.
>   (zzy,1996:199)

译文的基本节奏形式为抑扬格七音步。当然,这里所采用的并非单一的技巧。

四、首尾呼应法

同类词性、结构或语法功能的词语,若分别置于出句及对句英译的句首和句尾,使之首尾呼应,也可以产生一定的语言美,这就是首尾呼应法。这种方法也可以藉以补足对仗之美。例如:

j. 李白《塞下曲》"晓战随金鼓,宵眠抱玉鞍"两句译为:

>   By day, directed by the drum and gong men charge and fight;
>   With saddles grasp'd in arms they sleep with vigilance at night.
>   (zzy,1996:118)

"By day"及"at night"两个介词短语都用以指时间。一首一尾,相互呼应,不失为对仗翻译的技巧之一。

类似的例子还有:

k. 李清照《夏日绝句》"生当作人杰,死亦作鬼雄"两句译为:

>   Be a man of men with mettle while alive,
>   And a soul of souls even if doom'd to die!
>   (zzy,1996:232)

与上例不同的是,这两行是句首与句首呼应(以 man 对 soul)、句尾与句尾呼应(以生对死)。此外,两个并列句的状语都是省略句。

五、修辞补偿法

在译文中,若上下两句都使用同一修辞格,也能产生与对仗相近似的对称美。

由于英语辞格对偶(antithesis)与中文对仗颇为近似,在对仗的翻译中其应用尤为广泛。上文 d、e、f、g 各例都包含了对偶。再例如:

l. 李渔《衙署内署联》:

能与山水为缘,俗吏便成仙吏;
不受簿书束缚,忙人即是闲人。

译为:

Union with hills and rills lends a terrene official celestial pleasure;
Detachment from doctrinism brings a busy man unthought-of leisure.
(zzy,2011:102)

其中出句英译中的 terrene official 与 celestial pleasure 形成对偶,出句与对句的英译形成对偶。

其他修辞格也可酌情使用。例如:

m. 陆游《游山西村》的颈联"箫鼓追随春社近,衣冠简朴古风存"译为:

The simple clothing signifies traditional values;
The flutes and drums announce that Spring Offering's drawing near.
(zzy,1996:238)

就使用了拟人格(personification)signifies 与 announce,加诸其他技巧(如两行句式都是主、谓、宾结构),使译文在语言的美学价值方面与原文近似。

n. 杜甫绝句中的"窗含西岭千秋雪,门泊东吴万里船"两句的译文是:

My window does enframe the West Ridge clad in thousand-year snows clean;
My door enjoys the anchor'd ships prepar'd to sail to distant Wu.
(zzy,1996:133)

两行各使用了拟人格 enframe 和 enjoys。再如:

o. 文天祥《过零丁洋》的颔、颈二联:

山河破碎风飘絮,身世浮沉雨打萍。
惶恐滩头说惶恐,零丁洋里叹零丁。

译为:

Like the catkin in the wind land's being lost, which gives me pain;
While my life suggests the duckweed being spatter'd by the rain.
On the Panic shoal, remarks on being panic I forth sent;
Crossing the Lonely Bay, over loneliness I now lament.

(zzy,1996:258)

颔联出句的英译用了明喻(simile)，对句虽非明喻，却具有明喻的修辞效果；颈联出句的 the Panic Shoal 与对句英译的 the Lonely Bay 不但都是双关语(puns)，而且还各自与 panic 和 loneliness（与 lonely 同根）构成重复(repetition)。

第三节 小结

对仗英译的补偿方法往往必须综合运用，方能产生"群体效应"，建构起与对仗相当的美学价值体系，而单一的策略是难以尽对仗之美的。例如：

p. 李渔《芥子园杂联(其三)》"到门惟有竹，入室似无兰"的英译：

Greeting the eye outside the door are the bamboos green;
Feasting th' sense in the room is th' fragrant orchids unseen.
(zzy,2011:109)

就是修辞与音韵等补偿法的综合运用。

q. 李渔《庐山简寂观对联》"天下名山僧占多，也该留一二奇峰，栖吾道友；世间好语佛说尽，谁识得五千妙论，出我仙师"的英译：

　　The monks having occupi'd most of th' mounts sound and renown'd, shouldn't there be found for my fellow Taoists one or two grotesque peaks as their ground?
　　Buddha having employ'd all of the words kind and refin'd, who can now expound the Great Master's Five-Thousand-Character Scripture that's profound?
(zzy,2011:96)

就是音韵法(行内韵、尾韵)、平行结构法(独立主格结构、反意疑问句)和修辞法的综合运用。

值得一提的是，在重构对仗这一形式美的同时，必须注重原作内容的再现，切不可"得形忘神"。

译无常法。它可能因文而异，因时而异，因地而异，因人而异。对仗的英译也是如此，其方法是多种多样的，本章焉能穷其妙？这里只是抛砖引玉，以引起大家对于对仗英译方法问题的关注。

思考题

1. 本章认为,译无常法。你对此有何见解?
2. 对仗英译的补偿方法是多种多样的。你能否加以补充?

练习题

1. 比较陶渊明《归园田居》的各种版本在对仗翻译方面的不同处理方法:

    少无适俗韵,性本爱丘山。
    误落尘网中,一去三十年。
    羁鸟恋旧林,池鱼思故渊。
    开荒南野际,守拙归田园。
    方宅十余亩,草屋八九间。
    榆柳荫后檐,桃李罗堂前。
    暖暖远人村,依依墟里烟。
    狗吠深巷中,鸡鸣桑树颠。
    户庭无尘杂,虚室有余闲。
    久在樊笼中,复得反自然。

译文 1: *Retired Country Life*
Tao Yuanming

Of conformistic qualities I've deriv'd naught
From birth; while by nature my love for mounts is keen.
Since in the net of worldly affairs I got caught,
Alas, a good thirty years it's already been!
As a fish in the pool recalls his days in the lake,
So yearning for his woods is the bird that is cag'd.
Having retir'd to farming for character's sake,
In reclamation of th' southern wastes I'm engag'd.
Around my thatched house of nine rooms lies a track
Of land, which measures below twenty *mu* in all.

The elms and willows shade my house's eaves at th' back,
While peach and plum trees grow nicely in front of th' hall.
A village is located some distance away,
Above whose chimneys wisps of smoke are hanging low.
At times from the deep lanes the dogs will bark and bay,
And cocks atop mulberry trees will proudly crow.
My court's devoid of th' dust of secular concerns;
My plainly-furnish'd home signifies ease and peace.
Eventually to nature I've now return'd,
Like a pent-up animal obtaining release!
(zzy,1996:63)

译文 2: *Once More Fields and Gardens*

Even as a young man
I was out of tune with ordinary pleasures.
It was my nature to love the rooted hills,
The high hills which look upon the four edges of Heaven.
That folly to spend one's life like a dropped leave
Snared under the dust of streets,
But for thirteen years it was so I lived.
The caged bird longs for the fluttering of high leaves.
The fish in the garden pool languishes for the whirled water of meeting steams.
So I desired to clear and seed a patch of the wild southern moor.
And always a countryman at heart.
I have come back to the square enclosures of my fields
And to my walled garden with its quiet paths.
Mine is a little property of ten mou or so,
A thatched house of eight or nine rooms.
On the north side, the eaves are overhung
With the thick leaves of elm-trees,
And willow-trees break the strong force of the wind.
On the south, in front of the great hall,

Peach-trees and plum-trees spread a net of branches
Before the distant view.
The village is hazy, hazy,
And mist sucks over the open moor.
A dog barks ina sunken lane which runs through the village.
A cock crows, perched on a clipped mulberry.

There is no dust or clatter
In the courtyard before my house.
My private rooms are quiet,
And calm with the leisure of moonlight through an open door.

For a long time I lived in a cage;
Now I have returned.
For one must return
To fulfill one's nature.
(tr. A. L., from xyz, 1992:146—147)

译文 3: *Back to Nature*

Not to conform was I born, but with nature I am in tune. Unfortunately, I allowed myself to be enmeshed in public affairs; and for thirteen years I was a caged bird, a fish impounded, hourly yearning for my native woods and waters. Now I am once more a simple farmer, tilling the long abandoned soil.

A few thatched huts in modest acres standing, with a screen of elms and willows at the back, and in front, peach trees, plum trees, a fine array... this is my home. Neighbours I have, some distance away. That's their village — plumes of smoke rising from a dark mass of house, faintly visible in the twilight. Well within hearing, though — dogs barking up the alley, roosters crowing atop the mulberry trees.

No social callers to stir the dust at my door, no worldly cares to rob me of peace and leisure, back to nature at last, after long years of abject servitude!
(wxl,1985:3—4)

2. 比较分析杜甫《自京赴奉先县咏怀五百字》中"朱门酒肉臭,路有冻死骨"

两句的不同英译：

Behind red gates wine and meat go to waste;
On th' road those frozen to death lie in dirt.
(zzy,1996:122)

Behind vermilion portals meat is left to rot,
While out in the streets starving people are frozen todeath!
(lwj,1985:50—2)

3. 李商隐《无题》原文如下：

相见时难别亦难，东风无力百花残。
春蚕到死丝方尽，蜡炬成灰泪始干。
晓镜但愁云鬓改，夜吟应觉月光寒。
蓬山此去无多路，青鸟殷勤为探看。

该诗不同译文如下：

译文 1:A Titleless Poem

'Tis hard for us to meet, but separation's harder still.
When breezes lanquish, fall and wither all the flowers will.
The silkworm ceases not to spin her thread before she's dead;
Unless burnt to ashes endless tears a candle'll shed.
At dawn the mirror may betray your dread of aging hair;
Reciting poems at night I feel the moon's chill in the air.
As mount Penglai is not very long a distance away,
The Blackbird may be kind enough to you frequent, I pray!
(zzy,1996:188)

译文 2:To ...

Hard it was to see each other —
harder still to part!
The east wind has no force,
the hundred flowers wither.
The silkworm dies in spring
when her thread is spun;
The candle dries its tears only

when burnt to the end.
Grief at morning mirror —
cloud-like hair must change;
Verse hummed at night,
feeling the chill of moonlight...
Yet from here to Paradise
the way is not so far:
Helpful bluebird,
bring me news of her!
(I. H. ,from xyz,1992:312)

译文 3：*To One Unnamed*
It's difficult for us to meet and part;
The east wind is too weak to revive flowers dead.
Spring silkworm till its death spins silk from lovesick heart;
A candle but when burned up has no tears to shed.
At dawn I'm grieved to think yur mirrored hair turns grey;
At night you would feel cold while I croon by moonlight.
To the three fairy mountains it's not a long way.
Would the blue birds oft fly to see you on the height!
（xyz,2000:277）
试分析不同译文在对仗处理及审美效果方面的差异。

4. 搜集有关资料,在小组讨论中谈谈你所总结出的对仗在英译中补偿与重构的若干方法。

附录 译者及著作者姓名缩略形式与全称对照表

A. B.—Anne Birrell

A. L.—Amy Lowell

A. W.—Arthur Waley

B. W.—Burton Watson

C. H. B. T.—C. H. Brewitt-Taylor

CTED—《中国翻译》

czq—陈泽勤

D. H.—David Hawkes

dxy—丁新彦

dzx & B. R.—丁祖馨、拉菲尔（Burron Raffel）

F. A.—Florence Ayscouth

gjh—龚景浩

gzz—郭著章

H. A. G.—H. A. Giles

hhq—黄宏荃

I. H.—Innes Herdan

J. A. T.— John A. Turner

J. L.—James Legge

J. M.—John Minford

kkh—Kiang Kang-hu（江亢虎）

ksc—Kang-i Sun Chang

L. C. B.—L. Cranmer-Byng

lybs—香港联益书店

ljm—林键民

lzw—陆志伟

mxy—毛小雨

N. S.—N. Smith

R. A.—Rewi Alley

R. K.—R. Kotewell
R. P.—Robert Payne
S. J.—Soame Jenyns
sm—石民
sms—苏曼殊
S. O.—Shigeyoshi Obata
S. S.—Sidney Shapiro
ttk—T'sai Ting Kan
W. A. P. M.—W. A. P. Marttin
W. B.—Witter Bynner
wdl—王大濂
web & wyx—王恩保、王约西
W. J.—William Jennings
W. J. B. F.—W. J. B. Fletcher
wlw—王力伟
wrp—汪榕培
W. R. S.—William R. Schultz
wxl—翁显良
wzk—王章凯
xtxl—小畑熏良
xyz—许渊冲
xzj—徐忠杰
yxy & gy—杨宪益、戴乃迭
yzh—Yang Zhouhan
zzy—卓振英

主要参考文献

[1] Alley. R. Du Fu：Selected Poems. Beijing：Foreign Languages Press. 2001.
[2] Breslin，R. Translation [M]. New York：Gardner Press. 1976.
[3] Graham，A. C. Poems of the Late Tang [M]. Middlesex：Penguin Books. 1977.
[4] Hawkes，D. The Songs of the South [M]. Harmondsworth：Penguin Books Ltd. 1985.
[5] Newmark，P. A Textbook of Translation [M]. London：Prentice Hall. 1988.
[6] Venuti，L. Rethinking Translation：Discourse，Subjectivity，Ideology. London and New York：Routledge. 1992.
[7] 陈子展. 楚辞直解[M]. 苏州：江苏古籍出版社. 1988.
[8] 丁祖馨 拉菲尔. 中国诗歌精华[M]. 辽宁大学出版社. 1992：121.
[9] 高阳懿. 评秦观《鹊桥仙》的三种英译[J]. 四川外语学院学报. 1997(3)：92—96.
[10] 顾延龄. 刘重德教授的翻译观[J] 外国语. 1991(1).
[11] 郭著章等(选译注).《唐诗精品百首英译》[M]. 湖北教育出版社. 1994.
[12] 韩家权 柏敬泽. 翻译思维方法论[M]. 大连：大连出版社. 2003.
[13] 侯健(主编). 中国诗歌大辞典[Z]. 北京：作家出版社. 1990.
[14] 侯晶晶. 论翻译中的操控现象[J]. 外语与外语教学. 2001(7)：46—48.
[15] 黄宏荃. Anthology of Song-Dynasty Ci-poetry. 221. 北京：解放军出版社. 2001.
[16] 胡经之 王岳川(主编). 文艺学美学方法论[M]. 北京：北京大学出版社. 1994.
[17] 教育部社会科学委员会学风建设委员会(组编). 高校人文社会科学学术规范指南[M]. 北京：高等教育出版社. 2009.
[18] 康德，伊曼努尔. 判断力批判(上卷)[M]. 宗白华译. 北京：商务印书馆. 1964.
[19] 朗格，苏珊. 情感与形式[M]. 北京：中国社会科学出版社. 1986.
[20] 李欣."翻译研究"各流派的阐释与梳理——介绍《翻译研究的系统论视角》[J]. 外语教学与研究. 2001(2)：153—6.
[21] 连淑能. 论东西思维方式[J]. 外语与外语教学. 2002(2)：40—48.
[22] 梁守涛. 英诗格律浅说[M]. 北京：商务印书馆. 1979.
[23] 林健民. 中国古诗英译[M]. 北京：中国华侨出版公司. 1989.
[24] 林同华. 美学心理学[M]. 杭州：浙江人民出版社. 1987. 106.
[25] 刘宓庆. 文化翻译论纲[M]. 武汉：湖北教育出版社. 1999.
[26] 刘英凯. 关于"音美"理论的再商榷[A]. 转引自杨自俭 刘学云. 翻译新论[C]. 武

汉:湖北教育出版社.1996.
[27] 刘重德.《浑金璞玉集》[M]. 北京:中国对外翻译出版公司. 1994:29,39.
[28] 吕叔湘. 中诗英译比录[M]. 上海:外语教育出版社.1980.
[29] 卢军羽 席欢明. 汉语古诗词英译理论的构建:述评与展望[J]. 广东外语外贸大学学报.2008(2).
[30] 陆国强. 现代英语词汇学[M]. 上海:上海外语教育出版社.1983.
[31] 马茂元(主编). 楚辞注释[M]. 武汉:湖北人民出版社.1985.
[32] 马祖毅. 汉籍外译史[M]. 武汉:湖北教育出版社.1997.233.
[33] 毛小雨. 唐宋词[M]. 南昌:江西美术出版社.1997.
[34] 茅于美. 中西诗歌比较研究[M]. 北京:中国人民大学出版社.1987.
[35] 孟广龄. 翻译理论与技巧新编[M]. 北京:北京师范大学出版社.1990:12.
[36] 钱冠连. 人品向学品的正负迁移[A]. 张后尘. 外语名家论要[C]. 北京. 外语教学与研究出版社. 1999.
[37] 钱冠连. 有理据的范畴化过程[A]. 张后尘. 来自首届中国外语教授沙龙的报告[C]. 北京:商务印书馆. 2002:43.
[38] 孙大雨. 古诗文英译集[M]. 上海:外语教育出版社.1997.
[39] 覃乃昌 潘其旭 覃彩銮等. 布洛陀寻踪——广西田阳敢壮山布洛陀文化考察与研究[M]. 南宁:广西民族出版社. 2001,92—255.
[40] 童庆炳. 现代心理美学[M]. 北京:中国社会科学出版社.1993:346.
[41] 汪榕培. The Book of Poetry(《诗经》)[M]. 沈阳:辽宁教育出版社.1995.
[42] 汪镕培 李 冬.实用英语词汇学[M]. 沈阳:辽宁人民出版社.1983.
[43] 王东风. 翻译文学的文化地位与译者的文化态度[J]. 中国翻译. 2000(4):2—8.
[44] 王恩保 王约西. 古诗百首英译[M],北京:北京语言学院出版社,1994.
[45] 王宗炎,求知录[J]. 翻译通讯,1980(6):1.
[46] 丁新彦(选注) 王力伟(英译). 汉英古诗100首[M]. 石家庄:花山文艺出版社. 2000:186.
[47] 王宁. 全球化时代的文化研究和翻译研究[J]. 中国翻译. 2000(1):12—13.
[48] 王逸. 四库全书·楚辞章句[M]. 上海:上海人民出版社/迪志文化出版有限公司. 1999.
[49] 王岳川. 从"去中国化"到"再中国化"的文化战略——大国文化安全与新世纪中国文化的世界化[J]. 贵州社会科学. 2008(10).
[50] 王章恺(主编). 汉语口语(Spoken Chinese A B C)[M]. 广州:广东高等教育出版社.1989.
[51] 吴广平.白话楚辞[M]. 长沙:岳麓书社. 1996.
[52] 吴翔林. 英诗格律及自由诗[M]. 北京:商务印书馆. 1993.
[53] 夏征农(主编). 辞海[Z]. 上海:上海辞书出版社.1990.

[54] 谢榛.《历代诗话续编》(上)[M].北京:中华书局.1997.

[55] 徐长山 王德胜.科学研究艺术[M].北京:解放军出版社.1994.

[56] 徐忠杰.唐诗二百首英译[M].北京:北京语言学院出版社.1990:153,328,329.

[57] 徐忠杰.《词百首英译》[M].北京:北京语言学院出版社.1986.

[58] 许渊冲.唐宋词一百五十首[M].327.北京:北京大学出版社.1990.

[59] 许渊冲.中诗英韵探胜[M].北京:北京大学出版社.1992.

[60] Xu Yuanzhong. Song of the Immortals：An Anthology of Classical Chinese Poetry. Beijing：New World Press. 1994.

[61] 许渊冲. Gem of Classical Chinese Poetry. Beijing：Zhonghua Book Co. 2000.

[62] 许渊冲(英译),杨逢彬(编注).楚辞[M].长沙:湖南出版社.1994.

[63] 杨成虎 周洁.楚辞传播学与英语语境问题研究[M].北京:线装书局.2008.

[64] 杨宪益 戴乃迭.汉魏六朝诗文选[M].北京:外文出版社.2005.

[65] 杨宪益 戴乃迭.楚辞选[M].北京:外文出版社.2001.

[66] 杨自俭 刘学云.翻译新论[C].武汉:湖北教育出版社.1994.

[67] 杨自俭.小谈方法论[J].外语论坛.2002(1).

[68] 于连(François Jullien).新世纪对中国文化的挑战[J].二十一世纪(香港).1999(4).

[69] 余立三.英汉修辞比较与翻译[M].北京:商务印书馆.1985.

[70] 曾杰 张树相.社会思维学[M].北京:人民出版社.1996:111—152.

[71] 张后尘(主编).论文选粹[C].上海外语教育出版社.1997. 20.

[72] 张后尘.外语名家论要[C].北京:外语教学与研究出版社.1999.

[73]《中国翻译》编辑部 中国对外翻译出版公司(编).诗词翻译的艺术[C].北京:中国对外翻译出版公司.1987.

[74] 中国翻译词典编委会.中国翻译词典[M].武汉:湖北教育出版社.1997.

[75] 周汝昌等.唐宋词鉴赏辞典[Z].上海:上海辞书出版社.1988.

[76] 周仪罗平.翻译与批评[M].武汉:湖北教育出版社.1999.

[77] 朱熹.楚辞集注[M].扬州:江苏广陵古籍刻印社.1990.

[78] 卓振英 楚辞疑难新考[J].云梦学刊 2005(5):34—37.

[79] 卓振英.典籍英译中的考辨——以楚辞为例[J].中国翻译.2005(4):23—26.

[80] 卓振英.汉诗英译的总体审度与诗化[J].外语与外语教学.1997(4):44—46.

[81] 卓振英.汉诗英译论要[M].北京:中国科学文化出版社.2003. 主要参考资料.

[82] 卓振英.汉诗英译中的"借形传神"及变通[J].福建外语.2002(1):54—9.

[83] 卓振英.汉诗英译中的"炼词"[J].外语与外语教学. 1998(12):28—30.

[84] 卓振英.汉诗英译中的"移情"[J].外语与外语教学. 2001(1):53—55.

[85] 卓振英.华夏情怀——历代名诗英译及探微[M].广州:中山大学出版社. 1996.

[86] 卓振英.诗歌的模糊性及翻译的标准和方法[J].福建外语.1997(3):45—50.

[87] 卓振英.李渔诗赋楹联赏析[M].北京:外语教学与研究出版社.2011.

[88] 卓振英.英译宋词集萃[M].上海:上海外语教育出版社.2008.
[89] 卓振英.典籍英译:问题与对策[J].汕头大学学报.2002(3).
[90] 卓振英.汉诗英译方法比较研究[J].外语与外语教学.2002(10):32—6.
[91] 卓振英.汉诗英译中的风格变通[J].外语与外语教学.2003(10).
[92] 卓振英.壮族典籍英译的新纪元——试论壮族《麽经布洛陀》英译研究[J].广西民族研究.2008(4).